What Christian readers have said about
Becoming Like Jesus:

"*Elegantly written, creatively structured, and carefully re-searched. . . . Becoming Like Jesus bridges the gap be-tween the worlds of biblical scholarship and popular lit-erature. . . . Van Dyken gives us truths about love, joy, peace, patience, kindness, generosity, faithfulness, gentle-ness, and self-control garbed in human flesh, human anec-dotes, and practical wisdom.*"

—WILLIAM A. EVERTSBERG
senior pastor, Westminster Presbyterian Church,
Grand Rapids, MI

"*Becoming Like Jesus should be on every Christian lay-person's and minister's bookshelf. From the first line to the last, it is simply chock-full of insights on the meaning of the Christian life and how to live it.*"

—RALPH W. PETERSON
executive counsel, Ketchum Inc.,
Boston, MA

"*Very relevant and instructive. . . . This is a book that relates to the hurts and needs of us all. It gives one a Christian perspective to face tomorrow and make it better.*"

—RONALD L. CORNETET
president, F. R. Neuman Insurance Company,
Grand Rapids, MI

Becoming Like

JESUS

Nurturing the Virtues of Christ

The Fruit of the Spirit in Human Experience

Seymour Van Dyken

with

Barbara M. Van Dyken

WILLIAM B. EERDMANS PUBLISHING COMPANY
GRAND RAPIDS, MICHIGAN / CAMBRIDGE, U.K.

© 1996 Wm. B. Eerdmans Publishing Co.
255 Jefferson Ave. S.E., Grand Rapids, Michigan 49503 /
P.O. Box 163, Cambridge CB3 9PU U.K.
All rights reserved

Printed in the United States of America

01 00 99 98 97 96   7 6 5 4 3 2 1

Library of Congress Cataloging-in-Publication Data

Van Dyken, Seymour.
Becoming like Jesus: nurturing the virtues of Christ /
Seymour Van Dyken with Barbara M. Van Dyken
p.   cm.
ISBN 0-8028-4163-5 (alk. paper)
1. Fruit of the Spirit.   2. Christian life.
I. Van Dyken, Barbara.   II. Title.
BV4501.2.V4265 1996
241 — dc20   96-9148
CIP

To Ronald L. Cornetet
whose longtime friendship
and generous encouragement
have kept the flame of this theme alight

I am the vine, you are the branches. Those who abide in me and I in them bear much fruit.

John 15:5

The fruit of the Spirit is love, joy, peace, patience, kindness, generosity [goodness], faithfulness, gentleness, and self-control.

Galatians 5:22-23

And all of us, with unveiled faces, seeing the glory of the Lord as though reflected in a mirror, are being transformed into the same image from one degree of glory to another; for this comes from the Lord, the Spirit.

II Corinthians 3:18

This is how we can be sure that we are in union with God: whoever says that he remains in union with God should live just as Jesus Christ did.

I John 2:5-6 (Good News Bible)

Contents

CONTENTS

Foreword

This book by Dr. Seymour Van Dyken, with its pleasant appendage consisting of nine poems by Barbara Van Dyken, embodies, to use a medieval phrase, God's great plenty. Carefully marshalled arguments jostle with luminous insights based on Dr. Van Dyken's robust involvement in the life of our times; quotations, illustrations, and anecdotes reinforce his own observations; and the tapestry of his discourse is adorned with rich phrasing, apt metaphors, and rhetorical power derived from a long career of effective preaching.

The book has more. Its theology, thoroughly rooted in the Scriptures, is expressed in richly creative statement. It has warmth and life. It is highly practical. It deals with authentic human problems, struggles, anxieties, and temptations. It deals with the human condition. Dr. Van Dyken draws from authors past and present, expresses wisdom that spans the centuries, mingles the timeless insights universally acknowledged with the momentous issues of contemporary life. The book combines exegesis and homily, and relegates his taxonomy of our fallen state to the larger vision of ethical maturity available for our contemplation and emulation. The tone, always positive, calls for a contagious winsomeness, an attitude that kindles like qualities in the several communities one inhabits.

The organization is lodged firmly in the Scriptures themselves, particularly the Pauline catalog of virtues that life in Christ nourishes as we live out our commitment of faith. The book summons us to participate in the high drama of the Christian life — its burdens and glories, its anxieties and hopes, its frustrations and triumphs — and in so doing to experience the serendipitous joys and adventitious casualness of the mysterious workings of the Holy Spirit. The obligation of the Christian, suggests C. S. Lewis, is to practice the virtues. This book can provide substantial help. "Sir, we would see Jesus," said the Greeks to Philip. This book can serve as a good companion to lead us into the presence of the Master.

Barbara's poems have their own intrinsic worth, but they provide as well authentic commentary on the prose discourse. Like diamonds, they reflect nuances, flashes, darting thoughts in ways that only poetry can do.

STEVE J. VAN DER WEELE
Professor of English, Emeritus
Calvin College
Grand Rapids, Michigan

Acknowledgments

My thoughts have been shaped, molded, and conditioned by so many writers and speakers throughout my varied ministries, both those whom I can specify and the host of people whose names I cannot recall but whose ideas I have absorbed, that any list of acknowledgments must be necessarily incomplete.

I am supremely grateful to my loyal and committed companion and wife, Barbara, who initiated my study by leading a women's retreat on the fruit of the Spirit, and whose patience encouraged me to rewrite the book after the virtually completed earlier manuscript was stolen and destroyed. Most of the ideas we have shared with each other, and her incisive thought, treasured intuition, and deep devotion have been an inspiration.

In addition, I have received valuable advice from many friends and colleagues, particularly the following: Ronald L. Cornetet, Dr. Richard R. De Ridder, Rev. William A. Evertsberg, Dr. William D. Geoghegan, William and Betty Knowles, Dr. William H. Kooistra, Rev. Charles A. Lewis, Rev. Dewey A. Peterson, Ralph W. Peterson, Dr. Kenneth P. Smith, Dr. Alfred B. Swanson, and Dr. Steve Van Der Weele.

The staff of the libraries of Bowdoin College, Calvin College, Chicago Theological Seminary, Curtis Memorial Library (Brunswick, Maine), Princeton Theological Seminary, and Reigner Library of Union Theological Seminary (Richmond, Virginia) graciously assisted me in borrowing books and tapes and in arranging interlibrary loans.

Congregants and students have motivated me to endeavor to make the good news of God understandable and relevant to our ever-changing times. The monitory advice of C. S. Lewis, "If you can't turn your faith into the vernacular, then either you don't understand it or you don't believe it," has perennially mentored me.

Barbara Carlson, my secretary at East Congregational Church, carefully typed much of the original draft, and previous to her Esther Schulz did initial work on several concepts. My computer literate friend Adrianna De Ridder prepared the manuscript for the publisher.

I am also grateful for the personal interest and helpful advice of William B. Eerdmans, Jr., President of William B. Eerdmans Publishing Company; to Samuel Eerdmans, Vice President of Sales and Marketing; to Jennifer Hoffman, Assistant Managing Editor, and her assistants; to Ina M. Vondiziano, Publicist; and others on the staff for seeing the book through the process of publication.

SEYMOUR VAN DYKEN
Harpswell, Maine, and
Fort Myers Beach, Florida

Preface

This is a book about positive, practical Christian living. None of us is perfect; we are all flawed human beings. But we want to become better people. God intends this fulfillment of us. As Jesus said, "I came that they may have life, and have it more abundantly."

The reader will do well to think of this book as the spiritual biography of any Christian who passes through the range of human relationships one sustains throughout life. It is a book for lay people who wish to apply the gospel to these human relationships. It is for parents who wish to train their maturing children for a richer spiritual life. It is for ministers who hopefully will find it suggestive for sermons and study courses that will enable others to realize these goals. It is for seekers still outside a faith community, and for those who endeavor to interpret the good news to them. It is for all who want to know how to live out the robust adventures that inhere in the affirmations of the Christian faith.

We approach a new millennium with increased emphasis on spirituality. Society is in ferment, asking pointed questions about the meaning of life and how to live it more satisfyingly. People are concerned about reclaiming values that have been lost. Some are swimming in a sea of question marks, grasping for anything that seems to answer the yearnings of their souls. Too often, in our generation of seekers, the transcendent dimension has been overlooked as people luxuriate in narcissistic spirituality.

Spirituality is an elastic concept, a term used to embrace a wide range of ideas. Numerous books present a smorgasbord of spiritualities today. The spirituality I deal with has its base in the New Testament study of the fruit of the Spirit; it is enriched with insights from theology, philosophy, psychology, sociology, science, and everyday human experience.[1] Some readers will find their culturally conditioned ethics and spirituality to be less prescriptive than the biblical witness. What we believe, after all, influences our behavior. Dorothy Sayers has reminded us that without creed there is chaos. Christian dogma is not dull, but dramatic.

This is the good news of God. God is glad when we change our minds (repent), turn our lives around to live the Christ-life (convert), and cooperate with the Spirit in following Jesus (renew), in order to enrich our own personal experience and permeate society with winsome Christian influence. It is nothing less than a personal miracle when our flawed characters are gradually transformed into the likeness of Christ.

I have, accordingly, studded the work with illustrations from my own pastoral and teaching experience, personal anecdotes from friends and acquaintances, and biographies of people who can illuminate our human situation. Occasionally I have included the humor and wit of others. History is replete with examples of persons

---

1. A good standard work on biblically based theology is Hendrikus Berkhof, *Christian Faith: An Introduction to the Study of Faith* (Grand Rapids: William B. Eerdmans Publishing Co., 1979).

For a study in historical perspective, see the classic work of Heinrich Heppe, *Reformed Dogmatics,* ed. Ernst Bizer, trans. G. T. Thomson (repr. Grand Rapids: Baker Book House, 1978).

For centrist theological insights, use has been made of Gabriel Fackre, *Christian Basics: A Primer for Pilgrims* (Grand Rapids: William B. Eerdmans Publishing Co., 1991); *The Christian Story: A Narrative Interpretation of Basic Christian Doctrine,* rev. ed. (Grand Rapids: William B. Eerdmans Publishing Co., 1984); *The Christian Story: A Pastoral Systematics* (Grand Rapids: William B. Eerdmans Publishing Co., 1987); *Ecumenical Faith in Evangelical Perspective* (Grand Rapids: William B. Eerdmans Publishing Co., 1993). Perusal of Fackre's personal journey in the introduction to his *Pastoral Systematics* made me aware of how much of his thought I had absorbed by theological osmosis over the years.

Invaluable for psychological insights are *Baker Encyclopedia of Psychology,* ed. David G. Brenner (Grand Rapids: Baker Book House, 1985), and *The New Harvard Guide to Psychiatry,* ed. Armand M. Nicholi, Jr., M.D. (Cambridge, Mass.: Belknap Press of Harvard University Press, 1988).

who have experienced the amazing grace of Jesus Christ — people such as the apostle Paul, Augustine, John Wesley, Albert Schweitzer, Toyohiko Kagawa, Mother Teresa, C. S. Lewis, and Charles Colson, to name but a few. The stories of their lives enrich ours.

"You will know them by their fruits," said Jesus. In contrast to the perversity of flawed fallen nature, the apostle extols the harvest of the Spirit — the love, joy, peace, patience, kindness, generosity, faithfulness, gentleness, and self-control that the Spirit nurtures in us. In Christ we "become new"; we are "transformed into [his] image," we are letters written "with the Spirit of the living God," and, in the end, "we shall be like him" when we see him as he is.[2]

I have shared many of these ideas with responsive congregations in sermons and study classes. In some of the churches I served as senior minister, in others as interim minister, or as a guest preacher. The congregations are memorable, composed of devout, enthusiastic, and committed Christians. They have made Christ and the Holy Spirit more vivid and vital to me. The churches cover the spectrum of rural town, urban centers, and college and university communities. They have been small and large congregations with members of all vocations and professions, believers who have enjoyed a wide range of educational, economic, and social experience.

We are meant to reflect the fruit of the Spirit in all our human experiences. From childhood to old age, life is a holy pilgrimage that takes us from our earliest friendships through romance, marriage, family life, and church fellowship, into the social relationships of neighbors and citizens. In all these relationships, our progressively sanctified selves experience life as God's image, redeemed by Jesus Christ, and reoriented by the Holy Spirit, as we seek to follow and become like Jesus.

2. II Cor. 5:17; 3:18; Eph. 3:3; I John 3:2.

CHAPTER ONE

A Liberated Lover

It dawned on me one day with all the warm glow of a summer sunrise that God wants us to be little christs — not a Christ, but copies of Christ, those who are being transformed by the dynamic of the Spirit into his image. God is an artist. He has given us a self-portrait in Jesus Christ. Christ has been called "God with a human face." He is our eternal contemporary, eager to take up residence in every believing heart. The apostle Paul informs his Galatian friends that he is "in the pain of childbirth until Christ be formed in you" (Gal. 4:19). Phillips Brooks was so moved by this prospect that he made one of the lines of his Christmas carol a fervent prayer, "O Holy Child of Bethlehem! . . . be born in us today!" When this happens, it is no less a miracle than the incarnation and the resurrection, for the Jesus of history becomes the Christ of experience. From then on, our characters are spiritually colored by the personality of Jesus.

This is what happened to Japan's Toyohiko Kagawa as a high school lad through personal conversation with a mission teacher. He turned his back on a diplomatic career, a family inheritance, and his Buddhist faith to work for the poor in the slums, praying, "O God, make me like Christ."

The old Negro Spiritual expresses the sentiment in simple style:

Lord, I want to be a Christian in my heart . . .
Lord, I want to be more loving . . .
Lord, I want to be more holy . . .
Lord, I want to be like Jesus . . .

1

Why should one want to be like Jesus? Isn't it enough just to be decent? Why should we not be content to be simply human, guided by our conscience according to the law written in our hearts (Rom. 2:15)? The simple reason is that to be human is not good enough, for we are all flawed human beings. God wants to restore us to the divine intention of creation, re-create the original image, redeem us from sin, and renew us by the Spirit to become spiritual sons and daughters.

The big question is: how does one become more like Jesus? The answer is that we do not achieve this experience by our own effort: it is the work of the Spirit of Jesus. His Spirit initiates the new life within us, which enables us to cooperate in nurturing the fruits of the Spirit, the "virtues of Christ," in theologian Friedrich Schleiermacher's apt phrase. The apostle Paul listed them as love, joy, peace, patience, kindness, generosity, faithfulness, gentleness, and self-control (Gal. 5:22-23). The Greek word he uses for love is "agape," which we distinguish from all other expressions of love by calling it Christian love. Agapic love is the diapason of the Christian life. "Clothe yourselves with compassion, kindness, humility, meekness, and patience," writes Paul; "above all, clothe yourselves with love, which binds everything together in perfect harmony" (Col. 3:12, 14).[1] It is "the golden chain" of the fruit of the Spirit. All the other virtues are extensions and expressions of the Christlike love that all believers should yearn for.

In successive chapters, all of these fruits will illuminate love in its various forms as it expresses itself in the progressive stages of life's pilgrimage. In this way, we make the life of the invisible God visible. God is Spirit, and no one has ever seen God, nor is Jesus or the Spirit visible today. But as we incarnate the virtues of Christ in manifesting the fruit of the Spirit, our lives become visible witnesses to the life of God within us.

---

1. Cf. also J. B. Phillips's version.

The Primacy of Christlike Love

The thesis of this book is that by the energy of the Spirit we can become more like Jesus in our human relationships. Jesus himself, therefore, is our model. He has left us an example in whose steps we can follow (I Pet. 2:21). "He is not an optimal model simply to be copied in every detail," writes Hans Küng, "but a basic model to be realized in an infinite variety of ways according to time, place, and person. . . . If someone commits himself to Jesus as the standard, if he lets himself be determined by the person of Jesus Christ as the basic model for a view of life and a practice of life, this means the transformation of the whole man. For Jesus Christ is not only an external goal . . . he determines and influences man's life and conduct, not only externally, but from within."[2]

Jesus is to become incarnate within us. No one has demonstrated love's joy, peace, patience, kindness, goodness, faithfulness, gentleness, and self-control as he did. He did not love human beings in general, but individual persons in existential situations: the sinful, sick, sorrowing, hungry, hateful, haughty, and hopeless were all the beneficiaries of his compassionate love. For Jesus, it was never love in general but love in particular, not even a hint of "'embracing millions,' of a 'kiss for the whole world,' as in the poem of Schiller, turned by Beethoven in the Ninth Symphony into a great hymn of joy." Such a kiss, Küng continues, "costs nothing: it is not like kissing the one sick, imprisoned, underprivileged, starving man."[3] Humanistic love is less costly the more it is directed to all humankind rather than to the individual with personal needs.

In his contact with the people of Palestine, Jesus constantly reached out with the gentle touch of kindness. He touched the leper, and the leper was made clean. He touched Peter's sick mother-in-law, and the fever left her. He took little children in his arms and blessed them (Matt. 8:3, 15). How patient he was with the needy masses that surged around him.

2. Hans Küng, *On Being a Christian* (Garden City, N.Y.: Doubleday, 1976), p. 551.
3. Küng, p. 256.

At the climax of his tutorial ministry to his disciples, in the upper room, he bequeathed to them his joy and his peace. Truly he could say in his intercessory prayer with them that he had faithfully finished the work that God had given him to do. Even in that most trying situation before Pilate, how masterfully he maintained his self-control. These are the virtues we should cultivate if we would be more like Jesus.

One of the most Christlike personalities of our time is Mother Teresa of Calcutta. Educated to teach in an elite convent, she one day suddenly resolved to give her life to India's castaways. Her life among the poor outcasts is love in action. Her face shines with love, and her words and actions carry love wherever she goes, as she seeks to do "something beautiful for God." Each day she meets Jesus twice: first in Holy Communion at the altar, then in the streets among the suffering masses. In Holy Communion she finds the spiritual strength to minister to bodies and souls in the sick society. In a world of injustice and human hurts, this octogenarian bundle of energy, living with a heart condition that would keep most people sedentary, keeps on day after day gently caring for the discarded sick and dying. "The way you touch people," she says, "the way you give to people the love [of God] for one another is his love in action through us."

Every believer is a saint, as the greetings of Paul's epistles tell us. But Mother Teresa is one of the most winsome. To me, she exemplifies the virtues of Christ as the fruit of the Spirit more dramatically than anyone else of whom I know. Her love shines in the joy that causes her and her associates to smile so easily. She moves about with a grace that exudes peace. Patience is the hallmark of her labor. Kindness to the suffering, dying outcasts (especially children) makes their wretchedness more endurable. Her generous goodness is indefatigable as she faithfully serves her Lord in ministering to others. Her gentleness in dealing with the deprived never turns into exasperation, for she is inwardly self-controlled by the love of God and her response to it. She lives by the Spirit and is guided by the Spirit.

We must think specifically of the Spirit. When we speak of the virtues of Christ in human experience, no tenet of the Christian faith is harder to understand than the nature of the Holy Spirit. We can look about us at the world and think of God the Creator who fathered and mothered the cosmos. When we read the words of Jesus in the Gospels, he becomes very real to us as the compassionate savior, the way, the truth, and the life. But when we contemplate the Holy Spirit we seem to enter a mysterious world. Putting it briefly, the Spirit is God in action — in us personally and in the world. The Bible speaks of the Spirit interchangeably as the Spirit of Jesus or the Spirit of God. We all know people who have personal power; the Spirit has divine power in our lives. The Spirit makes God real to us, helps us to believe in Christ, and enables us to live the Christ-life. In short, the Spirit is the living presence of Christ in you and me.

The good news of the glad God is that, as the Spirit of Christ takes up residence in our hearts, the Spirit liberates us from the perversity of our lower natures to "the freedom of the glory of the children of God." Christians are liberated from bondage to what the apostle calls "the works of the flesh," the list of which resembles today's newspaper and TV newscast accounts: "fornication, impurity, licentiousness, idolatry, sorcery, enmities, strife, jealousy, anger, quarrels, dissensions, factions, envy, drunkenness, carousing, and things like these" (Gal. 5:19-21). William Bennett in a recent speech suggested that these propensities are still with us. "There is a coarseness, a callousness, a cynicism, a banality, and a vulgarity in our time," he said. "There are too many signs of decivilization — that is, civilization gone rotten." Paul's moral manifesto is for all times: live by the Spirit in order to produce the fruit of the Spirit.

Without these spiritual graces, life is devoid of value, a trivial affair. For far too long the media have been telling us a pack of thundering lies about how to find "the rich, full life" in secular and materialistic pursuits. People everywhere are hungering for more satisfying values. There is a quiet spiritual revival coursing through American culture. TV commentator Bill Moyers recently declared that "millions of Americans are searching for some clearer understanding of the core principles of religion and how they can be applied to the daily experience of living as well as to humanity's common destiny of this planet." Americans are experiencing a new fascination with spirituality.

5

Although there are hordes of depraved people in the world who still do horrendous things, there are also hosts of people who are being emancipated from these evil propensities to nurture the fruit of the Spirit. Throughout this book, explicitly and implicitly, we will recognize the various fruits as love in action in human experience. This chapter in an initial way conveys the sense of the whole, the main idea that the others amplify, that the root fruit of Christian love expresses itself in all the other fruits of the Spirit. In each progressive relationship the energizing Spirit enables us to nurture the virtues of Christ so that the personality of Jesus shines through us.

The Poetry of Agape

The possibility of enjoying a loftier life captivates people in every age. Anyone who can point the way to a nobler life has an eager audience. More than a century ago, in the year 1887, Henry Drummond, a young Scottish preacher, delivered an address at a conference in Northfield, Massachusetts, which so captivated his listeners that they besieged him with requests for copies. It was published, became a best-seller, was translated into many languages, and has never gone out of print. I picked up a copy of it just a few weeks ago in a bookstore. It is an exposition of the love-poem of I Corinthians 13, which Drummond entitled *The Greatest Thing in the World.* The address is about agape, the love that reflects God's self-giving love to us.

Drummond had to explain that "charity" in the King James Version means love. Since in our day the word *love* has become so woolly and elastic, we need to emphasize that the apostle did not have in mind love in general, and certainly not the lurid love of many current novels and films; he meant Christian love, love that seeks the highest good of others.

It is a pity that agape needs to be explained in a world that so freely uses scientific and technical terms. You will find the word in our dictionaries, but it still is not generally used in common speech, an acknowledgment that agape is in a class by itself. It is other-

6

regarding, sacrificial love. It is all giving. It embraces all our faculties. It is more than mere feeling; is informed by the mind and stabilized by the will. It is undiscourageable goodwill to others that seeks their highest good.

The stately Elizabethan diction of the King James Version, the noblest monument to English prose, still beloved by many, is perpetually poetic in its lilting phrases: "Though I speak with the tongues of men and of angels, and have not charity, I am become as sounding brass, or a tinkling cymbal." It has been superseded by new translations that reflect changes in our culture and language, but the rhapsodic exaltation of agape as the highest human virtue has not been lost. We still thrill to the graceful rhythms of contemporary language that have not altered the essential beauty and thought of the apostle's inspired poem.

Surely Paul was thinking of Jesus when he penned his poem. If you substitute "Christ" for "love" and then, as one who bears his name put in your own name, you will have a verbal portrait of the Christ-life that bears the fruit of the Spirit.

John is patient;
Mary is kind;
John is not envious or boastful or arrogant or rude;
Mary does not insist on [her] own way;
John is not irritable or resentful;
Mary does not rejoice in wrongdoing, but rejoices in the truth.
John/Mary bear all things, believe all things, endure all things.

I cannot recall the number of times brides and grooms have requested some part of this love-poem in their wedding ceremonies. Sometimes they prefer the lucid and flowing prose-poetry of J. B. Phillips's paraphrase: "This love of which I speak is slow to lose patience — it looks for a way of being constructive. It is not possessive: it is neither anxious to impress nor does it cherish inflated ideas of its own importance. Love has good manners and does not pursue selfish advantage. It is not touchy. It does not compile statistics of evil or gloat over the wickedness of other people. On the contrary, it is glad with all good men when Truth prevails. Love knows no

7

limit to its endurance, no end to its trust, no fading of its hope: it can outlast anything."[4]

Whatever the version, agape's translation retains its poetic beauty.

The Power of Love

Agapic love burst on the Greco-Roman world as a virtue more noble than anything human beings had ever known. The early Christians took this seldom-used word and gave it a new glory. It is a word "born within the bosom of revealed religion," writes linguist R. C. Trench. More accurately it was "reborn" within the Christian experience. This love, patterned on the sacrificial love of Christ, empowered the early believers to live so adventurously and unselfishly that the ancient world stood agape with wonder!

In agape-love we give ourselves to one another, writes Karl Barth, "with no expectation of a return, in a pure venture, even at the risk of ingratitude, and of that other person's refusal to make a response of love."[5]

The winsomeness of the early Christian fellowship so threatened the pagan powers of the empire that they sought to strangle the infant body of Christ in its Mediterranean crib. For three centuries, emperors sought to dismember it with ghastly persecutions. The early believers were imprisoned, scourged, thrown to the lions in the coliseum, even crucified. The followers of Jesus, however, "faithful unto death," were inspired by the cartoon language of the Revelation, the Easter book of the New Testament, and marched victoriously into the future with the trumpet notes of a Hallelujah Chorus sounding in their souls. Their faithfulness astounds us. Christians have been fiercely persecuted in other parts of the world in subsequent ages, but the early Christians were the spiritual pioneers of a new order, one that now encircles the globe.

4. J. B. Phillips, *Letters to Young Churches* (New York: Macmillan, 1954), chap. 13. Subsequently noted as Phillips.

5. Karl Barth, *Church Dogmatics*, IV/2, trans. G. W. Bromiley (Edinburgh: T. & T. Clark, 1958), p. 221; quoted by Michael Harper, *The Love Affair* (Grand Rapids: William B. Eerdmans Publishing Co., 1982), p. 89.

The transformation of Jesus' eleven cowering disciples into a courageous company of the committed defies naturalistic explanation and transcends psychological analysis. The secret? "The spring of our actions," says Paul, "is the love of Christ" (II Cor. 5:14, Phillips).

They initiated a revolution. "Revolution" often suggests aggressive violence, such as anti-monarchists storming the Bastille, repressed races ransacking the halls of government, or tattered mobs of frustrated masses rioting in the streets of the Middle East or Central America. The early Christians, however, overturned the ancient world, not with violence from without, but with quiet, transforming power from within.

Every revolution has had a battle cry that ignited the zeal of its devotees. In the American Revolution it was "No taxation without representation." In the French Revolution it was "Liberty, Equality, and Fraternity." In the First World War it was "Make the world safe for democracy." In the Second World War it was "The war to end all wars." For Christianity it was Christ's command, "Love one another!"

Unlike the catastrophic upheavals of our century — those of Vladimir Lenin in Russia, Adolf Hitler in Germany, Mao Tse-tung in China, Ayatollah Ruholla Khomeini in Iran, Saddam Hussein in Iraq, and others in Third World countries whose leaders have left a trail of carnage at home and terrorism abroad — the Christian revolution has been nonviolent. "My kingdom is not from this world," Jesus declared to Pilate. "If my kingdom were from this world, my followers would be fighting to keep me from being handed over" (John 18:36).[6]

It is the spiritual power of this pacific revolution which constitutes the secret of its long influence in the world. If Christians, and

---

6. As Hans Küng has noted, Jesus' home territory of Galilee was the center of the Zealot movement, one of his disciples (Simon the Zealot) had been a revolutionary at heart, and Judas Iscariot may have shared similar ideas. The religious leaders' charge that Jesus aspired to be "King of the Jews" played a decisive role in Pontius Pilate's decision to have Jesus executed by the Romans for political reasons. But, though Jesus preached a God who was not on the side of the rulers and the established authorities, the essence of his message was that of a God of redemptive liberation. He never indulged in polemics or agitation against the occupying Romans, nor stirred up anti-Roman feeling. Jesus' emphasis was on a nonviolent revolution that proceeded from the human heart into society. "Society had to be transformed through the transformation of the individual." *On Being a Christian,* trans. Edward Quinn (Garden City, N.Y.: Doubleday, 1976), pp. 183-91.

9

the Church, had fallen for the temptation to power that Jesus refused when he was tempted by the devil in the wilderness, we would not find any Christian influence alive today. It would have been crushed or decayed, as are all worldly kingdoms. As it is, however, there is no mightier power in the world today than that of the living Christ. In the United States, the Church of Jesus Christ exercises more power than the combined strength of our leading institutions. And it does this through the power of the Spirit expressing itself in love, joy, peace, patience, kindness, generosity, faithfulness, gentleness, and self-control.

Regrettably, Christians have not always lived up to Jesus' expectations. The conflicts that subsequently scandalized Christianity, especially the Crusades, the Inquisition, and the wars of religion, were not divinely inspired. They were the eruptions of unsanctified human nature, the back-eddies of unredeemed passion, not the mainstream of liberated Christian life.

Napoleon Bonaparte, scanning his career of conquest and devastation, reportedly confessed that he, Alexander, Caesar, and Charlemagne had built great empires, empires that depended on force. "But centuries ago Jesus started an empire that was built on love," he said, "and even to this day millions will die for him." Spiritual power, he acknowledges, ultimately is stronger than physical force. Stalin's sneer, "How many battalions does the Pope have?" now sounds ludicrous with the internal collapse of his vaunted communistic hegemony.

Love is still the greatest power in the world.

"What do you mean, the greatest power?" skeptics exclaim. In an age of moon landings, space probes, computer chips, genetic engineering, heart transplants, and a burgeoning list of human achievements, technology, they proclaim, is the greatest power. America is the birthplace of Thomas Edison, the Wright brothers, Jonas Salk, and the refuge of the likes of Albert Einstein and a host of other foreign scientific giants. Technology has power such as the world has never dreamed of. They point to nuclear fission and the limitless prospects of fusion. Billions of dollars' worth of space hardware scan military movements worldwide and search out the secrets of our solar system. Horticulturalists can make deserts blossom like

10

a rose, so that, if we decided to, we could feed the world. There is no limit to our control of virtually every aspect of human existence, from the cradle to the grave! So speaks a world come of age!

We are, of course, legitimately fascinated and overwhelmed by the technological achievement of our age. Within a few decades technocratic civilization has advanced further than any in all previous human history. Yesterday's marvels soon become tomorrow's museum pieces. Yet serious questions must be asked. During this time what has been happening to the character of humankind? Are these awesome powers autonomous, or are they instruments in the control of human minds and wills? And with what ethical standards shall we govern their use? The assumption that because we are better at things we are better people is an illusion. As atrocities continue to victimize millions, the battle against barbarism is never ending. Cultures and civilizations rise and fall for moral reasons. French lawyer and theologian Jacques Ellul in his classic *The Technological Society* gives a pessimistic appraisal of technical efficiency when regarded as an end in itself.[7] The hope of solving contemporary problems through technological, scientific, or political schemes, he asserts, is misplaced. Human efforts apart from God's grace will always be self-destructive.

As we approach the twenty-first century our great need is a new exploration of the human spirit. Technology and reason alone do not inspire confidence and trust. Authentic spirituality, in league with ethics and psychology, is beginning to move to center stage.[8] The longest journey, observed Dag Hammarskjöld, is the journey inward. The soul of improvement is the improvement of the soul.

The future of our lives, therefore, will be determined not by forces from without, but by forces operating within the human spirit. Whether mind-boggling scientific creations will be a bane or a blessing will be determined by the moral and spiritual qualities of the people who control them. Manipulated by revolutionary fanatics,

7. Jacques Ellul, *The Technological Society* (New York: Alfred A. Knopf, 1964).
8. Leander E. Keck, *The Church Confident* (Nashville: Abingdon Press, 1933), p. 99.

11

they inspire dread and fear, but employed by those who are morally sensitive, they inspire hope for all who live on planet earth.

We are weary of the incessant recital of bad news on morning and evening newscasts. We yearn for news that concentrates not on problems but on solutions. Love alone can curb crimes of violence, sever slavery's shackles, liberate labor's bondage, and achieve racial and gender equality. Christ can "break the power of canceled sin" and set the captives free. We rise to our highest stature as we join his redemptive program for the human race.

Bertrand Russell, renowned humanist, startled a Columbia University audience some years ago with a candid confession: "The root of the matter if we want a stable world," he declared, "is a very simple and old-fashioned thing, a thing so simple that I am almost ashamed to mention it, for fear of the derisive smiles with which cynics will greet my words. The thing I mean is love, Christian love. If you feel this, you have a motive for existence, a guide in action, a reason for courage, an imperative necessity for intellectual honesty."[9] He could not have been more right!

The Practice of Love

Christian love is more than an affectionate feeling or an abstract idea; it is an active force. Theological and philosophical treatises can describe it, but they cannot capture its grandeur. This is the reason why the Bible is so full of love stories. They are accounts of love in action.

A diplomat was once asked about his knowledge of French. "My French is excellent," he replied, "all except the verbs." That was a notable exception! Verbs are the sinews of speech. They carry the action. No verbs, no action. For Christians the nouns are superb: redeemer, savior, liberator. The adjectives are beautiful: gracious, sacrificial, forgiving. But if the verbs are missing there is no action. The New Testament, however, is full of verbs: believe, follow, love.

9. *The New York Times,* November 16, 1950, p. 29, quoted by Robert J. McCracken, *What Is Sin? What Is Virtue?* (New York: Harper & Row, 1966), pp. 91-92.

Profession and practice must go together. Creed must be married to conduct. A rather dour church officer once spoke of his great love for his church. Yet, in spite of his master's degree in engineering from a leading university and a position with a significant salary, his minuscule financial pledge did not match his profession, and I was not impressed.

Was not this Communism's perennial problem, that its performance never matched its propaganda? That this should be the case in a naturalistic society does not surprise us. In the society of Jesus it is nothing less than a tragic contradiction. We are not meant to be spiritual schizophrenics. Our actions should speak as loudly as our words.

As I write this, we have been celebrating the fiftieth anniversary of D-Day. One of the popular songs at that time had the phrase "accentuate the positive and eliminate the negative." The apostle Paul had something like this in mind when he composed his poem on love. Love, he says, accentuates two very positive fruits of the Christ-like spirit: it is patient, and it is kind.

Patience may not seem glamorous and exciting. Contrary to the thinking of some people, it is not weak and supine. It is tough. It has great strength. Patience never gives up on people, said William Barclay, however unreasonable they may be. How right he was! It is long-suffering. Many today know it as the power to see things through: a trying marriage, the loss of a job, getting on with difficult people.

Kindness is also one of the positive graces we want most from others, and that we should be most eager to show to others. We show kindness in so many different ways. Kindness is a dinner brought to a bereaved family, time listening to a troubled friend, gentle encouragement to one who is depressed. It may be pausing to give "Samaritan help" to an accident victim on a busy highway, or warning fellow travelers of danger ahead. Sometimes, to our embarrassment, we do not recognize the well-meant kindness of others. A dapper young man, cruising in his high-powered convertible, was rounding a curve on a hilly two-lane road, as a chic blond, also in a convertible, her long tresses streaming in the wind, zoomed around the curve from the opposite direction. "Pig!" she shouted at him. "Sow!" he contemptuously shouted back at her. And dashing around the bend he crashed into a pig standing in the middle of the road!

Love also eliminates the negative. It is not boastful, or arrogant, or rude. Jesus denounced the conceit and arrogance of the proud Pharisee who prayed, "Lord, I thank you that I am not like others. . . ." Nor does love "insist on its own way." It is not irritable, or touchy, or easily provoked. It does not harbor resentment, a trait that ultimately hurts the resenter more than the one resented. Resentment is acid poured on yesterday's wounds. Love keeps no record of wrongs. It is not "historical." Negatives such as these tell us almost as much about the distinctive quality of Christian love as the positives.

Love emphasizes the affirmative. "It does not rejoice in wrongdoing, but rejoices in the truth." Christian joy is a by-product of love. Where there is love, there is joy. This is so because both are people-oriented. Joy comes in loving people. And because of this "it bears all things, believes all things, hopes all things, endures all things. There is no limit to its faith, hope, and endurance." This sounds like a counsel of perfection for imperfect people. Love is hard work. Yet, Paul confidently asserted, "I can do all things through him who strengthens me!" We are in touch with illimitable reserves of power. No one has yet seen what the Spirit can do with a person who is wholly devoted to God!

Believers who make love and its attendant virtues the hallmark of their lives captivate us. Dr. Karl Menninger of the Menninger Clinic at Topeka, Kansas, endeavored to do just that. A devout Presbyterian, he believed that love is great spiritual energy. He announced that the work of the entire clinic was to be organized around active love by psychiatrists, nurses, electricians, and caretakers. The result: hospitalization time for most patients was cut in half. One woman had been sitting for three years in a rocking chair without saying a word. He called a nurse and said, "Mary, I am giving you Mrs. Brown as your patient. All I am asking you to do is to love her until she gets well." The nurse got a rocking chair just like Mrs. Brown's, sat alongside her, and loved her morning, noon, and night. The third day the patient spoke. In a week she was out of her shell and on the way to health. "Love is medicine for the sickness of mankind," says Dr. Menninger. We must love or perish.[10]

Christian love creates wholeness, the contemporary equivalent of the Hebrew word *shalom*. Shalom suggests harmony with oneself, other people, and the world about us. When we love in the agapic sense we enjoy peace (*eirene* in the Greek New Testament), peace that surpasses all understanding. It involves right relationships, with the goodness of kindness and gentleness as their hallmark. When we love people, we are also able to be patient with them even when circumstances become trying. Spouses, especially as they begin to show the signs of the breakdown of age, parents as they cope with growing children, and anyone who lives with idiosyncratic neighbors, can, and must, learn the beauty of the virtues of peace and patience. It may be hard work, but love has power.

In our contacts with others it may be the kind touch of a loving hand. It is not fortuitous that the New Testament prescribes the laying on of hands in the practice of Christian healing. The gentle touch while praying for the sick and aged communicates what words cannot express. Newborn babies who are deprived of a mother's or a nurse's touch will eventually die. Life atrophies when denied love. Love that is gentle and kind is a spiritual medicine.

Our glutted foster-care agencies grope to meet this basic need. Unfortunately, they are understaffed. The disastrous consequence of the deprivation of love comes out in poignant accounts of abused and abandoned children. At the age when most children are shy of strangers, youngsters who have been ill-treated cling to any caring person who comes near. An adult who momentarily sits is likely to be surrounded, in a matter of seconds, by toddlers wanting to be cuddled. "They just hold on to you," says one volunteer; "even if all they get is a foot, they're happy."

Recent scholarship has discovered that the skin, which was once regarded as little more than a body covering, is actually a significant sense organ. More than half a million sensory fibers flow from the skin through the spinal cord to the brain. As a sensory

---

10. Quoted by E. Stanley Jones, *Conversion* (Nashville, 1959), p. 72.

15

system it is our body's most important organ, a sophisticated communications network in the employ of love.

Increasingly, we are learning the beneficial effects of love. Such traditional risk factors as cholesterol, blood pressure, age, gender, genetics, smoking, diabetes, obesity, and a sedentary life explain only about 50 percent of heart disease. Scientists at Yale University School of Medicine found that the more we are loved and supported, the less coronary arteriosclerosis we will have at angiography, independent of the risk factors just cited. Why some people get heart disease and others do not is still only partially known. Physicians suspect that psychological and spiritual attitudes are important factors. Works such as Dr. Bernie S. Siegel's *Peace, Love and Healing* and his *Love, Medicine and Miracles* document the importance of these factors for health and happiness.[11]

Hostility and cynicism, on the other hand, are toxic. Resentment creates heart trouble. It harms the one that harbors it more than the person to whom it is directed. It is like a coiling cobra's poison. Christian love severs the chain that shackles us to yesterday's hurts.

Isolation and suppression of positive feelings can also lead to illness. Intimacy, social, and spiritual support are healing. If one suffers from high blood pressure, being a member of a church, according to some experts, can significantly decrease the risk of premature heart disease and death.

Adults who have no meaningful human contacts consult therapists, says Reality-psychologist William Glasser, in order to "buy a friend." He is not cynical. He is making a telling point. The art of listening is an act of love.

The need for love can become so excessive, however, that we develop a dependency syndrome. Healthy people need the support of others, but when these feelings become so dominant that they replace confidence in ourselves, we develop a passive-dependent personality disorder. When we think that we cannot live without a significant other nearby, or become depressed when we are separated,

11. Bernie S. Siegel, M.D., *Peace, Love and Healing* (New York: Harper & Row, 1989).

or sometimes become violently angry at being parted, we have become pathologically parasitic. Such feelings often can be traced back to the lack of parental love in infancy or early childhood. Whatever the cause, need-love must be balanced by give-love.

The counterfeit love promoted in superficial love lyrics, movies, TV soaps, pulp magazines, and lurid novels reflects love-yearnings at their lowest level. They never satisfy the deeper hungers of the soul. But to feed your mind with "whatever is true, whatever is honorable, whatever is just, whatever is pure, whatever is pleasing, whatever is commendable" — things that are excellent and worthy of praise (Phil. 4:7, 8) — is the finest advice one can heed.

There is a grace that is common to all, but to live at our best we need more than love in general; we need the agapic resources of the Spirit. The Bible, the devotional literature it inspires, biographies that recount experiences of grace, and music written for the glory of God (as J. S. Bach inscribed his manuscripts) carry us close to the heart of God and enable us to become agapic agents of the Spirit.

The Impartiality of Love

Unlike Aristotle and other Greek philosophers who taught that one should love only the attractive and the lovable, Jesus taught us that love does not discriminate. We are to love the educated and the uneducated, the rich and the poor, the socially prominent and the outcasts, the good and the bad, friends and even our enemies. In this way, we show that we are children of God, "for he makes his sun rise on the evil and the good, and sends rain on the righteous and on the unrighteous" (Matt. 5:45). Christian love impartially promotes the highest good of others.

We have developed, quite legitimately, a deep compassion for the poor. Their plight is tragic, especially in the bowels of our great cities and in the drought-stricken and violence-ridden countries of the world. The benevolent flow of healing drugs, food, and the basic necessities of life to these suffering folk is so well-publicized that it needs no elaboration here.

We do well to recognize that the rich also need our love. In Grand

Rapids, Michigan, a Roman Catholic priest from blue-collar Brooklyn knows how to live with the poor and downtrodden, but he has also rubbed elbows with such prominent people as Margaret Thatcher, Jean Kilpatrick, and William Buckley. He faithfully ministers to his flock at the Catholic Information Center, and in his free time he heads an organization that ministers to the wealthy. He knows the need of the impoverished, he has stuck ice packs under the armpits of overdosing people in Greenwich Village, and has had AIDS patients vomit on him — experiences that require the patience and kindness that only the Spirit can inspire. But in order to attend to the needs of the poor, he says: "We must also have the freedom to create wealth." The inner-city blight is no better today, despite massive federal aid and intervention. Those left behind by welfare cuts are being cared for by the church, not the government. Religious folk, he believes, must wake up to the creative possibilities of a free market. "I think I have found a niche," he says; "it has been astounding."

A church in suburban Minneapolis has an active ministry to executives. When Keith Tussing, one of its associate ministers, stepped into one of Minneapolis's largest department stores, he wasn't going shopping. He was making a parish call on the company's chief executive officer. And Arthur A. Rouner, Jr., the senior minister, started a six o'clock religious power breakfast called "The Businessmen's Round Table." "Business leaders have great impact on others' lives," he explains, "and they need help to make ethical decisions in the marketplace."

In instances such as these, Christlike love reaches out to "the poor [whom] you always have with you," as Jesus sadly remarked (John 12:8, Revised Standard Version), and to the upper class whose needs are spiritual needs.

In a distinctive way, Covenant House and other spiritual networks in our large cities from New York to Los Angeles seek out runaways and lonely prostitutes working the main streets, offering them sandwiches, coffee, and a place of acceptance and genuine love. Many are reclaimed; because a caring community shows love and concern, some return to the homes from which they had run away.

Such love is not soft and sentimental; it is sturdy and strong, fortified by the Spirit. It is working with the Comforter, as Jesus called the Holy Spirit, the one who stands alongside of us and in us, bracing us in the work of compassion. Such love is realistic and rigorous. Pallid platitudes trivialize love, as does the thin optimism of old-fashioned liberals and the syrupiness of pietists. Love dynamized by the Spirit also supplants manipulation; it quietly proffers the spiritual fruit of kindness and generous goodness.

Agapic love gives to others because of their needs; it is not something expressed to benefit ourselves. It is identification with the interests of another, writes Karl Barth, "in utter independence of the question of his attractiveness." Gene Outka, in devoting an authoritatively scholarly work entirely to agape, describes it with such shorthand phrases as "equal regard" and "self-sacrifice."[12] The apostle Paul had been a terrorist. A passionate persecutor of new disciples of Jesus, he drove himself from city to city, harrying them out of hiding to face torture and possible death. But in a dramatic moment of blinding insight on the Damascus Road he saw Jesus in a new light. Love replaced hostility as the master motive of his life. "I now live," he declared, "by faith in the Son of God, who loved me and gave himself for me" (Gal. 2:20).

The Pull of Love

The awareness of our need to love and to be loved arises out of a variety of experiences. For some of us it is an awakening in our own minds; for others it is a recognition of the world's great need.

---

12. Barth, IV/2, p. 745. Gene Outka, *Agape: An Ethical Analysis* (New Haven: Yale University Press, 1972), pp. 9-34. Barth put it succinctly in stating that it is identification with the interests of others. It shows neither favoritism nor aversion. It is personal love for another who is never a mere "It," a mere thing. It is never elitist, therefore. Outka brings into his scholarly net a representative group of thinkers that includes M. C. D'Arcy, Søren Kierkegaard, Reinhold Niebuhr, Anders Nygren, Paul Ramsey, Karl Barth, Emil Brunner, and Paul Tillich. In a more recent study, he extends his discussion of impartiality between self and others by emphasizing its universality in the sense that it includes regard for the self and all other humans. Gene Outka, "Universal Love and Impartiality," in Edmund N. Santurri and William Werpehowski, eds., *The Love Commandments: Essays in Christian Ethics and Moral Philosophy* (Washington, D.C.: Georgetown University Press, 1992).

I have often wondered what it was that sparked the desire in my young mind to become a minister. I came from a very religious home. God was very real to us. But social and psychological conditioning also did its part, I am sure. The ministers who called frequently at our home, often just to chat at the end of the day, were robust and good men who loved and were loved by my family. They were men whose lives reflected the Christlike virtues. They made a difference in the congregation and in the community. Subconsciously, they doubtlessly created a deep impression on me.

I vividly recall a day in the fourth grade in our public school when, perhaps to keep me out of mischief after I had finished the prescribed assignment, my teacher set me to drawing pictures of birds and animals. These she thumbtacked to the corkboard above the blackboard. Commenting on my "art" one day, in the way teachers do, she said, "Seymour, if you don't become an artist or an architect someday I will be disappointed." Without hesitating I replied, "No, Miss Johnson, I'm going to be a minister." She was obviously surprised; but she remembered it. Years later she encountered my mother in a supermarket, asked what I was doing, and when told that I was studying theology in a seminary, she recounted the incident, much to the amazement of my mother!

Looking back on it now, I am confident that besides growing up in a deeply religious home and in a caring church, it was a mix of wanting to serve God in what I considered a high calling, as well as wanting to love and be loved, that influenced my vocational choice.

Many psychiatrists enter their profession, a practitioner friend confided to me at a party one night, in order to solve their own neuroses, an experience that in turn leads them to be a greater help to others. Why do people choose to become teachers, physicians, scientists, or social workers? The specific reasons are many and varied, but in many instances the motivating desire is to love and be loved.

A violent thunderstorm drove the terrified Martin Luther into a monastery to save his soul. He desperately needed love. There, through much anguish, self-abnegation, counseling by superiors, reading the church fathers, and study of the Scriptures, he finally emerged into the sunlight of the grace of God. God used him to spark the long-sought reformation of the Church and to bless succeeding generations with the good news of the glad God.

Others have come to the conviction that they needed to love more, not because of the winsomeness of others, but through an awareness of the world's great need. An American soldier pointedly inscribed this resolution in his war journal: "Last night I lay awake and thought of all the inhumanity of it, the beastliness of the war. I remembered all the brutal things I had seen since I came overseas. . . . This morning when I rose, tired and distraught from death, I knew that in order to survive this time I must love more. There is no other way."[13]

Love for others sent Albert Schweitzer, with doctorates in medicine, music, and theology, to minister to the natives of Africa. It took hold of Charles Colson, of Watergate notoriety, and sent him back to prison after his own release to minister to the inmates through his Prison Fellowship. It led Jimmy and Rosalyn Carter, after the presidency, to take up hammers to work for Habitat for Humanity and establish the Carter Center. Such unselfish work for others brings joy and peace to their own hearts, and their gentle kindness and faithful goodness are an inspiration to others.

There is an art to loving, it is said. There is, but it is more than an art. An art, like a skill, can be learned. If the practice of loving were only a matter of mastery, we could achieve it as we do many skills. We would do our research, learn by trial and error, and eventually succeed in the enterprise.

When I built a boathouse at our island cottage on the coast of Maine many years ago, I knew nothing about carpentry. But I went to the bookstore, purchased a builder's manual, studied it carefully, and went to work. The end-product was an amateurish structure, to be sure, but I learned in the process how to build. So, some suggest, we build love-relationships. Life is education. We learn by doing. What makes a good musician? Or an artist? Or a poet? Practice. In the same way, they say, we develop the art of loving.

Practice should not be minimized. Christlike virtues do develop

13. Robert J. McCracken, "Commitment Unlimited," in Clyde E. Fant, Jr., and William A. Pinson, Jr., eds., *Twenty Centuries of Great Preaching* (Waco: Word Books, 1971), vol. 12, p. 89.

and grow by practice. Physical exercise makes strong bodies; spiritual exercise makes good character. We become more patient by cultivating patience. Kindness and gentleness become more natural to us when we endeavor to make them regular expressions of our love. Self-control obviously requires great discipline. Every fruit of the Spirit grows by being nurtured. Biblical counsel and encouragement would be meaningless unless they were put into practice. C. S. Lewis remarked that even when certain personality traits do not come naturally we should "act as if," and eventually they will become a part of us.

The good news of the gospel, however, is that God has given us more than a striver's manual. We do not create the fruit of the Spirit solely by our own efforts. We nurture it with the grace of God, but it is produced within us by the Spirit. To nurture what the Spirit creates is hard work. It requires disciplined wills, minds, and affections. The biblical word for the unity of all these faculties is heart. "Keep your heart with all diligence," says Proverbs, "for from it flow the springs of life" (Prov. 4:23).

To do this, we need help. We need the grace that empowers us to live redemptively. The world has never been a friend to grace and, living in an increasingly secularized world, we desperately need this gift of God. Grace liberates us to love and bear the spiritual fruit that reflects the personality of Jesus.

We have come to associate the word *grace* with the dramatic experience of John Newton. Converted from being a slave-ship captain, one of the most inhumane vocations, he became a compelling and distinguished minister in the evangelical curacy of the church at Olney, England. Out of the joyous experience of liberation came what is perhaps the best known of his three hundred hymns, "Amazing Grace! (how sweet the sound!) that saved a wretch like me! I once was lost, but now am found, was blind and now I see." Grace has brought me safe thus far, he wrote, and grace will lead me home.

The Prism of Love

Liberated from the "works of the flesh," those who seek to be more like Jesus show their gratitude by nurturing the "fruit of the Spirit."

Love, the preeminent fruit, expresses itself in a plethora of other Christlike virtues. Like a many-faceted diamond that prismatically refracts its light, we reflect the Christ-life in human experiences.

We can become spiritually fruitful, however, only by being intimately linked with Jesus as the true vine. United with him by faith, we produce the unbroken cluster of virtues: love, joy, peace, patience, kindness, generosity, faithfulness, gentleness, and self-control (Gal. 5:22-23).[14] If we lack love, the whole cluster withers.

Some categorize these virtues into three groups: love, joy, and peace relating to God; patience, kindness, generosity, and loyalty relating to our fellow human beings; and gentleness and self-control relating to ourselves. This schematization is artificial and misleading. All are ethical qualities that refer to every human relationship, and all emanate from love.

As we trace our spiritual journey through life in the following chapters, we will note how the living Christ progressively nurtures the fruit of his Spirit. He does this in friendship, romance, marriage, family life, church fellowship, neighborliness, and world citizenship. The good news of the glad God is that the Spirit can refashion us into winsome Christians who reflect the grace of our Lord Jesus Christ, the love of God, and the fellowship of the Spirit.

14. Hendrikus Berkhof discusses at length the progress in the struggle for renewal. "The same Paul who speaks so much about struggle knows also of a growing, a going forward, a pressing on, a straining toward what lies ahead, a growing stronger. Some passages in the New Testament even seem to say that in this life conformity with Christ lies within the believer's reach." He cites John Calvin, who writes: "with continuous effort striving toward this end: that we may surpass ourselves in goodness until we attain to goodness itself." The fruits of faith, writes Berkhof, "are such that they can be visible to the believer himself and to the outside world." *Christian Faith: An Introduction to the Study of Faith* (Grand Rapids: William B. Eerdmans Publishing Co., 1979), pp. 471, 472, 474.

CHAPTER TWO

A Faithful Friend

Napoleon Bonaparte once said, "I love nobody, not even my brothers." Little wonder, then, that at the end of his life, on the desolate island to which he had been banished, he lamented, "I wonder if there is anyone in the world who really loves me." But we are not surprised. His ruthless egomania had created a ghastly trail of death in homes and cities and nations, and rivers of blood that flowed from the Pyrenees to Moscow.

Everyone wants a friend. But the only way to have a friend is to be one. Some people find it easy to make friends; others find it more difficult. It depends on the way you give yourself and on the capacity of others to receive your love. Friendship at its best is a matter of spirit. It is not created by wealth or intelligence or looks; nor is it confined to certain personality traits — whether one is an extrovert, for example, or an introvert. You may be the life of the party but still be lonely, whereas someone more reticent may be genuinely loved because she is a sensitive and caring person. The magnetic qualities of friendship vary as widely as persons differ among themselves.

In our fast-paced, technocratic society we hunger for warm personal attachment. Thoughtful writers throughout the ages have praised it. English poet and critic Samuel Coleridge once wrote to his young godson that among life's greatest blessings was to be a Christian and to have kind, faithful, and loving friends. Most of us would agree. A friend is like a second self. A friend loves me for myself, not my circumstances. Genuine friends enrich life, making prosperity brighter and adversity lighter. A faithful friend is the medicine of life. Yet, such friends are like melons: you must try a hundred to find one that is good. Aristotle thought that without friends, though one had all other possessions, one would choose not to live.

The Epitome of Friendship

The supreme virtues of Christian friendship (*philia*) are faithfulness, kindness, and patience, qualities that make friendship a joy.

In our quest to be more like Jesus in our friendships, we have a perfect example of friendship in Jesus himself. Being human, and sharing our common lot, he also needed, quite obviously, the companionship and love of friends. He was a friend to a broad range of people. He selected certain people, however, to be his favorites. Among his best friends, whom we might call retreat friends, were Mary, Martha, and their brother Lazarus. Their home was a haven of rest in his busy ministry, a sanctuary where he could relax from the pressures of his mission. Many of us have known such spiritual oases where the strains of public life are assuaged by the pleasures of propinquity.

One day a message came to Jesus that Lazarus had fallen ill and died. After pausing for a day or two, Jesus announced that he was going to "awaken him." As he stood outside the sepulcher he "began to weep," and the crowd surrounding the tomb murmured, "See how he loved him!" (John 11:11, 36). Then with resolute voice he cried, "Lazarus, come out!" As he emerged from the tomb Jesus commanded them to unwrap him, and he was restored to their fellowship. His friendship for Lazarus was more than the hail-fellow-well-met of our weekly service club luncheons. In his intimacy with Lazarus, Mary, and Martha, "deep called to deep."

Jesus also befriended the outcasts of society. His sociability with internal revenue agents of the Roman government elicited the sneers of the religious establishment that he was "a friend of tax collectors and sinners." The self-styled religious elite did not understand that his redemptive mission was for all, including such social fringe

25

people as the tree-climbing extortioner Zaccheus. Taking leave of him, Jesus said, "Today salvation has come to this house." At another time a sinful "woman in the city" quietly slipped into a dinner at a prominent Pharisee's house and anointed his feet with expensive perfume. The host was mortified, but with gentle kindness Jesus declared: "Her sins, which were many, have been forgiven; hence she has shown great love" (Luke 7:34; 19:9; 7:36-47).

His most intimate friends were the twelve disciples whom he chose "to be with him." He opened his heart to them, revealing as much as they had the capacity to comprehend at the time. In the upper room before his crucifixion, as they had the last supper together, Jesus said to his disciples, "I have called you friends, because I have made known to you everything that I have heard from my Father" (John 15:15). Of the twelve, three were an inner circle: Peter, James, and John; and among these John, doubtless because of his dedication and loyalty, was called "the disciple whom Jesus loved." John was the only one at first to enter the courtyard of the high priest when Jesus was arrested, and John was the only one who stood at the foot of the cross alongside Mary the mother of Jesus, to whom Jesus said, "Woman, here is your son," and to John, "Here is your mother" (John 19:26-27).

Even when Judas, disillusioned because Jesus did not fulfill his hopes for a political Messiah, led a band of brigands to the garden of Gethsemane to apprehend him, Jesus greeted him, "Friend . . ." (Matt. 26:50). How heartbreaking, commented Kierkegaard, "that Christ, who is the teacher of love, is betrayed — with a kiss."

The Way Friendship Grows

Our very first associations with others are with those who parent us, especially mothers. But those associations are involuntary; we did not choose to be born. Our friendships, however, are voluntary choices. Already as toddlers we learn to get on in life as we respond positively to others.

It was always a fascinating experience for me to leave my church study and visit that part of the parish house where we maintained a preschool for the children of the community. There, often because of the prickles and peculiarities of temperament, skilled directors and teachers mediated occasional disputes, perhaps over the possession of a toy. The children learned something that some adults never learn, that you do not pick up your marbles and run if you don't get your way. They learned how to be tolerant, patient, and kind.

The spiral of socialization widened as our parents enrolled us in schools. In Sunday School, we learned to sing "Jesus loves me," but also "Jesus loves all the children of the world." Where day schools became educational jungles, parents often chose private schools for their children's best development. One of the main reasons why parents prefer private to public education, writes Episcopalian law professor Stephen L. Carter in his provocative book *The Culture of Disbelief*, "is our determination to educate our children in an environment that celebrates, not demeans, their religious beliefs, one that is responsive to our concerns about morality and parental responsibility."[1] Moral and spiritual values are matters of importance in an increasingly secularized society. The friendships we form in early school life are crucial for our spiritual and psychological development.

Family life is also inestimably important in helping children and young people form good friendships. Christian parents talk with their children about the right and wrong of things, and about where to draw the line in ambiguous situations. Goodness is encouraged as a Christlike virtue. When as teenagers we cut the psychological umbilical cord and became involved in social relationships with which we did not know how to cope, we subconsciously wanted our parents to help us to say "No." We were also encouraged to participate in youth fellowships at church. As I write this, memories come flooding back of the enriching times we shared together in the days of ardent youth.

In many of our homes there was, to adapt a phrase of the apostle Paul, "the church in [our] house" (Philem. 1:2; Rom. 16:5; I Cor. 16:17), with family devotions a regular part of the daily

1. Stephen L. Carter, *The Culture of Disbelief* (New York: Harper Collins, Basic Books, 1993), p. 185.

schedule. On the subject of friendship, I vividly recall readings with comments from the Proverbs, in which the wise man counsels that companions can be either constructive or detrimental, that immoral pleasures are frighteningly dangerous, that promiscuity is foolish and leads to disease, social stigma, a bad conscience, as well as the loss of wealth and self-respect. Volatile tempers are a no-no, and flying into a rage to gain selfish advantage is injudicious, for "one who is slow to anger is better than the mighty" (Prov. 16:32). Long before Paul wrote of the conflict between the flesh and the spirit, the Proverbs writer extolled the virtues of goodness, patience, loyalty, and self-control.

The good friendships we thus formed also taught us a great deal about ourselves. Our friends were mirrors that enabled us to see our likable and unlikable traits. We learned that attitudes and actions that were not winsome often left strained or fractured relationships in their wake. We learned to accentuate the positive and eliminate the negative.

The Anatomy of *Philia*

The love of friendship is something we experience, not something that we spend a great deal of time discussing or writing about. And yet there are certain attributes of friendship that, when noted, make friendship better understood.

1. Friendship is first of all selective. We chose this person to be our friend, not that one. Ben Jonson was right: "True happiness consists not in the multitude of friends, but in the worth and the choice."[2]

For a Christian, there is something mystical about the forces of attraction. "A secret master of ceremonies has been at work," according to C. S. Lewis. "Just as Christ said to his disciples, 'You have not chosen me but I have chosen you,' so he can truly say to every group of Christian friends, 'You have not chosen one another but I have

---

2. *Cynthia's Revels* (1600), act 3, scene 2; quoted in John Bartlett, *Familiar Quotations* (Boston: Little, Brown, 1980), p. 255.

chosen you for one another.'"[3] The observation is unique, based not on rational grounds, but on faith. To be sure, our own wills, minds, and emotions, activated by the Spirit, also certainly influence our choice of friends.

However discriminating we may be in the choice of a friend, no one person can fulfill all our needs, for we encompass many interests. To be a friend to more than one person avoids the peril of overcrowding. Clutching behavior overloads a relationship. Beware of the person who feels threatened by your relationship with others, for jealousy is a green-eyed monster that has ruined many a friendship.

2. Secondly, friendship is enhanced by the enjoyment of mutual interests. "Friendship of a kind that cannot easily be reversed tomorrow," writes Barbara Tuchman, "must have its roots in common interests and shared beliefs." At its best it is shared spirituality. Unlike lovers who delight in looking at each other, friends are always looking away at something they enjoy in common — a concert, a play, the ballet, golf, or tennis (or TV football!). We delight in conversation about the little things of life, but the more profound the friendship the more we gravitate toward matters of significance such as religion, theology, philosophy, history, the arts, politics, or the economy. Mutuality, however, should not cancel out individuality. "Iron sharpens iron, and one person sharpens the wits of another" (Prov. 27:17).

Mutuality is important, for through it we enrich each other's lives. "Love does not insist on its own way." Self-centeredness is a blight. Opportunism and manipulation are fatal. Aristotle spoke of three kinds of friends: utility friends, pleasure friends, and genuine friends. I am sure that all three elements blend in any worthwhile friendship, but when the first two become dominant the relationship is headed for trouble. Friends are obviously useful to each other, and they do give each other pleasure. If, however, someone is a friend only because of what she can get from you, or the pleasure you can afford her, she is using you. If we call on friends only when we need them, the relationship disintegrates into a quid pro quo of bartered

3. C. S. Lewis, *The Four Loves* (New York: Harcourt, Brace and Company, 1960).

assistance. An executive, told that a friend had telephoned, responded, "I wonder what she wants now." That is utilitarianism.

People of position, power, and possessions must ever be on guard against opportunists. "Wealth brings many friends . . . many seek the favor of a generous man, and everyone is the friend of a man who gives gifts" (Prov. 19:4, 6). People who cultivate friendly relations with others as long as it promotes their interests and jettison the relationship when the person is no longer needed are self-centered, opportunistic, and miss the joy of loyalty.

3. Friendship, moreover, is voluntary. Unlike marriage, we do not solemnize our relationship with a special ceremony and vow lasting friendship. Life's changing circumstances, a move to a more distant place, or the development of new interests may cause a friendship to gradually fade. Shallow and fickle persons will be readily influenced by such alterations. People of character, however, who invest a great deal of energy, time, and personality in the relationship often find that friendship does not alter when it alteration finds. They contrive ways to maintain friendship. As we shall see, forever-friends do exist.

The Felicity of Faithfulness

Some claim that the voluntary nature of friendship precludes faithfulness. Yet life and history furnish us with many examples of loyal friendship, of relationships that grow and deepen throughout the years.

One of the most notable is that of David and Jonathan. David was a simple shepherd boy who became a hero by felling with a slingshot the Philistine giant Goliath who had been terrorizing the army of Israel. He had learned the art of using this simple weapon while protecting his father's sheep from wild animals. The day David saved the army of Israel, Jonathan, King Saul's son, was "bound to the soul of David, and Jonathan loved him as his own soul" (I Sam. 18:1, 3, 4). Jonathan loved David so much that he made a covenant with him, and gave him his robe, his armor, and his weapons. Though Jonathan was heir to the throne, David's nobility, patriotism, and character led them to become fast friends. Jonathan, in a sense, had everything to lose by making David a friend, but they were loyal friends because they admired and respected each other and ministered to each other's needs. David's heroic exploit promoted his candidacy for king among the populace, but it did not jeopardize their friendship.

David's life, from that time on, was at risk. Saul's manic temperament tried to destroy him. More than once, when summoned to play his harp to calm Saul's unruly spirit, he had to dodge Saul's spear as he tried to pin him to the wall. But Jonathan, at the risk of his own life, contrived ways to protect him, so deep was their friendship.

In a later battle with the Philistines, the tide turned against Israel and Jonathan was killed. David's poignant lamentation says it all:

> Jonathan lies slain upon your high places.
>   I am distressed for you, my brother Jonathan;
> greatly beloved were you to me;
>   your love to me was wonderful,
>   passing the love of women. (II Sam. 1:25b-26)

Although David did become king by popular acclaim, he never forgot Jonathan. Aware that had it not been for the loyal love of his friend he never would have risen from humble circumstances to the throne of Israel, he asked, "Is there still anyone left of the house of Saul to whom I may show kindness for Jonathan's sake?" (II Sam. 9:1). A search discovered Mephibosheth, Jonathan's handicapped son, crippled in both feet. To him David restored the lands that belonged to Saul. He also insisted that Mephibosheth should always eat at the royal table "for Jonathan's sake." His friendship had a moral memory.

David and Jonathan did not play at friendship. Theirs is a notable example of kindness and faithfulness through trying circumstances. Their friendship had the character of "a true friend [who] sticks closer than one's nearest kin" (Prov. 18:24).

Not all friendships are that virtuous. Consider by contrast that of David's oldest son Amnon who became infatuated with his beautiful half-sister, Tamar. His frustrated passion so tormented him that

31

he became ill. "But Amnon had a friend whose name was Jonadab . . . a very crafty man," who counseled Amnon on how to lure Tamar into his house under the guise of preparing a meal for him, and then seducing her. So Tamar came to feed him, but his libidinous hunger was stronger than his appetite for cakes, and, against her anguished protests, he raped her. The predictable psychological reaction was immediate. Satisfied lust turned to loathing, and he ordered her to "Get out!" (II Sam. 13:1-15).

"Making love," as psychiatrists point out, is not necessarily an act of love. M. Scott Peck describes it as the collapse of ego boundaries in a moment of ecstasy, but as soon as the ego boundaries have snapped back into place, one becomes devoid of every shred of affection.[4]

"Amnon had a friend." But what a friend! Good friends make good people better; bad friends make bad people worse. Better to choose solitude with a good conscience than a friend who leads us to compromise our character.

The friends of Job also give us a glimpse into the complexities of friendship. Their visit to comfort Job in the time of his calamities was well-intentioned but pathetically misinformed. Their thinking was captive to the religious thought of the time: God rewarded good and punished evil. In losing his possessions, his children, and his health, Job was, so they charged, obviously receiving just chastisement for some evil he had committed. With lengthy speeches they endeavored to induce Job to acknowledge his sin, confess it, and be healed. "Job's friends do everything in their power to contribute to his moral torments," writes psychologist C. J. Jung, "and instead of giving him . . . their warm-hearted support, they moralize in an all-too-human manner, that is, in the stupidest fashion imaginable, and 'fill him with wrinkles.'"[5] Distraught, Job lamented: "In trouble

4. M. Scott Peck, *The Road Less Traveled: A New Psychology of Love, Traditional Values and Spiritual Growth* (New York: Simon & Schuster, 1978).

5. C. J. Jung, *Answer to Job,* trans. R. F. C. Hull (Princeton: Princeton University Press, 1973), p. 14.

like this I need loyal friends, whether I have forsaken God or not. . . . Have pity on me, O you my friends" (Job 6:14; 19:21).

They had come to "comfort and console" Job in his afflictions, but even though for seven days they sat dumbfounded at the pathos of Job's affliction, when they began to speak they showed everything but patience, kindness, and gentleness. They spoke with the rigid theological orthodoxy of their time. They had not yet come to understand the kindness and gentleness of agapic love.

The story is a theodicy, a treatise written to show that, however enigmatic and mysterious the ways of divine providence, God did not forsake Job. The appropriate human response to God's majestic omnipotence is humble faith. Job's friends were rebuked, and God restored to Job double of all that he had lost.

The vast difference between the friendship of David and Jonathan and that of Job and his friends graphically points up the felicity of faithfulness in friendship. The apocryphal writer of *Ecclesiasticus* (or *The Wisdom of Jesus Son of Sirach*) extols its virtue.

> Faithful friends are a sturdy shelter:
> > whoever finds one has found a treasure.
> Faithful friends are beyond price;
> > no amount can balance their worth.
> Faithful friends are life-saving medicine;
> > and those who fear the Lord will find them.
> Those who fear the Lord direct their friendship aright;
> > for as they are, so are their neighbors also. (Ecclus. 6:14-17)

The Many Faces of Friendship

"I have so many friends," a church secretary confided in me one day. "I have music friends, intellectual friends, spiritual friends, hobby and craft friends, as well as a friend who walks the beach and takes bicycle rides with me." She is an enviable person.

During the span of a lifetime we enjoy a spectrum of diverse friendships. First there are chums, neighborhood playmates. By the time we get to college, we have developed relationships that are deeper in spirit. As adults, we have many casual friends, people with whom we visit only occasionally — often at parties, perhaps a big bash around the Christmas holidays (a convenient way to repay our social obligations in one swoop!). We also become club friends at our weekly service organizations, or at town and country clubs. Professionally, we enjoy collegial friends, perhaps in intimate groups where we take turns presenting and discussing papers on subjects such as theology, medicine, dentistry, law, science, or business, exercises that enable us to pursue our work more knowledgeably and effectively.

Cross-sex friends are common as women increasingly enter vocations and professions that traditionally have been held by men. Some, like C. S. Lewis in his earlier days, could not envision the possibility of such relationships existing without becoming erotic, but if Jesus and the apostle Paul could do so licitly, by the grace of the Spirit we can do so also, and myriad instances confirm the possibility.

A disturbing side effect of gender liberation for some business and professional women, however, is "corporation casualty." In the cross-sexual mix, when success comes to one and not to the other, friendship-casualty is sometimes the result. As women vie with women and women with men, much as men compete, the sisterhood finds that rivalry and envy become the price of success. As they rise in the corporate power structure, some discover to their dismay that success with its attendant recognition and power deals a death blow to earlier friendships. Yet not all are "barracudas" maneuvering their way around corporate reefs; some within the competitive complexity of the same company continue to be best friends. There may be rapier thrusts, but also hugs. The apostolic advice is healthy: "outdo one another in showing honor" (Rom. 12:10).

A number of commentators note the difference in gender language and style of leadership as women bosses relate to their secretaries. They are more egalitarian and less demanding. Women often use language that to them seems more polite and appropriate but which to men seems to reveal a measure of insecurity. New arrangements call for new understandings between men and women. Men and women need not speak the same way, but understand each other they should. When a woman tells a man about a problem, she may receive a barrage of advice that she may interpret as criticism, whereas the man may think that he is being helpful.[6]

People who have church friends are best equipped to meet the social challenges of life. Spirituality gives depth and significance to life. Over the years women especially have found rewarding associations in their guilds and circles. "Never underestimate the importance of the guilds!" my wife once counseled me. The members bond in heart and service, rejoice in each other's happiness, encourage each other in trial and bereavement, and stand with each other in times of need.

Best of all are close friends. It is said of Dag Hammarskjöld, thrice-elected Secretary-General of the United Nations, a deeply religious man and a lifelong bachelor, that he did not have numerous friends, but that those he had he treasured greatly.

It seems that today a great deal of close friendship is created in playing golf. For most, the all-consuming interest in the sport is trying to get a little white ball into a little round hole with the fewest strokes. For several years, until the pressure of working on a Ph.D. program claimed much of my time, I found it to be an enjoyable and healthful hobby. Friends keep trying to induce me to take it up again. They make it sound alluring. They talk about teeing up with friends, enjoying intimate conversation in the open air on a luxuriant green, bantering over shanked chips, approach shots that drop sweetly onto the green, difficult putts that lip the hole and roll inches beyond, an occasional slice, flubbed shots and yipped putts, and then refreshment and more friendly conversation in the clubhouse before they head home. Rusty as I am, I am tempted to take it up again, for not only according to Paul does "bodily fitness have a certain value," but intimate friendship is important.

It takes a great deal of time and trust, as well as grace, to grow

---

6. Among the many books dealing with the subject, see such popular works as Deborah Tannen, *Talking from 9 to 5: How Women's and Men's Styles Affect Who Gets Heard, Who Gets Credit, and What Gets Done at Work* (New York: William Morrow, 1994); *You Just Don't Understand: Women and Men in Conversation* (New York: Ballantine Books, 1990); and John Gray, *Men Are from Mars, Women Are from Venus* (New York: Harper Collins, 1993).

deep and loyal friendship. We treasure friendships that we formed many years ago, warm friendships that time and its passing do not diminish. Such friendships engage our total personalities. They have character because we share spiritual and social values. My wife and I continue to enjoy the friendship of wonderful people whom we met years ago. We eagerly look forward to being with them even though we have scattered to widely separated parts of the country. We celebrate birthdays and anniversaries, rejoice in their joys, and feel their hurts in our hearts. Since "you are what you remember," it is a blessed thing to enrich life by continually adding new experiences to the bank of memory. "The capacity to form and maintain durable relationships," writes senior research professor Wayne Oates, "is a mark of maturity and a test of character."[7]

Several former parishioners, as well as college and seminary classmates, are among my most treasured friends. We may see each other only occasionally, but how we enjoy those times together! One special friend recently experienced a health crisis involving a heart condition and a crippling stroke that affected his hands, feet, and eyes. But, as in the case of the apostle Paul's thorn in the flesh, this trial revealed his incredible faith and strong will. A magazine article about his return to health was entitled "The Walking Miracle." Though he has suffered Job-like trials, he retains an infectious sense of humor. He is one of the finest Christians I know, and I am happy we are friends.

Martin Buber, in his *I and Thou,* casts an illuminating ray on the special quality of loyal friendship. Whenever an I meets a Thou, he writes, something of the I goes into the Thou, and something of the Thou goes into the I, so that the I is no longer the same I and the Thou is no longer the same Thou, for the Thou has I in it and the I has Thou in it. This relationship is vastly different from our relationship with an It, for an It can never respond as an I or a Thou. A computer, for instance, can never become a friend.

A friend once received a note that said, "I feel so richly blessed to have a friend who stands beside me, who takes an interest in the things I do, a friend whose strength I lean upon, whose wisdom

7. Wayne E. Oates, "A Long Friendship," *The Christian Century,* January 19, 1994, p. 38.

helps to guide me, whose faith and trust will always see me through." She concluded, "I feel so blessed to have a friend who adds such joy to living, and I just pray that I'll be worthy of this friend who is so good to me, so thoughtful, kind and giving. This friend I'll always treasure, always love."

A faithful friend is one of life's choice blessings.

Kindness in Friendship

True friends know how to reach out to relieve in times of distress and how to reach out to receive in times of need. Friendship-love is two-sided: it is give-love and need-love. In a special way it is colored by the personality of Jesus.

Reach Out to Relieve

1. Real friends reach out to befriend the lonely. Loneliness, said John Milton, "is the first thing which God nam'd not good." It has become one of the most painful human wounds in today's society, writes Fr. Henri Nouwen. People who as children were laughed at because of the way they dressed, who as teenagers were the last ones chosen on a softball team, who as students were not selected for the debate team or the choir, who in business feel their personalities are out of sync with their associates' social mores can feel dreadfully lonely. Competition and rivalry create a sense of isolation. Even at parties they can at times feel utterly alone. Deep down they cannot escape the feeling that nobody cares.

Loneliness, of course, must not be confused with solitude. Solitude can be a fulfilling experience, an experience a busy person welcomes in order to get in touch with one's real self and God. Jesus, for example, frequently retreated to the mountaintop to commune with God. In solitude we review life's blessings and accomplishments, relive the happy moments that are stored in the vault of memory, and project plans for the future. A lonely person, on the other hand, frequently falls into the trap of recalling the faults and failures of the past and lets the mind gravitate toward guilt rather than grace.

People who find it difficult to adapt to an uncongenial environment do all sorts of things to escape the painful experience. The story is told of a British army officer some years ago who sat drinking at a bar. He had consumed a considerable quantity of liquor. A fellow officer suggested that he was drinking too much. As he lifted his glass he replied, "This is the fastest way out of India!" Others resort to overeating, drugs, illicit sex, even suicide.

The Bible vividly describes the feeling that psychology has only recently explored in depth. David, penitent for his sin, lamented: "My friends and companions stand aloof from my affliction, and my neighbors stand afar off" (Ps. 38:11). He felt like an ostracized leper, a quarantined transgressor, a social outcast, alone and forsaken.

Chronic feelings of loneliness and inability to relate to others can often be traced to early family rejection. Divorce, business moves, and early retirement can also create a sense of loss akin to bereavement. The experience is rendered even more acute by our impersonal technological society.

When you befriend the lonely, however, recognize that they have feelings that they must first work through on their own. Intrusiveness is counterproductive. But be available. Stand alongside. Do not get in the way. Never befriend another because it makes you feel good, or because you feel you are fulfilling an obligation and a duty. Keep the friend's needs uppermost in your mind. Only then can you gently move closer step by step.

Also ask yourself a few questions. Am I the kind of person who is needed? Do our personalities resonate at this point? Do I have the spiritual and psychological resources to sustain myself in the process? Or am I relying on my own battery power? M. Scott Peck, a Christian psychiatrist, encourages us in this in his book *Further Along the Road Less Traveled*: "As we grow spiritually, we can take on more and more of other people's pain, and then the most amazing thing happens. The more pain you are willing to take on, the more joy you will also begin to feel. And this is truly good news of what makes the journey ultimately worthwhile."[8] God can do wonderful things for your

8. M. Scott Peck, *Further Along the Road Less Traveled: The Unending Journey Toward Spiritual Growth* (New York: Simon & Schuster, 1993), p. 28.

friend when you rely not on yourself alone, but on the grace and wisdom and tact that the Holy Spirit inspires.

It is noteworthy that Dr. Peck speaks of the spiritual joy that you will feel in ministering to another. Is this what Jesus felt when he found joy in being busy doing God's will, and being active in God's service? I believe it is. This is what he meant when he said, "My joy I give unto you."

2. Befriend the bereaved. When we go through painful surgery, the healing process takes time. What surgery is to the body the loss of a dear one is to the soul and psyche of the bereaved. At such a time an understanding friend can be medicine for the soul.

Jesus showed deep empathy for his grieving friends Mary and Martha when their brother Lazarus died. At his graveside he wept (John 11:1-43). On another occasion he was met at the gate of the town of Nain by a funeral procession of a young man who was his mother's only son, and she was a widow. When the Lord saw her, he had compassion for her and said, "Do not weep." He raised the young man to new life (Luke 7:11-17). Jesus seemed to have a special and tender concern for women. Jesus went about doing good. He epitomized gentle kindness.

Grief involves acute psychological pain and emotional turmoil. When I was a young minister, Dr. Elisabeth Kübler-Ross enhanced my understanding of grief as she outlined the stages she had observed in dying patients and their survivors. She spoke of the process of denial, anger, bargaining, depression, and, finally, acceptance. Her schematization was helpful, but the process is not that orderly at all times. Sometimes it is emotionally chaotic. It varies from person to person and on the friend's emotional and spiritual state. The nature of the loss also influences a friend's reactions. Death of an aged relative after long-term illness is quite different from death by accident or suicide. Frederick Buechner, for example, in an autobiographical work, shares the secret of his own long-delayed coming to terms with the suicide of his alcoholic father when he was only a boy.[9]

Understanding the dynamics of the grieving process helps us

9. Frederick Buechner, *Telling Secrets* (New York: Harper San Francisco, 1991).

to share our friend's pain. We also need to reassure our friend that grief is a natural reaction to loss, and that one must pass through it, not around it. In the meantime we stand alongside. Christians have a great advantage in being able to assure the grieving friend of God's present love and our eternal hope. Jesus is the resurrection and the life; therefore we can say to our friend: "Do not let your heart be troubled" (John 14:1; cf. Rom. 8).

Allow your friends to talk out feelings. Often they feel self-pity, sometimes anger and indignation. The last thing they need to hear is the bland affirmation that "time heals everything." Time never healed anything. Love heals. But sometimes it does take time for love to do its healing work. Love knows how to "share . . . the sorrow of those who are sad" (Rom. 12:15, Phillips).

Empathy is the best gift. Sympathy is feeling with a person. Empathy is strong identification. Halford Luccock described it as "your pain in my heart." When your love has been tempered by the fire of similar experience, you will know best what to be and do and say.

3. Befriend the depressed. Depression can cause sufferers to walk about aimlessly, often wringing their hands, their minds like a broken record playing and replaying phrases from a symphony of sorrow. Some despairing souls crawl into bed, locking their bodies in fetal positions, trying to retreat to the womb of forgetfulness. At church, at work, on the street, they look in face after face for the merest flicker of human warmth. Life becomes a roadside ditch with busy human traffic passing unnoticingly by as they sink ever more deeply into the mire of melancholy. The last thing they want is for a superior-acting person to throw them the rope of encouraging words from above. They look for someone to get close to them and understand what they are going through. Like Ezekiel, who sat stunned with the captives in Babylon, we need to sit where they sit (Ezek. 3:15).

If it is patient, kind, and gentle, love is like a medicine. An untrained minister once told a devout but depressed parishioner to "snap out of it." It was a cruel thing to say. At that moment, the person hoped that he would never come back. Our love must reflect the Great Physician's heart. When Paul felt abandoned by his friends at his first arraignment, he said, "The Lord stood by me and gave me strength" (II Tim. 4:17).

God gives grace, but grace does not fall like manna from heaven; it often comes through caring friends. Especially a best friend. Often that best friend is a husband or a wife.

4. Befriend the dependent. We begin life utterly dependent, and as we grow we continue to count on family and friends. When natural feelings of dependence overdevelop, however, and deprive one of a sense of autonomy and independence, the condition is detrimental to one's wholeness and sense of self-love. A friend who becomes so attached to another that she loses her inner reserves for making decisions develops a dependency syndrome, a psychological disorder that is pathologically parasitic. When this becomes apparent, a good friend will endeavor to help her to rediscover her autonomy. A friend's dependency may flatter the ego of a person of position and power, but candor is more Christian than control. What is friendship for, if not to encourage each other's personal growth?

In all these varied circumstances the first and best thing to do is to practice the art of listening. We are often disposed to talk, to give advice, to counsel, when the primary need of our friend is to have us listen. A ministerial colleague tells the techniques he employs in his listening-training groups. Silent response, listening with your eyes, giving attention to your friend's body, smiles, tears, and gestures — all these are important. Echoing what you hear with questions or statements confirms your interest in your friend's feelings. Only then is one ready to ask, "Do you want to talk about it?" There are times when advice is in order, but advice given too quickly is not good listening. "A receptive attitude toward others, self, and God, which is the essence of listening," he says, "is a central aspect of spiritual practice."[10]

Communications experts estimate that only ten percent of our communication is represented by the words we say, that another thirty percent is represented by our sounds, and sixty percent by our body language. "In empathic listening," comments Stephen R. Covey, "you listen with your ears, but you also, and more importantly, listen with your eyes and with your heart. You listen for feeling, for

10. H. William Gregory, *Faith Before Faithfulness: Centering the Inclusive Church* (Cleveland: Pilgrim Press, 1992), pp. 83-97.

meaning. You listen for behavior. You use your right brain as well as your left. You sense, you intuit, you feel."[11]

Etienne De Grellet put it thoughtfully: "I will pass through this world but once. If, therefore, there be any kindness I can show or any good thing I can do, let me do it now; let me not defer it or neglect it, for I shall not pass this way again."

Reach Out to Receive

The supportive companionship of friends enables us to become our own best selves. Friends help us move beyond family dependencies into the complex relationships of the wider world. In quiet or in overt ways, friends, sharing our successes and failures, our happiness and disappointments, help us to fashion our individual identities. Introverts are often more hesitant to reach out to receive than are gregarious souls, but it is all right to be an introvert. We each need what the other can give.

Men especially need to be encouraged to reach out. "The American male," says Dr. Roy Menninger, President of the Menninger Foundation, "sees himself as a very high-powered piece of machinery rather than as a human need system." Self-reliance, from our country's beginning, has been regarded as a preeminent virtue. But carried too far, it shuts us off from other people. In imagined self-sufficiency, we become cold, unattractive, and isolated. Afraid to admit our vulnerability, we miss out on the joy of a friend's help.

There is something magnetic about the words, "I need you." Women tend to admit this need more readily than men, but men are just as needy. There is much truth in the old maxim: "If you want to win someone as a friend, ask a favor."

When the wife of *Christian Century*'s editor Martin E. Marty underwent a radical mastectomy, he commented that to theologians who like to write on the large and important topics of the day, "friendship seems bland." We take friends for granted in daily life,

11. Stephen R. Covey, *The Seven Habits of Highly Successful People: Restoring the Character Ethic* (New York: Simon & Schuster, 1989), p. 241.

he wrote, "but when daily life disintegrates, their sustenance guards and guides our being."[12] Prayers, visits, cards, and letters suddenly take on new value.

We who minister are called upon so often to give encouragement, comfort, and help to others that we are tempted to assume a professional pose of never needing help. We are the givers, we suppose, not the receivers. Physicians, psychiatrists, and others in the caring professions have the same propensity. It has taken me time to realize that it is healthier and more honest to acknowledge that I am as needy and vulnerable as others, and that I am most effective with others when they know this truth about myself.

One of our associate ministers came into my study one day and said, "Sy, we often come to you with our problems and you try to help us. Whom do you have to go to?" I was happy to tell him that I have a devout and helpful wife and a few confidential friends, but that I also found inspiration in daily devotions, especially in the classics of devotional literature.[13] Worship with its prayers, lessons, hymns, and anthems, I told him, has exalting powers. Our Lord is a present help in trouble. He passed through all the experiences that try us. We can, therefore, "approach the throne of grace with all boldness, so that we may receive mercy and find grace to help in time of need" (Heb. 4:16).

Help is available for all. Reach out to receive it.

Bandaging the Bruises

Even the best of friends occasionally hurt each other by mistakes and misunderstandings. When this happens, it is healthy to face the facts openly. We need to bandage the bruises.

12. "M.E.M.O.," *The Christian Century*, May 30, 1979, p. 623.
13. Devotional literature is abundant. Among those I have most frequently used are the following: John Baillie, *A Diary of Private Prayer* (New York: Charles Scribner's Sons, 1954); William Barclay, *A Guide to Daily Prayer* (New York: Harper & Row Publishers, 1962); Malcolm Boyd, *Are You Running With Me, Jesus?* (New York: Holt, Rinehart and Winston, 1965); and *The Private Devotions of Lancelot Andrewes* (New York: Meridian Books, 1961).

We don't limp along the highway with our automobile when a tire goes flat, nor doggedly push on when the warning signal flashes on the dashboard computer screen. We head for the nearest service center. We don't junk a momentarily temperamental car; we try to repair it.

Friendship is much more valuable and eminently worth preserving. "A man, sir, should keep his friendship in constant repair," observed Samuel Johnson.[14] Like flowering plants, friendships wither and die if they are not constantly attended to.

In the movie *Love Story,* Ali MacGraw and Ryan O'Neal popularized the saying "Love means never having to say you're sorry." They were dead wrong. We all make mistakes. To apologize, to say "I'm sorry," is the most Christian thing to say when that happens, whether in a friendship, love relationship, or marriage. A true apology, Norman Vincent Peale once aptly remarked, is more than just an acknowledgment of a mistake; it is a recognition that something you have said or done has damaged the relationship and that you care enough about the relationship to want it repaired and restored. To apologize is not a sign of weakness. It takes moral strength to say, "I was wrong."

When Friendship Fades

Friendship, being voluntary, can fade and die in spite of good intentions. Unlike marriage, we do not vow that our friendship will last for life. David voices the feelings of all of us in his lament: "Even my bosom friend in whom I trusted, who ate of my bread, has lifted the heel against me" (Ps. 41:9). In ancient times, eating bread together was not only a sign of hospitality; it was a sacrament of friendship. To abandon such a friend was the unkindest cut of all.

There was another time when David was hurt deeply by the betrayal of an intimate friend. "It is not enemies who taunt me. I could bear that," he grieves; "it is you, my equal, my companion,

14. James Boswell, *Life of Johnson* (1791), in John Bartlett, *Familiar Quotations* (Boston: Little, Brown, 1980), p. 354:4.

my familiar friend, with whom I kept pleasant company; we walked in the house of God with the throng" (Ps. 55:12-14). He anticipates the experiences of our Lord himself, cut even more deeply by Judas's kiss of betrayal.

Nor was the apostle Paul a stranger to this experience. He enjoyed the encouraging assistance of several companions in his mission. But late in life he writes from a prison cell in Rome to Timothy, "Do your best to come to me soon, for Demas, in love with this present world, has deserted me and gone to Thessalonica" (II Tim. 4:9).

When George Matheson was going blind, his fiancée told him that she would not marry him. His world temporarily collapsed. In that dark hour faith in God came to the rescue. He picked up his pen and composed the moving words of the hymn,

> O Love that wilt not let me go,
>   I rest my weary soul in Thee.
> I give Thee back the life I owe,
>   That in its ocean depths its flow,
> May richer, fuller be.

Spiritual friendships are not readily broken. Two friends plus Christ make for a strong relationship. "A cord of three strands is not quickly snapped" (Eccl. 4:12, Revised English Bible). Dietrich Bonhoeffer claimed that there are no direct Christian relationships. We go through Christ to each other, and the friendship is stronger than if Christ were in one alone. Mutual commitments form strong bonds.

A hyphen friendship develops when one person wants to continue the friendship and the other wishes to let it slip by. Like a hyphenated word, writes Kierkegaard, one friend keeps the first part with the hyphen, while the other drops the second part of the word. Social, cultural, psychological, or religious differences may develop and become wedges that separate. These are ruptures that grace can restore, but if one does not choose to deal with them redemptively, friendship dissipates into neglect and avoidance.

Deepening Friendship

Make Friends a Priority

A worthy friendship deserves constant nurture. Good friends take time for each other. They visit, telephone, write letters, and share experiences. All this takes time, but it makes for happiness. John Wesley, "The Lord's Horseman," traveled thousands of miles on horseback throughout England and America preaching spiritual renewal. He was a driven evangelist, always ministering to the sound of a ticking clock. James Boswell tells us that Samuel Johnson once remarked, "John Wesley's conversation is good, but he is never at leisure, he is always obliged to go at a certain hour. This is very disagreeable to a man who loves to fold his legs and have his talk, as I do."[15] Busy ministers know Wesley's feelings, and many needy parishioners echo those of Johnson. People in caring professions pressured by arbitrary schedules are often prevented from enjoying the fine pleasure of relaxed time with a friend.

Few things are more "happifying" than a spur-of-the-minute telephone call from a friend asking, "Are you free for lunch?" I can't imagine Jesus sending a messenger to Mary, Martha, and Lazarus requesting permission to visit. Life is vastly different today, of course, but good friends know how to find room in their schedules for time with each other.

Don't wait for things to happen; make them happen. Take the initiative. Write a letter without waiting for a reply. Telephone when the spirit prompts. A few days ago I was surprised by a long-distance telephone call from a former secretary who had worked very closely with me. While waiting in a physician's office she read a magazine article that said something to the effect that if you have been waiting to write someone for a long time but haven't gotten around to it, don't wait any longer. Pick up your telephone and make a personal call now. And she did just that. We talked on and on about family, church, travels, and a host of things. The call was costly, but she felt good about doing it "now," and I was elated.

15. Boswell, *Life of Johnson* (1791).

46

We give attention to our health, wealth, homes, and clothing, writes Emerson, "but who provides wisely that he shall not be wanting in the best property of all — friends?" We do well to make friends a priority.

Learn to Open Up

Let your friend know how you think and feel. To do this you must be strong, strong enough to be vulnerable. In today's society this is not easy. We are conditioned from youth to protect ourselves. We mask our feelings and hide behind facades. But listen to this from George Eliot: "Oh, the comfort, the inexpressible comfort of feeling safe with a person, having neither to weigh thoughts nor measure words, but to pour them out, just as it is, chaff and grain together, knowing that a faithful hand will take and sift them, keeping what is worth keeping, and then, with the breath of knowledge, blow the rest away."

People who are afraid of being known too intimately suspect that if they were truly known their friendship might end or, almost as bad, become superficial. So they keep thoughts and feelings hidden for fear of censorious judgment. But friends who fear being honest about themselves, or put up pretenses, keep friendship from becoming truly authentic.

Jesus showed us the way. All other friendships pale in comparison with the openness of his friendship with his disciples and, by extension, with us. He trusted his followers, and opened his heart to them with no secretiveness. "I have called you friends," he said, "because I have made known to you everything that I heard from my Father" (John 15:15). His was a friendship that had depth. And he never doubted their loyalty. It is to this warm and wholehearted openness with him and others that he calls us.

Breaching trust, of course, creates almost irreparable damage. Anything that could be injurious to a friend's reputation if made public ought to remain a private matter forever. Some friends, therefore, share with each other only what their friends would approve of, implicitly or explicitly. Loyal friends, of course, trust each other.

Early in my ministry I read virtually every book by the Swiss

47

psychiatrist Paul Tournier that I could lay my hands on. I was impressed with his profound insights into human nature and his Christian commitment to his profession. He tells us that early in his career as a physician he attended a small meeting of people who honestly and simply shared their feelings about their life experiences — their hurts, their joys, their excesses. He was a religious person, but this experience, he says, was a spiritual transformation for him. He returned to his medical practice with the resolve to take the time to talk with his patients, opening up to them and letting them open up to him. It led him to appreciate the importance of the psychiatric dimension of people's illnesses. The change inaugurated a distinguished career that has influenced practitioners in the healing and counseling professions on many continents, as well as the reading public, leading thousands to new health and wholeness of body, mind, and spirit.

Be Kind and Gentle in Criticism

Dare to be candid with each other, but remember that constructive criticism is most helpful when it is perceived as being motivated by a kindly concern for the best interests of a friend.

Benjamin Franklin, as ambassador to France, was one of the most sought-after men in Paris, but he had to learn to be a gentleman. He tells how a Quaker friend early helped him to improve his manners. The friend gently informed him that, not content with being right when discussing a point, he often was overbearing and insolent. Franklin resolved to change all this. He no longer pointed out the absurdity of another's errors but simply observed what to him "appear'd or seem'd" a difference. "Conversations," he soon found out, went on "more pleasantly."[16]

Although intrusiveness should always be gentle and kind, if a friend develops a problem that affects your friendship — overeating, or addiction to drugs, for instance — interest in his welfare will require the exercise of unusual tact and wisdom. How graciously intrusive

16. *The Autobiography of Benjamin Franklin* (New Haven: Yale University Press, 1969), p. 159.

48

Jesus was with the woman with a moral problem whom he met at the well at Sychar. How gentle he was in restoring Peter at the seaside breakfast after his resurrection. Because of his tact, I am sure Peter preached better every time he heard the crowing of a cock. "Always be ready to make your defense to anyone who demands from you an accounting for the hope that is in you," he wrote later, "yet do it with gentleness and reverence" (I Pet. 3:15-16a). The apostle Paul also had a record that he was not proud of and, speaking of other transgressors, wrote, "you who have received the Spirit should restore such a one in a spirit of gentleness" (Gal. 6:1).

If it is painful for you to criticize your friend, you are safe in doing so. But if you take the slightest pleasure in exposing his flaws, hold your tongue.

Forgive

General Oglethorpe of Georgia said to John Wesley on one of his preaching missions to America, "I never forgive and I never forget." To which Wesley responded, "Then, sir, I hope you never sin." In the prayer Jesus taught us, "Forgive us our sins as we forgive those who sin against us," the implication is plain. You can measure the forgiveness God gives you by the way in which you forgive others. The Proverbs writer was right: "One who forgives an affront fosters friendship, but one who dwells on disputes alienates a friend" (Prov. 17:4). Forgiveness is an act of incredible strength, not a sign of weakness.

Be a Friend to Yourself

A low self-image is not a friend to grace. It projects unloving attitudes toward others. You are created, redeemed, renewed, and accepted by God. You should, therefore, accept yourself. It was said of a certain woman, "She has a circle of friends; too bad it doesn't include herself."

CHAPTER THREE

A Religious Romantic

I would like to say a good word for romance. Romance or eros has often been misunderstood, confused with infatuation, and limited to short-term relationships. Eros is much more than sexual attraction; it can be an elevating lifetime experience, one that grows beyond friendship into courtship and lifelong marriage. Healthy romance is more than ecstatic emotion; it includes a sound mind and a resolute will. It is realistic and religious and reflects the virtues of kindness, goodness, faithfulness, and self-control. Consequently, it is an experience of great joy. In this way, the Spirit colors romantic love with the personality of Jesus.

In Praise of Romance

Romance is the poetry of life. It is love between a man and a woman who love each other in a way they do not care to love anyone else. At its best, it has a spiritual glow that is simultaneously sentimental, ecstatic, and stable. It is more than roses on Valentine's Day; it is a life of expectation, experience, and surprise — one serendipity after another.

As a young minister closely associated with young people, I found that virtually all of them dreamed of falling in love with a beautiful or handsome person of good character and enjoying an exciting relationship that would culminate in the happiness of lifelong marriage. They all knew that many did not realize this possibility, but they confidently believed that for them it would be different. Most of them, fortunately, did achieve fulfilling marriages, in spite of the vicissitudes of "want," "sorrow," and "sickness." Unlike the fantasy world of movies, television, and many novels, they were infused with the spiritual ingredient that "believes all things, hopes all things, [and] endures all things."

In dealing with young married couples who began to feel their early ardor becoming tepid, I endeavored to help them understand that life is a complex mix of mind and will as well as emotion, and that romance is not dependent upon glamour. Ravishingly beautiful brides may be uncoupled by divorce within a few years of marriage, whereas more ordinary couples often enjoy a lifetime of happiness. Inner character is more important than outer beauty. The road of life is not an uninterrupted ascent to lofty peaks of ecstasy; it also descends into the valleys of trial and traverses level plains of routine. It is like a picturesque northern New England way that winds up and down hills with magnificent forest vistas laced with roaring rapids and placid ponds, with occasional potholes of unexpected crises that bump them awake to the fact that life can sometimes be rough but not ruinous.

Romantic love has inspired more sonnets and poems than any other experience. There came a day when Robert Browning discovered a volume of poems of a new writer by the name of Elizabeth Barrett. Even though she was four years his senior and a reclusive invalid, he fell in love with her as well as her poems. Their love had healing power. It made her well. After they married, she composed a series of poems, perhaps the most endearing being the one that has the lines:

How do I love thee? Let me count the ways.
I love thee to the depth and breadth and height
My soul can reach, when feeling out of sight
For the ends of Being and ideal Grace.
I love thee with the breath,
Smiles, tears, of all my life! — and, if God choose,
I shall but love thee better after death.[1]

1. Elizabeth Barrett Browning, *Sonnets from the Portuguese* (1850), no. 1.

Unrealistic Romance

There are those who think less optimistically about romantic love. Among them are some of today's prominent psychiatrists and philosophers. M. Scott Peck in his *The Road Less Traveled* deprecates romantic love as a "myth." He is thinking of people who immediately feel they are meant for each other, fall madly in love, and often just as quickly out of it. Clinical experience with disillusioned patients prompts him to dismiss romantic love as a "dreadful lie."[2]

Peck is correct in his contention that masses of people live in a world of illusion. They are in love with the idea of love. But to assert that all romantic love is a delusion is going a step too far. He himself admits that romantic love contains a grain of truth and may be very close to real love, that it is part of the mysterious scheme that introduces us to mystical ecstasy. In his later work, *Further Along the Road Less Traveled,* he reasserts his belief that it is an illusion, a form of narcissism, a looking at one's spouse or lover as a kind of god who creates a kind of heaven on earth. "And it never works."[3]

Romance equated with the euphoria of infatuation will understandably be short-lived. Infatuation is passion that flames like a booster rocket until it burns out. Its emotional intensity creates sleepless nights, restless days, daydreaming, and broken concentration. Its pounding pulse propels one into foolish risk-taking, addiction to senseless sentiment, compulsive sexual obsession, and tormenting regrets. Unrealistic romance is indeed a tragic illusion.

The New York Times recently carried a story of a fifty-four-year-old New Jersey truck driver who went to the airport to meet his fiancée, a forty-two-year-old Russian mail order prospective bride whom he had charmed with two years of romantic correspondence. He had written about his love of nature, of his love for his two

2. M. Scott Peck, *The Road Less Traveled: The Unending Journey Toward Spiritual Growth* (New York: Simon & Schuster, 1978), pp. 91-92.

3. M. Scott Peck, *Further Along the Road Less Traveled: A New Psychology of Love, Traditional Values and Spiritual Growth* (New York: Simon & Schuster, 1993), p. 224. Eric Fromm, similarly, says that "falling in love" is a contradiction in terms, that it does not reckon with the importance of an active mind and will. *To Have or to Be* (New York: Harper & Row, 1976), p. 457.

sons, and about traveling. "I love you. I need you," he reassured her. She responded, "I'm romantic; I dream to look at the world. . . . I think this man must be good." She brought with her a three-year-old daughter. One month after they met, the intended bride and her daughter were living in a shelter for the homeless. She had complained constantly about American food, was suspicious when he took a shower before going to work, and became enraged by his frequent telephone conversations with his injured eighty-seven-year-old mother. He, in turn, was irritated by her daughter's continual crying during the night and by the woman's stealing his treasured possessions and pretending she was pregnant, though he had had a vasectomy. She had also "propositioned" his twenty-seven-year-old son. "It was a complete disaster," he lamented; "not a minor but a major disaster." To her it was like love for a puppy that did not live up to expectations and was put back on the street. "Every marriage is like a song," was her reaction; "you sing it and it's finished. You begin another song." Such romantic love truly is a "myth" and "a dreadful lie."

A plethora of pulp magazines panders to the popular hunger for such quirky, twisted love stories. The steady stream of passion thrillers and enticing paperbacks that keep bookstore sales booming, as well as the tabloids that clutter our supermarket checkout counters, reveals that even in our jaded era people can't get enough of make-believe romance. A best-seller portrays a passionate if unlikely love affair between a staid Iowa farm wife and a *National Geographic* photographer who appears at her doorstep to ask directions. A top-grossing movie features a high-roller billionaire offering an ostensibly happily married woman a million dollars for a one-night stand. Fake romances "take you out of the normal day-to-day pattern of life," explains social psychologist Arthur Aron of the University of Southern California. "The more you are familiar with the unusual, it is no longer usual," writes Ruthie Stein; "it has got to be unusual compared to what you vicariously experienced before."[4]

---

4. Ruthie Stein, *The San Francisco Chronicle*, reprinted in *The Times Record* [Brunswick, Maine], April 30, 1993, p. 27.

Some scholars trace the advent of romantic love to the late medieval era. Denis de Rougemont in his book *Love in the Western World* pinpoints its beginnings at A.D. 1118, in the letters between theologian Abelard and Heloise, who became pregnant during their amorous tutorial sessions. Marrying secretly, they so enraged his uncle, who had arranged the educational relationship, that he hired thugs to castrate Abelard and banished him to a succession of monasteries. Those who cite this case, however, overlook the important fact that their romance was not only real but religiously based. Their correspondence continued. When he died on his way to Rome to defend his theological views, his body was given to Heloise for burial. She arranged to have herself buried beside him when she died. Today they lie entombed together in Paris.

Medieval courtly love, a highly ritualized love convention, however, was a rebellion against the rigidity of the system that arranged marriages, often when the partners were still young children, for political and social reasons. Marriage was maintained to perpetuate the purity of the family line, but amour flourished in parallel adventures. The love between a lover and his lady, as expressed in the poetry of the troubadours of southern France at the end of the eleventh century, spread widely throughout Europe as expressed in an epidemic of love sonnets. The lover always addressed the wife of another in the semi-religious secrecy of service to the god of love and his lady-saint.

Other researchers, however, contend that it is preposterous to trace romantic love to the troubadours, knights, and poets of the eleventh to the thirteenth century. It was far more ancient and widespread in other cultures. A survey of 168 cultures evidences the existence of romantic love in 87 percent of them, among people living as far back as the first and sixth centuries in India, China, and Japan, as well as among the eastern Cherokees, Polynesians, inhabitants of New Guinea, and the Tiv of Africa.[5]

5. Cf. Helen Fisher, *The Anatomy of Love* (New York: W. W. Norton, 1992), pp. 49, 50.

Religion and Romance

Genuine romance, authentically religious, also is much older than medieval times. It can be traced back to early experiences of the Hebrew people.

One of the most beautiful romances is that of Jacob and Rachel. In his early days Jacob was a schemer who tricked his virile brother Esau out of his birthright blessing. Jacob was his mother's favorite, and with her assistance he fled from Esau's murderous anger to her ancestral homeland, ostensibly out of Isaac and Rebecca's desire that he find a wife there rather than fall for one of the pagan Hittite women. On his arrival, he met Rachel coming to a well to water her father's flocks. He was attracted to her the moment he saw her. In a moment of rare strength he rolled the great stone from the mouth of the well and watered her sheep. Then, breaking with the tradition of arranged marriages, he himself informed her father Laban of his reason for coming and bargained for her hand in marriage.

The story is complex. In brief, since he had no property for a dowry, he agreed to work seven years to marry her. On the day of the wedding, however, Laban surreptitiously presented him with her veiled older sister, Leah, for the custom of the region was that the oldest sister should marry first. Though piqued by this, Jacob agreed to work another span of years for Rachel, whom he married one week later. Seven additional years he worked for Rachel, "and they seemed to him but a few days because of the love he had for her" (Gen. 29:20).

Jacob is one with true lovers of all times. Rachel was the center of his life's devotion, the bright spot in a very checkered career. Their two children, Joseph and Benjamin, were Jacob's favorites among his twelve sons. When Rachel died at the birth of Benjamin, Jacob buried her at what is now Bethlehem and set up a great pillar at her grave, a marker that remained standing for centuries.

Those who categorically deprecate romantic love will also have to deal with the Bible's Song of Songs. As a love poem it is unmatched in Hebrew biblical literature. The lovers' desire is expressed in a doxology that brides and grooms still request for their wedding ceremonies.

> Set me as a seal upon your heart,
>   as a seal upon your arm; . . .
> Many waters cannot quench love,
>   neither can floods drown it.
> If one offered for love
>   all the wealth of his house,
>   it would be utterly scorned. (Song of Songs 8:6-7)

Such love is not mawkishly sentimental, but robust and resilient.

The Song is neither prudish nor priggish. Its explicit expressions of passionate love celebrate romantic attraction in a way Victorians and pietists could not understand.

> Let him kiss me with the kisses of his mouth!
> For your love is better than wine. . . .
> He brought me to the banqueting house,
>   and his intention toward me was love.
> Sustain me with raisins,
>   refresh me with apples;
>   for I am faint with love.
> O that his left hand were under my head,
>   and that his right hand embraced me! . . .
> How fair and pleasant you are,
>   O loved one, delectable maiden!
> You are stately as a palm tree,
>   and your breasts are like its clusters.
> I say I will climb the palm tree
>   and lay hold of its branches.
> Oh, may your breasts be like
>   clusters of the vine,
>   and the scent of your breath like apples,
> and your kisses like the best wine
>   that goes down smoothly,
>   gliding over lips and teeth.

I am my beloved's,
  and his desire is for me. (Song of Songs 1:1; 2:4-6; 7:6-10)

The love of the Song is not all sweetness and light, however; it knows the bittersweet of lovesickness and heartache of separation. Its rhapsodies are interspersed with the throbs of pathos at being apart and lost. Ecstasy, impatient for consummation, suffers elusive pangs, not of unrequited love, nor of infidelity, but of rapture restrained and postponed.

Many have wondered how a book of lyric poetry so full of sensuous symbols could have been canonized. It has been allegorized and spiritualized, therefore, some making God, others Christ, the lover. The ancient church father Origen, for instance, taught that on the moral level the Song represents the love of Christ and his church, and on the mystical level the union of souls with the divine Word. The tradition continues to this day. Recently I picked up a new Roman Catholic publication employing the same hermeneutic. For these interpreters, the story is a reflection of spiritual truths. Authoritative commentators, however, recognize it as a song in praise of the enduring romantic love of a humble shepherd for a beautiful country girl, love that is passionate and pure, "hungry as the sea." He is her man, her own Solomon, and she is his princess, his queen.

Romance Defiled

Flawed human nature, however, can defile the romantic love even of religious persons. In contrast to romance that is pure, Hebrew storytelling at its best gives us the racy account of the life of Samson. It is a story of dedication desecrated. Born to be a morally strict Nazarite and elevated to be a judge of Israel, he delivered his people from the oppression of the Philistines as long as he lived a consecrated life. This meant touching no defiling body, drinking no strong drink, and not shaving his symbolically long hair.

But he was brought down by a series of illicit affairs with pagan women. He came back from a visit to Philistia one day with the demand, "I saw a Philistine woman at Timna; now get her for me as my wife." His father and mother remonstrated: "Is there not a woman among your kin, or among all your people, that you must go to take a wife from the uncircumcised Philistines?" But Samson was insistent. "Get her for me, because she pleases me" (Judg. 14:1-3). He married her at a great feast in Philistia, but the affair soon ended in disaster. His religious commitment had become merely formal, and with the loss of spiritual fervor he descended into one erotic venture after another.

A prostitute of Gaza became his next romantic affair. The entanglement climaxed with the Philistines closing the gates of the city, intending to kill him. But Samson crept out at midnight and, with amazing strength, picked up the entire gate assembly and deposited it on a mountaintop. He had escaped the blandishments of a fickle woman and the snare of the Philistines, but not the clamor of his perverted passions.

We discover him next in the seductive arms of Delilah in the Philistine valley of Sorek. "Three times and out," we say, and so it was. The story is involved, but, in brief, the Philistines bribed Delilah to get him to reveal the secret of his great strength. She beguiled him with her charms and tearful reproaches, "Samson, you don't love me! How can you say you do and keep on mocking me?" He finally capitulated and revealed that the secret was in keeping his head unshaven. With flattery, caresses, and wine she put him to sleep in her lap, then called the Philistines, who sheared his long locks. When he awoke, powerless, a captive, they seared out his eyes with hot irons, fettered him with brass rings, and tied him in a mill to work as an animal grinding corn. John Milton's *Samson Agonistes* voices the pathetic regrets of one who unfaithfully has gone back on God and his mission.

> Then swollen with pride, into the snare I fell
> Of fair fallacious looks, venereal trains,
> Softened with pleasure and voluptuous life,
> At length to lay my head and hallowed pledge
> Of all my strength in the lascivious lap
> Of a deceitful Concubine, who shore me

Like a tame wether, all my precious fleece,
Then turn'd me out ridiculous, despoiled,
Shaven, and disarm'd among my enemies.

Milton has Delilah visit Samson in prison, who, in reply to his charges of betrayal, responds, "Ere I to thee, thou to thy self was cruel."

Samson's dramatic career ends with his being brought into the temple of Dagon as entertainment for a throng at a huge celebration banquet. His hair has again grown long, his strength has returned. He asks his attendant to let him rest against the two central pillars that supported the great structure, and then beseeches God to give him strength once more. With a surge of power he pulls the pillars together, causing the whole edifice to collapse upon the Philistines and himself. Thus he wreaked vengeance upon his oppressors, killing more in one final act than he had done in his whole life before (Judg.16:23-31).

Was Samson the victim of feminine wiles? It is generally thought that men are the initiators in love. A German ethnologist, however, from a purely secular point of view, notes a universal pattern in women's flirting behavior that initiates human courting ploys. Her smile, lifting of the eyebrows, tilting her head, shy looks, use of voice, slight touch, and body synchrony are all part of a standard repertoire of gestures to attract a mate. Such body talk he finds in all cultures.[6] Were they the ploys that his Philistine women used to ensnare and seduce Samson? Was he victim or victimizer? Mystery has eluded studies and still beclouds the process of attraction and attachment. "The way of a man with a maid" remained an inexplicable experience for the writer of Proverbs as well.

In the Hebrew Bible, Samson wears no halo for his libidinous escapades. His inclusion in faith's Hall of Fame in Hebrews 11 is hard to understand, except for the fact that in the end he repented of his lascivious life and prayed that God would use him once more as an instrument of deliverance. Understood in this manner, it is a powerful tale of eros defiled becoming eros redeemed.

6. Cited by Fisher, pp. 20-36.

The Hollywood Hoax

Romantic love is vitiated today by Hollywood. The glitterati models for today's sensate populace are screen stars who create headline news with their "romances." The storied love affair of Woody Allen with Soon-Yi, the twenty-one-year-old adopted daughter of his love-liaison Mia Farrow, for instance, shocked the moral sensitivity of millions. Even in a sensate society he had gone too far. He had obviously violated propriety. Was the romance also incest? Woody and Mia, living with and separately from each other, simultaneously created a child out of wedlock and produced movies together. After they married, Woody developed a romantic attachment with Mia's adopted daughter Soon-Yi, and his reel and real life with Mia became a war. Mia had other children, and Soon-Yi in her siblings' eyes tumbled from child-woman to other-woman. Tabloid newspapers feasted on the fracas. Journalists became garbologists. Thoughtful people, sickened by the spectacle, reacted to the immoral dalliance with distaste, and noted that many of his films dealt with middle-aged men falling in love with teenagers. Was he uncovering in them the dark forest of his own heart? Woody himself casually white-washed the affair with, "The heart wants what it wants. There is no logic to such things. You meet someone and you fall in love, and that's that." The heart may want what it wants, but the glands do not have to give it everything it asks for. It was his id that wanted what it wanted. Even the media called it lust-romance.

In the conflict between the flesh and the spirit that the apostle Paul describes, lust reflects the "works of the flesh," and stands in stark contrast with the "fruit of the Spirit."

Lust (*epithymia* in Greek) is naturalism. It is a self-centered philosophy of life that luxuriates in self-gratification. It says we are animals who have evolved from other animals, and thus all physical gratification is morally neutral. Our endocrine glands determine how we behave. In a sensate culture, "let us eat, drink, and be merry" with no questions asked, for hedonists get the most enjoyment out of life. It is the prevailing philosophy of our time.

Naturalism's lust knows nothing of the nobility of friendship's philia, nor the self-giving of agape. Lust is Venus, says C. S. Lewis, who contrasts it with Eros. Eros wants the Beloved, he says, not just a woman. A person who wants just a woman wants merely the pleasure for which the woman happens to be "the necessary piece of apparatus." The ways one feels a few minutes after being satisfied is the gauge of whether one thinks of another as a person or a thing. "One does not keep the carton after one has smoked the cigarettes." On the other hand, we are the products of Eros, the king of creative pleasures. But even for Eros, pleasure is a by-product that needs God's rule lest it become a demon.[7]

The Hollywood hoax is that the essence of romance is ecstatic sex, an experience that is dependent on the beauty, charm, and allure of women and the strong physiques of handsome men. Most people, however, are not endowed with smooth skins, shining white teeth, and alluring smiles. Even the centerfolds of sex magazines are a fake. Look at the faces: they are blank, detached, and expressionless.

Lust undermines human dignity. It impersonalizes and abuses both men and women. The infamous Navy Tailhook debacle at Las Vegas, at which male pilots formed a gauntlet down which they passed, pawed, and stripped women pilots, has slapped popular consciousness awake to the horrors of sexual abuse.

The Bible denounces all illicit desire and vagrant sex. It may not be the greatest sin, as C. S. Lewis reminds us, but it is a vitiating vice. We are all potentially lustful, if not in deed, at least in thought. Jesus exposed the self-righteousness of the legalists who had dragged a sinful woman into his presence with, "Let anyone among you who is without sin be the first to throw a stone at her." With that they all slipped away, beginning with the oldest. Then, redemptively Jesus said to the repentant daughter of Eve, "Go, and . . . do not sin again."

Jesus, however, never shut his eyes to errant romance. The morality of Jesus was stringent. For offending eyes and hands he recommended radical surgery: "pluck them out!"; "cut them off!" What he meant was: if your eyes rove ravishingly, flip off the optic

7. C. S. Lewis, *The Four Loves* (New York: Harcourt, Brace and Co., 1960), pp. 134, 135, 160.

power supply; if your hand in its exploratory adventures leads you to indiscretion, pull the mental switch that controls its motor nerves.

The apostles reiterated his moral teaching. The new Christians of Greece and Asia Minor were exhorted to renounce the pornographic rituals of the pagan temples. Spiritual sincerity and sordid love are incompatible. A Christian, in taking a wife, some ancient scriptural manuscripts advise, should control his body in holiness and honor (I Thess. 4:4-5 [note]).

In our "respectable" churches we have too long avoided speaking about "indelicate" subjects. But if the church has muted its voice, the publishing world has capitalized on it. Several years ago when I first read Malcolm Muggeridge's book *Christ and the Media,* a blistering condemnation of the British television industry, I had the impression that his statement was overdrawn. I now believe he had a legitimate point, one long overdue.

More recently Michael Medved, a practicing Jew with high moral standards, has written a devastating critique of today's amorality in his book *Hollywood vs. America.* He fearlessly exposes the film industry's deliberate attempt to shock the public with sensuality, violence, and cruelty, in spite of the fact that a general media poll by The Associated Press shows that 80 percent of Americans think there is too much offensive language in films, that 82 percent think there is too much violence, and that 72 percent think there is too much illicit sex. The only kind of sex that seems forbidden on TV and in the movies, says Medved, is sex between husbands and wives. Sex outside of marriage is portrayed fourteen times more commonly than sex inside marriage, in spite of the fact that studies show that married people enjoy sex more frequently than single people. Hollywood is perversely and unrealistically driven to shock society as a self-appointed heretic. It is frozen in a degenerate adolescent attitude. Medved has been savagely criticized by the news media as being shrill, sanctimonious, a closet Christian, and a tool of the religious right, but his message is getting through.

The media's impact on the illicit lifestyle is hard to exaggerate. Casual encounters and temporary relationships are portrayed as the normal expressions of fulfilled life. Sexual athletes go through disposable women who make no demands beyond the moment. It is estimated that people who watch television for two or three hours a day are exposed to 14,000 sexual encounters a year. The mendacious media induce the young to go for too much too soon, bombard young adults with portrayals of fantastic sex, tempt the middle-aged to go for a last fling, and deceive the old with thundering lies about missed adventures.

One ray of hope on the moral horizon is the demise of the Playboy Clubs. Several decades ago, the founder, a minister's son in a failing-fifties marriage birthed a new magazine by printing nude pictures of Marilyn Monroe. Seven years later in Chicago, men lined up to get a key to the opening of his Playboy Club Kingdom. As the sexual revolution bloomed, centerfolds of his magazine titillated the curious with a monthly parade of nymphets pandering to the new popular permissiveness. "Variety, vitality and adventure of experience," he unabashedly admitted, "are more meaningful to me than the security of marriage." Marriage for him killed romance. Over his threshold he hung a Latin saying, "If you don't swing, don't ring." A few years ago, however, on a Saturday night in a garish hotel room in Lansing, Michigan, the last Playboy Bunny in America encased herself in her costume and did the final Bunny dip as the last Playboy Club in America closed.

But it has not ended the era of retail romance. Magazine racks still stock his monthly magazines as well as a new generation of competitors, plus pulp magazines with come-on titles such as *Real Romances, True Romance,* and a host of variants.

Romance without religion lacks the high morality fostered by the harvest of the Spirit, and often reflects the catalogue of the works of the flesh that precedes the apostle Paul's enumeration of the fruit of the Spirit. It reduces people to objects.

So much for the sensualist.

Enter the scientist.

Chemistry and Commitment

Those who once considered romantic love too emotional to be researched in the laboratory have changed their minds in recent decades. Romantic feeling now fascinates them as something bred into our biology, a panhuman characteristic embracing all cultures. Romantic love, they are now convinced, can be explained by biology and chemistry. You may not be thrilled by the purely scientific analysis of love, but for what it is worth, this is the way some scientists explain it.

Lovers captivated by a meeting of the eyes, a touch of the skin, or an aphrodisiac scent, they claim, are carried away by a flood of chemicals released in the brain that race along the nerves and into the blood. The brain is revved up by phenylethylamine (PEA), dopamine, and norepinephrine, all natural amphetamines that produce euphoria and elation. The result is amorous attraction. Attraction is followed by attachment, as larger amounts of endorphins flow into the brain. The brain's pituitary gland then secretes oxytocin, which produces feelings of satisfaction and attachment. Just how this causes one person to fall in love with another is somewhat mysterious, but each person carries in his or her mind a unique subliminal guide to the ideal partner, a love map, a record of the enticing and exciting, disturbing and disgusting experiences of childhood and adolescence imprinted in the brain's circuitry.[8]

So, there you have it. Satisfied? Probably not. To most people love will always be more than the sum of its natural parts. It's a mingling of body and soul. It involves more than glands and chemistry; it includes the action of mind, will, and emotion.

We are more than puppets of our genes, nor are our personalities solely determined by cranial chemistry and cultural compulsions. These are real, but we are more than the sum of them. They do not explain the unique ethical character of long-lived Christian romantic love. Enduring romantic love includes the ingredient of commitment. The joy of this commitment protects religious romantics from the specter of boredom and the flux of desires that tempt many to escape into unrealistic romance.

8. Cf. Fisher, pp. 37-58, 317.

Romance Redeemed

Romance without religion can be morally ruinous. But errant romantics can be redeemed. No one needs to remain a prisoner of prodigal passion. The good news for those who have compromised their commitments and who live with a conscience that stings, is that they can be transformed by what Thomas Chalmers called "the expulsive power of a new affection."

Many a time in dealing with persons with moral problems I pointed to a sturdy oak tree outside my church study window. It was one of the last trees to let go of its leaves in the fall, and some of its scarred leaves clung to the branches through the ice and wind of howling winter storms. But, come springtime, the vital sap began to creep up its trunk and into its branches, bringing with it new life for new leaves. A budding new leaf would say to an old battered and disreputable remnant of the previous year, "Pardon me, but this is now my place." And the new leaf would push the old one off. It was nature's expulsive power of new life. Countless delinquent saints know this spiritual experience.

One of the most intriguing instances of Jesus' intrusive grace is his dealing with the woman of many romances whom he met at Jacob's well at Sychar in Samaria (John 4:1-43). She came alone to draw water, for she was shunned by the respectable women of the town. She was a marginal person living in a marginalized society. When Jesus met her she had three strikes against her: she was foreign, female, and fallen. He startled her with a gentle request, "Please give me a drink." Astounded, she ejaculated, "What! You a Jew ask a drink of me a Samaritan, and a woman at that!" Jesus' psychology is fascinating. Tired and thirsty himself, he knew that she was tired of her way of life and thirsting for a new chance to really live. Needing to do her a favor, he begins by asking a favor.

Gradually it dawned on her that he was not interested in her body but in her soul. There followed a form of theological tennis, a series of assertions and counter-assertions, questions and counter-questions about race relations and worship. Sensing that he might be a prophet, she responded with a bit of theological one-upmanship: "The Messiah is coming, and when he comes he will tell us everything." Like a thunderclap Jesus replied, "I who speak with you am he!" Forgetting her thirst, she left her water pitcher behind and ran into the city to announce her great discovery. The whole town turned out to meet him. They listened. Then they invited him to stay with them, which he did for two days, and many believed.

Redemption may come in a moment, like switching on a light, or it may come gradually like the rheostat of the dawn. It can be an intellectual awakening, a decisive act of the will, or a profound emotional experience. One psychologist, shunning the word *regeneration,* speaks of instantaneous reorientation. Call it what you will, in instances such as this it is a radical change of one's mind and the direction of one's life.

Kindness and gentleness are winsome spiritual forces in leading the lapsed back to the bread of the Father's house. Jesus is our model. The familiar hymn sums it well: "To those who fall, how kind thou art! How good to those who seek."

The story of the church, from the beginning until now, is replete with examples of similar redemption. The classic case is that of St. Augustine, the greatest of the early church fathers, whose religious experience still influences theological thought today.

Born in Tagaste, Numidia (now Algeria), North Africa, in 354, he reflected the contrasting characters of his parents, his father's passionate and sensuous nature, and his mother's prayerful devoutness.

A precocious student, he was sent to Madaura, then to Carthage, to study rhetoric. Already at seventeen he was enthralled by the allurements of pagan culture. "Frenzy gripped me," he confides in his *Confessions,* "and I surrendered myself entirely to lust." At nineteen, he took a mistress to satisfy his "restless passions," and with her he had a son whom he named Adeodatus (a gift of God!). After fifteen years he dismissed her, at the urging of friends, in order to be socially correct and marry. His fiancée was only twelve, however, and the imposed legal delay so frustrated him that in his impatience he struck up another romance and took another mistress.

He had traveled from Carthage to Rome to Milan in advancing his teaching career, but more fascinating was the pilgrimage of his mind and heart. He moved restlessly from one philosophy to another until, under the eloquent preaching of Bishop Ambrose, he entertained thoughts of becoming a Christian. He began to pray, though not without ambiguities, "Give me chastity and continence, but not yet."

The climax of his soul struggle came in a garden to which he had retreated to meditate. He prayed, "How long shall I go on saying 'tomorrow,' 'tomorrow'? Why not now? Why not make an end of my ugly sins now?" In the distance he heard a child's voice chanting, "Take and read." Interpreting this as a divine command to turn to the Scriptures, he read the first passage his eyes fell on: "let us live honorably as in the day, . . . not in debauchery and licentiousness. Instead, put on the Lord Jesus Christ, and make no provision for the flesh, to gratify its desires" (Rom. 12:13-14). Immediately, he says, "it was as though the light of confidence flooded into my heart and all the darkness and doubt was dispelled." Throughout the following week, he tells us, "I was lost in wonder and in joy."

He was baptized with his son by Ambrose on Easter, the Feast of the Resurrection, in 387. At the age of thirty-three, a dramatically changed person, he began a new life. He returned to Africa and devoted the second half of his life to the work of the Spirit. He was ordained to the priesthood, and four years later was made Bishop of Hippo. In a celebrated confession he prayed, "Thou hast made us for thyself, and our hearts are restless until they rest in thee."

For his restless heart it was peace at last.

There is no peace, says Isaiah, for the wicked. Peace of soul is a fruit of the Spirit, a gift to those who turn from the "works of the flesh" to live for him who "died to make us good." Without repentance and conversion, there can be no experience of the renewal that the Spirit gives, and those who do not desire and seek goodness have no right to peace of mind and never find peace of soul.

In addition to peace, Augustine says, "I was lost in wonder and in joy." It was the joy of a returning prodigal, a banquet of rejoicing. Such joy is a thread of bliss that runs through countless biographies.

The kingdom of God, says Paul, is righteousness and peace and joy in the Holy Spirit.

Obviously, his new life required the constant energy of self-control. He did not achieve this by native resources alone. It was possible only with the spiritual power that Christ gives. Paul affirmed that he could do all things through Christ who strengthened him. Augustine, as the great interpreter of Paul, confessed the same. He had to learn to be patient in spiritual growth as he nurtured goodness, kindness, and gentleness. In all this he was above all a faithful servant of Jesus Christ. Like his great mentor, Paul, he could say that he was not disobedient to the heavenly vision.

Augustine has over the years been recognized as a dedicated pastor, a preeminent preacher, theologian, and apologist of the Christian religion.[9] His spiritual autobiography, a classic of religious experience, is the story of amazing grace. Today St. Augustine travels on the Internet in a course that stretches from a classroom at the University of Pennsylvania down the main artery of the information superhighway from North America to Australia, from Great Britain to South Africa, from Turkey to Thailand.

The point I have been making is that the religious romances of Jacob and Rachel and the lovers of the *Song of Songs* are an inspiring contrast to the unseemly compromises of Samson, as well as the lewdness of the culture influenced by Hollywood. The good news is that romance defiled can be redeemed by Jesus Christ, as the cases of the woman of Sychar and Augustine illustrate. Romantic love at its best reveres goodness, kindness, faithfulness, and self-control, virtues that create great joy. Religion makes genuine romance radiant. It can be celebrated as something real.

9. Augustine's *Confessions,* written about A.D. 400, have been retranslated and republished in many editions. For a recent translation see that of Henry Bettenson, 1972, reprinted by Penguin Books, 1984. The sections referred to here are 2.2, 4.2, 6.15, 8.7, and 8.12 (cf. Rom. 13:13; 9:6; 1:1).

Celebrating Religious Romance:
C. S. Lewis and Joy Davidman

In our century one of the most remarkable instances of the flowering of romantic love is the story of C. S. Lewis and Joy Davidman.[10] It was a most unlikely romance, but it has gripped the imagination and feelings of millions. Lewis was a tweedy Oxford don, a sixty-year-old bachelor who was a professor of literature at Magdalen College, Oxford. Joy Davidman (Mrs. William Gresham) was a Jewish American poet, a former member of the Communist party, who was experiencing a crisis in marriage with a psychopathic and alcoholic husband. In her disillusionment, she discovered the books of C. S. Lewis. His fantasy literature, together with his *The Great Divorce* and *The Screwtape Letters,* had a major influence upon her. As she read Lewis and Francis Thompson, God came in. She had turned from Judaism to investigate other religions, but only one gave her an understanding of grace and repentance and love and the Redeemer whose personality she would have recognized among ten thousand. He was Jesus.

Christianity outshone all other religions as "the sun outshines smoky torches," she wrote. She and her two sons were baptized in a Presbyterian Church. Chad Walsh was a spiritual encouragement, and introduced her by letter to Lewis. Her own letter to Lewis caught his attention, and soon he and Joy were enjoying regular correspondence as "pen pals."

To get away from her philandering husband and to consult one of the clearest thinkers she knew for help, she moved to London. In 1952, she invited Lewis to have lunch with her at the Eastgate Hotel

---

10. There are more books written about C. S. Lewis than the number of his own works, and also a large number of books about Lewis and Joy Davidman. I have found the following to be the most informative and interesting, and I am indebted to them for much in this section: Brian Sibley, *C. S. Lewis through the Shadowlands: The Real Story of His Life with Joy Davidman* (Grand Rapids: Fleming H. Revell, 1994); Chad Walsh, *C. S. Lewis: Apostle to the Skeptics* (New York: Macmillan, 1949), and *The Literary Legacy of C. S. Lewis* (New York: Harcourt, Brace, Jovanovich, 1979); and Lyle W. Dorsett, *And God Came In: The Extraordinary Story of Joy Davidman* (New York: Macmillan, 1983).

opposite Magdalen College. Lewis obviously enjoyed their meeting and reciprocated her hospitality by inviting her and a woman friend to join him and his friends at Magdalen for lunch.

Their friendship flourished as Lewis (known as Jack) discovered in Joy the very qualities she admired in him. They read each other's writings, visited all the best pubs, and saw all the traditional tourist attractions of Oxford. Lewis was oblivious of the fact that his kindness could be misinterpreted, since his experience with women had been limited. Joy fell in love with him.

As the time approached for her return to America, she received notice from her husband that he had fallen in love with her cousin and wanted a divorce. She immediately turned to Jack for advice, and, surprisingly, he advised her to divorce him. After a short, fruitless return to America, she came back to England and took up residence in London with her two sons.

Lewis visited her several times in London, and in her financial destitution sent money for her support and her children's education. He urged her to move to Oxford, found a house for her a mile away from his own, and began to see her every day. Chad Walsh, visiting Joy, "smelt marriage in the air." By the time *Surprised by Joy* was published (he had started it a few years before) Oxford was percolating with gossip about him and Joy. He had been oblivious to the double meaning of the title, but many were not, and joked about the fact that Jack HAD been "surprised" by Joy. In a later book, *The Four Loves,* he wrote that "what is offered as Friendship on one side may be mistaken for Eros on the other with painful and embarrassing results, or what begins as Friendship in both may become also Eros." And so it did.

When the British Home Office in 1956 refused to renew Joy's visitor's visa, it meant that she would have to return to America unless she married a British citizen. Lewis decided to marry Joy as "a pure matter of friendship and expediency." She continued to live in her own house but increasingly suspected that her reputation was suffering from Jack's presence in her house every day, often staying until eleven at night. When her lease on the house terminated, Jack decided that she and her children should move into his and his brother's house.

Disaster struck when one day she fell and broke her leg. It had become brittle with cancer. A malignant lump was also discovered in her breast. It was the hour of decision. "No one can mark the exact moment at which friendship becomes love," Lewis had written earlier, but at that moment it happened to him. He had never regarded the civil ceremony a Christian marriage and now resolved that his relationship with Joy should not become an adulterous one. He approached the Bishop of Oxford to grant permission for them to receive Christian marriage, but he refused on the ground that the Church of England regarded remarriage by a divorced person to be adultery. Lewis then resolved to publish notice of their marriage. On Christmas Eve he placed a carefully crafted notice in the *Times*: "A marriage has taken place between Professor C. S. Lewis, of Magdalen College, Cambridge, and Mrs. Joy Gresham, now a patient in Churchill Hospital, Oxford. It is requested that no letters be sent."

As Joy's condition worsened, Peter Reid, a friend and former student of Lewis, now a priest in the Church of England, agreed to marry them according to the service of the Church of England, that it might bring peace at the end to both of them. As Joy lay propped up on pillows with Jack at her bedside, they exchanged vows, promising to be faithful to each other "for better for worse, for richer for poorer, in sickness and in health, to love and to cherish till death do us part." Father Reid, believing in faith healing, laid his hand on Joy and prayed for her recovery. Amazingly, she did begin to recover, and soon returned to their home.

Joy wrote to a friend: "You'd think we were a honeymoon couple in our early twenties, rather than our middle-aged selves." They went on a few days' trip together, and Jack remarked: "I'm such a confirmed old bachelor that I couldn't help feeling I was being rather naughty ('staying with a woman at a hotel! Just like people in the newspapers!')" As their love became more intense he told old friends, "I never thought I would have in my sixties the happiness that passed me by in my twenties." They took a belated honeymoon to Wales and Ireland and then, sometime later, a trip to Greece that Joy had always dreamed of. But when they returned, Jack wrote to Chad Walsh that they came back "in a 'nunc dimittis' frame of mind."

When the end drew near, a friend, Father Austin Farrar, gave

Joy final absolution: "Almighty God, our heavenly Father, who of his great mercy hath promised forgiveness of sins to all of them that with hearty repentance and true faith turn to him: Have mercy upon you; pardon and deliver you for all your sins; confirm and strengthen you in all goodness; and bring you to everlasting life, through Jesus Christ our Lord." Turning to Jack, Joy said, "You have made me happy."

She died that evening at 10:15. Lewis later recalled, "She said not to me but to the chaplain, 'I am at peace with God.' She smiled, but not at me."

CHAPTER FOUR

A Suitable Spouse

Prelude to the Wedding

Romance blossoms into courtship, a time of discovery and decision, a pivotal period in one's life journey. Persons of faith will have already made a prior decision that equips them, "armed with Christlike graces," to face the vicissitudes of life victoriously. As they explore each other's personalities, they will find that their relationship is colored with the personality of Jesus. They will experience the ecstasy of joy and peace in their deepening intimacy as well as patience with each other's foibles. They will be eager to show kindness and will become gentle and faithful with each other. Courtship will challenge them to exercise self-control, for they will want to seek each other's good as they seek to enhance their love for each other.

Courtships should never be hasty. Short courtships and impulsive decisions to marry can be devastating. Those who marry too young often divorce too readily. Mature lovers experience mounting affinities. The better you understand each other, your strengths and weaknesses, your likes and dislikes, the better you will relate to each other. You will talk with each other and about each other, often. Like attracts like, but we are as individual as our fingerprints, and subtle differences also enrich life. "Vive le différence!" exclaim the French.

Exciting talk, however, is never enough. Lovers need to be with each other and do things together, for shared experiences build up a fund of memories and fuel the flame of fervor. Many factors cooperate to create a strong bond. "All you need is love," sang the

Beatles. Nonsense! Bonding engages the mind, will, and emotions. If attraction is mainly physical, you will miss many of the steps that make for a strong union.

In counseling prospective brides and grooms, I have often used the metaphor of welding. A good welder establishes as many bonding points as possible. Lovers who are religiously, psychologically, and socially akin forge a strong union. How important it is to share similar ideals and values! If one comes from a wealthy suburb and the other from a depressed inner city; if one is optimistic and enthusiastic about life while the other is disillusioned and depressed; if one likes symphony concerts, ballet, and good books, while the other is interested mainly in rock music and TV soaps; if one cannot live without regular worship while the other finds little value in it, they are headed for trouble. Only a good match makes for a promising future.

Marriage is not a missionary venture. It's risky to assume that you can transform another's personality, alter character, or make an unhappy person happy. Adjustments are possible, but only God can change human nature.

Important questions need to be answered. Who are you? How do you think of each other? When men think mainly of the bodies of their beloved, tragedy lurks. Women who flaunt their own in order to manipulate their men are courting disaster.

What about former sweethearts? Do they still linger in your memories, inhibiting concentration on your present love? If so, they must be jettisoned. The door on the past should be closed. Whatever the quality of previous relationships, it is best for a couple to forget the things that are behind, to take each other for what they are, and press forward to the goal of committed union.

A similar attitude applies to family dependency. A charming young couple during counseling about their wedding plans found themselves referring frequently to the young woman's attachment to her mother. Although he loved his fiancée dearly, this dependence was troublesome to him. He had to learn that family ties are precious. She had to learn that her deepest allegiance was now to her fiance, to grow free from mother-father dependency in order to deeply love each other. The psychological umbilical cord had to be severed.

Family backgrounds, nonetheless, do play an influential role in the lives of those who marry. If your parents loved each other, and you as children, there is good reason to believe that you, too, will be tuned to love. We have learned a great deal in recent times about the influence of genetic heritage and social conditioning. Loving, happy, patient, kind, loyal, and self-controlled parents are powerful role models.

The religious climate of home life will have left an important imprint on your personalities and characters. If God is important in your lives, you will be less tempted to idolize each other. To do so is risky, for idols often are found to have feet of clay.

Some are prepared for the wedding but not for the marriage. Preparation for marriage involves vastly more than consulting personality-characteristic files or receiving a physical examination. Premarital counseling fosters happy fulfillment. Professionally and religiously informed counseling canvasses a wide range of important aspects of life, especially the religious and psychological dimensions. Most couples seek out ministers for this service. Clergy in mainline churches have received intensive training in seminary and in special seminars that equip them to help people understand the dynamics of successful marriage. Knowledgeable ministers will often cooperate with professional psychologists who are religiously oriented to augment their counseling. Sophisticated tests are available today that in individual, conjoint, or group encounters open lovers' eyes to hidden realities. Group retreats that canvas the implications and responsibilities of marriage offer invaluable insights. Anxieties, questions, and doubts, ventilated in a relaxed atmosphere, clear the path to greater bliss.

Expectation, experience, and happy realization create marital serendipity. Unfortunate surprises, however, can be devastating, the closest thing to hell on earth.

Since over one-third of all engagements are broken off, it is important to face the basic question: "Should we marry?" Some are still finding their way. It has never been pleasant to suggest that lovers wait a bit longer, but it may be the kindest thing to do. Facing the question honestly may result in a decision to postpone the wedding, or, in rare situations, even terminate the relationship.

75

Marriage is made in heaven, it is said, but marriages are not. To become truly one is ecstasy, but "quiet desperation" is the unhappy lot of those who are unprepared for the costly joys of conjugal love.

Courtship can be an exciting processional to adventuresome marriage. To move through friendship, romance, and courtship to committed marriage, nurturing the Christlike fruit of the Spirit, is to embark on a pilgrimage that promises serendipitous fulfillment.

Cohabitation: Cul-de-sac?

Before elaborating on the virtues of Christian marriage, pause briefly to consider a contemporary alternative. Cohabitation is in vogue today. Many women and men think of it as the first step toward marriage; many others seek mainly intimate companionship. Uncertainty prompts still others to test their compatibility. Some are skeptical about marriage. "Why tie yourself down with demanding commitments?" they ask. "Why not just live together?" Over six million people in the United States are doing just that. Whenever feelings change, they feel free to split, without the trauma of separation. Yet breaking up can be as painful as divorce.

The movement that began in the liberal lifestyle of the San Francisco area now seeks to legalize relationships between consenting intimate singles, whether heterosexual or homosexual. New terms are being coined as the contest for naming these nontraditional arrangements in our pluralistic culture continues: Significant others? Roommates? Lovers? Domestic partners?

In spite of lingering social stigma, living-together arrangements have become increasingly socially acceptable, mainly because some of the benefits lovers would seek in marriage are more readily available to them — intimate companionship, and independent financial security. It is the climate of today's culture.

Religious leaders (Jewish, Roman Catholic, and Protestant evangelical) have not been slow to react to these alternative lifestyles. Such relationships are more than variations in society's ideas of marriage, they declare. They attack and undermine marriage and family.

76

Cohabitation is commitment to be uncommitted. Today, half of all men and women under thirty cohabit before marriage. In signing the marriage licenses of people I have married in the last couple of decades, I have noted that many brides and grooms listed the same address. They assume that it is better to experiment before they leap.

Cohabitation, as well as intimacy before marriage, is common among Christians today. The cultural impact on male-female relationships within the last few decades has been revolutionary. Many devout persons no longer consider it deviant.

An executive Roman Catholic wife who attends church every Sunday with her family and sends her children to a Christian school tells me that she lived with her fiancé for four years before they married. After their honeymoon their life together continued just as it had before. They had cared about each other, intended to marry, and found it to be a natural way to live. She knew that she was flagrantly disregarding papal precepts. Yet she is a person who seeks high religious and moral values for her children and exhibits in every way the virtues of a godly life. She is not exceptional in today's culture.

Many are unaware, however, of how disastrous it can be. Virtually half of those who cohabit are more likely to divorce than those who do not. Another sorry corollary is that these arrangements are frequently more violent, with higher levels of aggression that result in psychological stress, broken bones, and hospitalization. The kindness, gentleness, and self-control of committed love too often are the casualties of cohabitation. If the couple is isolated from their relatives, their violence is often less noticed by caring people who might intervene.

Some of those who have tried such "freedom" are telling us that it doesn't work without commitment. A student in a college class erupted: "I have lived through three or four of these so-called relationships. I am here to tell you there is no way for them to be open, trusting, loving, and caring, no way in hell without a promise. I hurt some good people in order to find that out. I wish the church had told me." Doubtless, the church had told him, but he had not listened. He learned wretchedness by experience.

The Bible's counsels on marriage are not arbitrary; they are guidelines for the happiest and most fulfilling life. The good news of the glad God is that high fulfillment is possible for all. It was for the Samaritan woman whom Jesus encountered at the well who had had five husbands and now was just living with a man. Jesus did not exclude any seeking soul from his kingdom.

Spiritually sensitive people will reflect the same gentle grace of Christ toward those who have chosen alternatives to the ideal. Jesus said that he came not to condemn but to save. It is so easy to be judgmental rather than to exercise his intrusive grace. Ever since Constantine, writes Philip Yancey, the church has faced the temptation of becoming the "morals police" of society. The Catholic church in the Middle Ages, Calvin's Geneva, Cromwell's England, Winthrop's New England, the Russian Orthodox Church — "each of these has attempted to legislate a form of Christian morality, and each has in its own way found it hard to communicate grace."[1] We are called to be contagious Christians who witness to the high calling in Christ. There are many situations in all our lives in which it will be well to recall the word of the apostle that where sin increased, grace abounded all the more. It is grace that is the heart of the good news.

The Special Qualities of Christian Marriage

Conjugal love is so unique that it prompted poet W. H. Auden to remark that "any marriage, however prosaic, is more interesting than any romance, however passionate." For many it is the best of all worlds. "There is no more lovely, friendly and charming relationship, communion or company," affirmed Martin Luther, "than a good marriage."

Husbands should love their wives in the same way that Christ loves his Church: he "gave himself up for her" (Eph. 5:25b). Parity of reasoning today includes wives in this reciprocal relationship. Christian marriage eschews "the works of the flesh," and, by the inspiration of the Spirit, begets "love, joy, peace, patience, kindness, goodness, faithfulness, gentleness, and self-control." Ideal marriage is a process more than a *fait accompli*. Its high joy has at least three special ingredients.

1. "Jesus and the Virtue Squad," *Christianity Today*, February 6, 1995, p. 104.

1. Marriage at its best is, first of all, *convivial companionship.* Marriage has its roots in creation, not redemption, but for Christians it has a spiritual quality. In the biblical story of human beginnings, God says, "It is not good for the man to live alone. I will make him a suitable companion to help him."[2] Eve was his first date, and he married her. The divine prescription for marriage is that "a man should leave his father and mother and be joined to his wife, and the two shall become one flesh" (Mark 10:6-8). "One flesh" in Hebrew does not refer primarily to physical relationship; it connotes psychological unity.

Companionship is mainly psychological. Lewis Smedes tells of a young man who experienced the casualty of "a virus nobody talks about [which] invaded [his] loins and knocked his sexual faculties out of connubial commission," yet lived happily with his wife in noncoital marriage for fifteen years because they loved and respected each other and shared good memories together.[3] Helen E. Fisher describes this elegant feeling of loving attachment as "a sense of contentment, of sharing, of oneness with another human being," as you walk together holding hands, sit with each other reading in the evening, laugh simultaneously at a movie, or stroll through a park or on the beach, your souls united in a world that is your paradise.[4] Psychologist Alan Loy McGinnis contends that the experience of kindness can cause as much joy as the most intimate sex.[5] One plus one equals one — such is the divine arithmetic. In convivial companionship, eros is married to agape. Suitable spouses seek the spiritual, psychological, and physical good of each other.

"Rejoice in the wife of your youth," counsels the wise man. "Let her be your companion; her love will satisfy you at all times and wrap you round continually" (Prov. 5:18-19).

2. Gen. 2:18, Good News Bible. The Revised English Bible translates it "a partner suited to him."

3. Lewis Smedes, *Caring and Commitment* (San Francisco: Harper & Row, 1988), pp. 27, 33.

4. Helen E. Fisher, *The Anatomy of Love* (New York: W. W. Norton, 1992), pp. 162-63.

5. Alan Loy McGinnis, *The Romance Factor* (New York: Harper Collins, 1990), p. 163.

Lovers themselves create this convivial union. They marry each other. No one else can "marry" them. At the wedding at Cana our Lord did not perform the ceremony; he was one of the guests. Whoever officiated did only what ministers and other authorized officials do today. They officiate at the ceremony; they do not create the marriage. Two people marooned on a deserted island could validly marry each other. It would be exceptional, but not illegitimate. We use legal and ceremonial forms for the sake of society. Laws regulate the validity of marriage, rituals sanctify it, and ceremonies celebrate it. Both church and state agree on the basic fact that two people link their lives by mutual vows and pledges.

A wedding may held in a stately church, attended by sartorially elegant guests, accompanied by exalting music, and conducted by colorfully vested clergy who use elevated language, creating a beautiful ceremony (sometimes a show); but however spectacular it may be, the extravagance does not make a marriage. Genuinely Christian spouses are the happiest, for they live not solely on the "batteries" of their own native resources but draw on the energy of the Spirit. Marriage is enhanced by the virtues of love, joy, peace, patience, kindness, goodness, faithfulness, gentleness, and self-control.

Such marriage is "as close as human beings may come to know the reality of heaven this side of the grave," declares Episcopal theologian Edward Stone Gleason. It is a balm that eases the hurts of the sorrows and difficulties of life and fosters a sense of self-worth. It demands discipline, but the payoff is a fusion of all loves — friendship, affection, passion, and agapic unselfishness.

Although this high view may seem unrealistic to cynics, it harbors mysteries that invite one to a lifetime of surprising exploration. Even after a lifetime together, convivial companions surmise that they have not come near exhausting life's possibilities.

The Hebrew and Christian understanding of life is not, contrary to medieval thinkers' emphases, ascetic and antisexual. "It is the curse of 'Christian morality,'" wrote Emil Brunner, "that it always regards the most negativistic view as the 'most serious.'" Marriage images the divine life of the Trinity. Perhaps this is why we are tempted to use the language of worship in saying we "adore" and "revere" our dearest love.

2. Marriage is not only convivially companionable; it also involves *covenanted commitment*. In the marriage service I have used over the years, brides and grooms "promise and covenant, before God and these witnesses, to be your loving and faithful husband [or wife]. . . ." To covenant means more than a signing a contract. Contract has a legal tone. Covenant has a spiritual ring. To covenant is to bind yourselves in enduring loyalty. The important Old Testament word here is *chesed,* which, translated, is covenant-love.

A woman of seventy-six went to see a psychologist to talk about her terrible marriage situation. She had married her husband "for better for worse," but she didn't envision that it would become "this much worse." A few years after he retired, her husband had suddenly become senile. At night when he couldn't sleep, he went from room to room babbling like a child. His personality had changed overnight from that of a mild-mannered person to one who swore, smoked, and drank to excess. All the physicians she had consulted recommended putting him in some institution. The psychologist himself was about to suggest a similar remedy, and was struggling to find the right words to make her feel free to put him away or divorce him. But when he began to talk about these possibilities, her eyes shot fire, and he suddenly realized that she had not come to discuss such radical solutions but only to vent her emotions, which were at the breaking point. Once relieved, she intended to return to her husband to give him the love and tenderness she had promised when they married. He was sick, but she had made a covenant with him and intended to keep it.[6] Christlike commitment is kind and gentle as well as supremely loyal. In difficult times, it knows how to marshal the spiritual power of self-control.

As feelings rise and fall, commitment is the faithful bond that holds marriages together. It is an act of the will that holds us steady during the oscillations of the mind and the emotions. Commitment makes us dependable, even in the incidental events of our lives.

When my wife and I were quite young, we purchased a small island with a honeymoon-like summer cottage on the rocky coast of

---

6. I am indebted to McGinnis, pp. 183-89, for this account of his personal experience.

Maine, way down east. It was a prized possession. A few years later, we arrived one early July day to find that the porch and kitchen had been damaged by fire. A young lad, angry at his parents for not taking him along to the airport to meet a friend, in reactionary rebellion had set the fire. The damage called for immediate repair. We had heard that it was difficult to pin down local workmen to specific times, and when I told a neighbor on the mainland that I was going into town to hire a carpenter, his sobering reply was, "Good luck!" After inquiring at various places, I was referred to a semi-retired carpenter with a good reputation and went to engage him. After hearing my hard-luck story he agreed to meet me at the precise time at the head of the cove when the tide was right in order to cross to the island by skiff. I was elated to have such a commitment. As I shook hands in taking leave, he said, "Yes sir, this Saturday at two o'clock — if nothing happens."

If nothing happens! What would happen to marriages if our commitments were no more dependable than that? And, yet, that is the quality of many marriage commitments today. They are conditional. Robert Bellah and his University of Southern California associates in their sociological study *Habits of the Heart* applaud commitment in a society that magnifies individualism.[7] Individualists who no longer give or find satisfaction and fulfillment feel free to go their own way. Christian love, however, "does not insist on its own way." It is faithful, and knows how to keep promises.

More than half of today's marriages break up. Rather than join the doomsters with another jeremiad, however, let us salute the half that does maintain lifelong commitment. Applaud the couple that leaves the wedding altar to the accompaniment of a triumphant recessional, but save your more fervent congratulations for those who see life through to its end together. Most of the people I know have managed to keep covenant and commitment intact. Their commitment to the Lord of life is an important factor in their loyalty and faithfulness. They promise to "love each other as long as we both

7. Robert Bellah, Richard Madsen, William M. Sullivan, Ann Swidler, and Stephen M. Tipton, *Habits of the Heart* (New York: Harper & Row Publishers, 1985).

shall live," which is quite different from Hollywood's "to live with each other as long as both shall love."

3. Faithful spouses are not only convivial companions and covenantally committed; they are *compatible complements* to each other. Ideal marriage is not a 50/50 arrangement, like a company partnership in which each owns an equal share of stock. It is a 100/100 union in which both give their all to each other. It does not cancel individuality; it encourages creative cooperation. It values differences as it builds on strengths and compensates for weaknesses. Husbands and wives are physically different, but they also reflect psychological, social, and emotional differences. They do not want to be clones, nor do they want to remake each other in their own image. Humble enough to recognize their own limitations, they appreciate the resources of a complementary spouse, one who adds to the other's knowledge, understanding of reality, and spiritual experience.

This relationship, according to Stephen R. Covey, is synergy.[8] Just as the roots of two plants growing close together strengthen and improve the quality of the soil so that both plants grow better together than separated, and just as two pieces of wood firmly bound hold more weight than the two separated, two complementary persons add strength to their union. "One plus one equals three or more." The challenge is to apply these natural principles socially to marriage. Married life provides many opportunities to practice synergy. Sameness is not oneness; uniformity is not unity. Sameness is uncreative and boring. Synergy values differences as each partner respectfully and tolerantly contributes to one of life's most intimate, joyful, and fulfilling relationships.

Catherine Marshall tells of the diversity in unity she enjoyed with her famous husband, the popular minister of New York Avenue Presbyterian Church in Washington, D.C., and chaplain of the Senate during the years of World War II. "The years brought many changes for Peter and me," she says. "Into our marriage came an ever-deepening fusion of heart and mind, though never a static peace. It was

8. Stephen R. Covey, *The Seven Habits of Highly Successful People: Restoring the Character Ethic* (New York: Simon & Schuster, 1989), pp. 189, 263, 274, 277.

a harmony growing out of diversity in unity, the most melodious harmony there is."[9]

Coping with Crises

Is there room for conflict in Christian marriage? Of course! Arguments? Yes! "Seldom, perhaps never, does marriage develop into an individual relationship smoothly, or without crises," writes psychiatrist Carl Gustav Jung.[10] Be sure that your confrontations are fair, however, and without malice. A medical study of 180 newlyweds shows that harsh arguing can be unhealthy. Reasoned disputes are helpful, says the survey, but sarcasm and put-downs can result in elevated blood pressure and a weakened immune system. Bitter arguments are also bad for the spiritual heart. Because you love each other, you should be each other's best critics, but, rather than being person-directed, your conflicts should focus on issues. Issues can be resolved; people can be permanently hurt.

I have always been a bit suspicious about couples who at their fiftieth wedding anniversaries said to me, "You know, in all our married life we never had a fight!" Either someone is lying, I think to myself, or one partner has so dominated the other that all individuality has been crushed. Life is like the weather: if it is all sunshine, it creates a desert. Though storms are natural in marriage, one can trace the rainbow of hope through the tears of reconciliation.

Some couples are so well attuned to each other, however, that they seldom have vigorous disagreements. Such rare couples are especially endowed with the graces of patience and kindness.

Other people so dislike conflict that they quietly absorb everything negative. Perhaps their parents quarreled excessively, and they decided that they would never allow such confrontations in their own marriages. Repression, however, can have serious psychological

9. Catherine Marshall, *A Man Called Peter* (Englewood Cliffs, N.J.: McGraw-Hill, 1952), p. 227.
10. Carl Gustav Jung, *Contributions of Analytical Psychology,* trans. H. D. and Cary F. Baynes (London: Routledge & Kegan Paul, 1948), p. 193.

consequences. Anger is a normal emotion. If partners can express their anger without letting it get out of control, the ventilation bodes well for the future of their love. Arguments in which either spouse becomes defensive or stubborn, whines or withdraws, are destructive. If one seeks to understand and be understood, differences can often be easily resolved. By drawing on spiritual resources, one is enabled to focus on solutions, heal the hurts, forgive and forget.

Learn to say, "I'm sorry." Grace empowers us to acknowledge that we are wrong. "Be angry but do not sin; do not let the sun go down on your anger" (Eph. 4:26). Never go to sleep without making up. Never leave home without being reconciled. Tragedy may lurk around the corner. A friend left home for an early morning meeting and without warning suddenly slumped lifeless over the table, the victim of a massive heart attack. He died without speaking or hearing the forgiving and redeeming word.

Battering and violence within marriage, prevalent in society at large, have no place within Christian marriage. Our flawed natures may create sharp disagreements, but wife-husband abuse is inconsistent with Christian love. Yet, sadly, instances of mistreatment by church members, even church leaders, are well known. It is estimated that ten out of every sixty women in church on any given Sunday suffer verbal abuse, and, of these, two or three have also suffered physical attacks. Such disrespectful conduct exhibits an alarming lack of the spiritual fruit of patience, kindness, and gentleness. "He who loves his wife loves himself" (Eph. 5:25, 28).

Over the years I have been a voracious reader of Christian Swiss psychiatrist Paul Tournier. In his book *The Violence Within,* he surprises us with a confession that on occasion he had spoken to his wife in wounding terms and that he had also slapped her. I was shocked. Reflecting on this moral aberration, he did not excuse himself but frankly admitted that in his heart he was much more violent than he liked to acknowledge. Fortunately, he also wrote the book *Guilt and Grace,* a masterful exposition of the secret of redemptive living.

Gentleness is a crowning virtue in marriage. Some biblical versions translate the Greek word *prautes* as meekness, and both in the popular mind suggest weakness and supineness. The nineteenth-century image of "gentle Jesus meek and mild" becomes for many the model of considerate marriage. But such docility does not engender feelings of enthusiastic self-esteem. It is a distortion of the meaning of gentleness. The Greek word the apostle used is hard to translate into English; I think it can be understood best as strength in self-control — like a Rolls Royce traveling down a sparsely traveled western Interstate highway at 55 miles an hour, or a strong father lifting his infant child. It is the very opposite of physical and psychological abuse. Basic to gentleness is respect for another and appropriate regard for oneself, all as children of God. It takes the inspiration of the Spirit to treat another person with dignity, and this is why it is named a fruit of the Spirit. Gentleness, as an expression of love, "does not insist on its own way; it is not irritable or resentful; . . . it bears all things, believes all things, hopes all things, and endures all things" (I Cor. 13:5-7). It knows how to "show courtesy to everyone" (Tit. 3:2), and it makes up with those who have done wrong "in a spirit of gentleness" (Gal. 6:1).

Gender differences, we now recognize, play a significant role in the way we manage conflicts. Men and women express their feelings and negotiate conflicts differently. Men are conditioned by society to argue in order to win; women are generally more interested in gaining love and approval. The result is that while men press for quick solutions, women care more about the process of expressing their feelings in the search for solutions. While greater recognition of our androgyny is slowly changing this, the basic pattern is still discernible.

Why men tend to withdraw from lengthy discussions is still clouded with ambiguity. Some experts claim that men are uncomfortable with intimate conversations that involve their feelings because their work world traditionally accentuates the competitive spirit that masks vulnerability. As women increasingly assume their legitimate vocational positions with men, research specialists anticipate the development of similar attitudes on their part. Today's social flux, therefore, presents Christian marriage with new challenges.

Besides conflict, compromise can become a serious crisis. We are all flawed. Even the best of us, says the Heidelberg Catechism, the gem of Protestant statements of faith, make only small beginnings in goodness and, one may add, in faithfulness.

King David, "the man after God's own heart," pacing restlessly on the rooftop of his palace as his army was engaged in battle, was ravished by the sight of Bathsheba taking her bath on her rooftop a short distance away. Since her husband was fighting at the front, David summoned her to the palace. Shortly afterward she announced that she was pregnant. In an attempt to mask the illicit affair, David brought her husband home on leave. Mindful of his embattled comrades, however, Uriah insisted on sleeping alone. Whereupon David returned him to the battle with sealed orders that he be placed on the front line, where he was soon killed.

But this was not the end of the story. The prophet Nathan appeared before him with a poignant parable about a rich man who stole and butchered a poor man's lamb to entertain a friend. The dreadful deed aroused David's anger. With pointed finger Nathan then declared, "You are the man!" (II Sam. 11–12).

At that moment, grace came into play. Like the prodigal son, David "came to himself," confessed his sin, and prayed, "Have mercy on me, O God . . . according to your abundant mercy blot out my transgressions. . . . Create in me a clean heart, O God, and put a new and right spirit within me . . . do not take your Holy Spirit from me. Restore to me the joy of your salvation" (Ps. 51:1, 10-11).

David has been variously called the great lover, the great rogue, and the great saint. Here he acted like a Christian before Christ. He had compromised his loyalty to the Lord. But he offered no excuses, no mitigating circumstances, nothing to suggest that he was under the influence of mysterious psychological forces, no attempt at exculpation. To be sure, he was at the moment under intense mental pressure, so intense that he was inattentive to the inner voice of conscience, but he did nothing to lessen or attempt to lessen the seriousness of his transgression. His prayer that the Holy Spirit might not be taken from him evidences that the Spirit was still very much alive in his life. In sharing his penitence with us, he has spiritually influenced countless lives. If David could experience forgiveness and reaffirm his loyalties, there is hope for every sin-sick soul.

Psychiatrists, in taking the lid off our minds, do not discover gossamer angel wings but a swarming world of lizard-like desires, "a zoo of lusts," as C. S. Lewis concedes. The good news is that "if we confess our sins, God is faithful and just and will forgive our sins and cleanse us from all unrighteousness" (I John 1:9). This is the good news of the glad God. There is joy in heaven every time a sinner repents, said Jesus. "Where sin increased, grace abounded all the more," writes Paul (Rom. 5:20). Such is the miracle of redemption that enables troubled consciences to find new peace and joy.

Some people have no right to speak of peace. They have ruined relationships and lives. Until they make their confessions and ask for forgiveness, they forfeit the right to enjoy peace of mind and soul.

Retaining rectitude is not easy in a world that so flagrantly entices us with the pleasures of sin. In Bangkok several years ago, my wife and I noticed in riding the elevators of our hotel a number of prosperous middle-aged European men accompanying extraordinarily beautiful younger Thai women. A few weeks later in Western Europe we saw television advertisements unabashedly promoting business-pleasure trips to Thailand. Although in counseling students and parishioners for many years I had become acquainted with virtually every irregular relationship, those blatant enticements caught me by surprise. Some years later, an executive of a major electronics firm told me that in walking through a Bangkok park he was approached by a young girl who asked, "Would you like to have me for fifty cents?" But whatever his colleagues fell for, he said, not once in his travels without his wife did he have the slightest urge to compromise. Genuine commitment in our kind of world creates great loyalties.

By contrast, I recalled calling on a young couple who had recently been married and joined the church. Conspicuously displayed on their coffee table was George and Nena O'Neill's book *Open Marriage.* This, they said, was their philosophy of life. Both, with the consent of the other, had the freedom to expand their relationships with someone else. Their marriage lasted only a couple of years. Later I learned that the O'Neills themselves had retracted many of the emancipated ideas.

A friend who ministers to a large liberal downtown church tells of how he and his wife were asked to speak to a group on "What

Makes a Successful Marriage." Together they discussed the question and prepared the presentation, but later concluded that speaking to the group was a stupid mistake. Not only did it appear that they were bragging, but there had been absolutely no communication with the audience. "In an era of individualism," he said, "we were promoting sharing and togetherness. In an era of immediate rewards, we were promoting long-term sacrifice. In an era of writing a contract, we were promoting the making of a vow." They were utterly frustrated. How does one speak of obligation to people who want only freedom and independence? How does one speak of will and intention to people who want only easy gratification? In their audience's eyes, they seemed to be prehistoric creatures, hopelessly out of step in a "brave new world."

Patient Loyalty

"Love suffers long," says the King James Version. The Greek word is *macrothymia* (*macros,* "long," *thymos,* "temper"). Christian love is long-tempered or, as our more recent translations put it, "patient" (I Cor. 13:14; Gal. 5:22). The incarnation of the patience of Christ fosters this virtue. Christian spouses sometimes do patiently "suffer long" with alcoholic, ill-tempered, disloyal, or psychopathic mates. Spiritually shallow partners quickly throw in the towel and call it quits; devout mates have the power to see it through.

Depression and disease in one's spouse often require an unusually large resource of spiritual strength on the part of the other. I have known several large-spirited persons who have stood alongside their husbands or wives as they passed through this dark night of the soul. Eros gives up too quickly; agapic love alone enables them to endure. Patience is not self-centered; it is other-directed. Spouses who patiently suffer long do so because they have covenanted with each other and wait for their restoration. They are the truly magnanimous who have earned their halos.

When our circumstances, culture, and characters change, the love of spiritually energized spouses does not quickly alter. It is uniquely wedded to patience and loyalty.

At the wedding of Prince Charles and Lady Diana Spencer in St. Paul's, London, the Archbishop of Canterbury, Robert A. K. Runcie, declared: "Marriage is first of all a new creation for the partners themselves. . . . As husband and wife live out their vows, loving and cherishing one another, sharing life's splendors and miseries, achievements and setbacks, they are transformed in the process." A good marriage is a life, as poet Edwin Muir says:

> Where each asks from each
> What each wants most to give
> And each awakes in each
> What else would never be.

Fairy tales, he went on to say, usually end with the simple phrase "They lived happily ever after." But fairy tales, he declared, regard marriage as an anti-climax after romance and courtship. That is not the Christian view. "Our faith sees the wedding day not as the place of arrival," he said, "but the place where the adventure really begins." Alas, how "miseries" and "setbacks," rather than "splendors" and "achievements," destroy many relationships that had a promising beginning.

In contrast, here is a wife who carefully selects just the right anniversary, birthday, and Christmas cards for her husband, and for more than forty years signs them "Faithfully yours, with love."

A woman once wrote popular advice dispenser Abigail Van Buren, asking why the most plain women seemed to have the best marriages, whereas outstanding beauties frequently divorced, remarried, and divorced again — unable to make a success of marriage. Abby replied, believe it or not, that beauty can be a handicap. Some beauties rely on their looks to get everything they want, including capturing their man, all the while neglecting to develop the more durable and important inner qualities. Unless she knows how to give her man more than the pleasure of looking at her, she may not keep him long.

Loyalty sometimes takes on surprising forms. There is a story of an old man and his grown children who gathered in the living room after the funeral of his elderly wife. They waited to bury her in a grave on the farm. While the sheriff was around they could not go ahead; it was against the law. When he left, the family walked outside to decide what to do. The farmer remembered 1920, when Inge came from Norway, where she had fled from Germany after her family was killed in the war. She had worked for his parents and made an agreement to come to the United States to marry him. She faithfully kept her promise. He remembered their first meeting and their immediate trip to the courthouse to be married, where they were refused the marriage ceremony because she did not have the proper citizenship papers. Undaunted, they stayed overnight in separate rooms in a hotel, then returned to his hometown for marriage. The judge there was equally adamant. She was German. Americans had just fought the Germans. She would have to get letters from Europe as credentials. Frustrated, they went back to his farm, and he slept in the hayloft so she could have the bedroom. Finally the letters came, but the judge considered the evidence insufficient. That night she came to him in the hayloft, and for forty-five years they lived loyally together in common-law marriage. His wife never forgot the raw treatment from the judges and chose never to become a citizen. She remained "without file or number, nonexistent to federal, state, or local record." She was real, Olaf thought, only to those who knew her, who loved her. And that, Olaf suddenly understood, was the way she would remain. "As in her life, so in her death." So they buried her that night, not in a grave near the house but in the middle of the field of wheat stubble. "Reverently they lowered her, and then, along with the dirt, they put a whole loader-shovel of manure and two bags of fertilizer for good measure on top of the coffin." The sons plowed the field so no one would know the grave. But Olaf knew, and ever after there would be a spot near the center of the field "where the wheat would grow greener, taller, and more golden than all the rest. It would be a gravestone made of wheat."[11] They made promises to each other early in life, and they kept them faithfully to the end.

11. Bill Weaver, "A Gravestone Made of Wheat," in the *Minneapolis Star Tribune,* February 12, 1989; reprinted by Martin E. Marty, *Context,* July 15, 1991, p. 6.

When Love Dies

Marriages today experience great stress and strain. Ministers spend increasing time counseling husbands and wives near the psychological breaking point. We often refer them to specialists in marriage counseling in the hope that a deeper understanding of the dynamics of their relationship will relieve the tensions and open the door to new affirmations. There are times when the cleavage is so great, however, that virtually all prospects of continuing the union have been shattered.

The Bible is not reticent about the tragedy of difficult marriages. Note two instances, one from the Old Testament, the other from the New. Churlish Nabal insultingly refused provisions for David and his troops, even though they had protected his large flocks from marauding Bedouins. He was saved from violent retribution only by the intercession of his sensible wife, Abigail, who secretly sent a lavish gift of food to David and openly admitted that her husband was ill-natured and foolish. The next morning when she told him about it, he suffered a stroke that, within days, claimed his life. David then married Abigail. In early New Testament times, Paul had to deal at length with the unhappy problems of mixed marriages in the church of Corinth that sometimes led to separation and divorce. There was also lewdness. "It is actually reported that there is sexual immorality among you," he writes, "and of a kind that is not found even among pagans; for a man is living with his father's wife. And you are arrogant!" (I Cor. 6:12-16; 5:1-2).

Today in America marriage is also in crisis. The picture is not pretty. Only one in three marriages, according to conservative estimates, is expected to last. Some say one out of every two. Some partners simply separate; most of them eventually divorce. Though marital instability seems to have plateaued, we still have the lowest percentage of successful marriages in our history. Cynics suggest that the institution of marriage is dying.

As love atrophies and dies, marriages of Christians break up as well as those of others. Protestants and Roman Catholics divorce almost as often as the non-devout. Roman Christians often resort to annulment ("Catholic divorce"), and liberal Protestants utilize "incompatibility" as an easy out. Both during and after the rupture, however, all family members suffer — husbands and wives, children, and the extended family. To leave a spouse is hard; there is no easy way to do it well.

Marriages disintegrate for many reasons: bitter quarrels, lack of communication, cruelty, alcoholism, sexual rejection — the list goes on and on. The social revolution that enables women to be psychologically and financially more independent, and a vigorous feminism (rightly emphasizing equality), causing threatened men to react with old-fashioned domination, has fueled the divorce explosion.

Some couples are manifestly mismated. Take, for instance, the case of a young couple who came to my study for premarital counseling. She was a beautiful, confident, ebullient, and highly capable person. He seemed only average in ability and bland in personality. Since they both seemed to understand the meaning and implications of marriage, I proceeded to plan their wedding with them. During the months after their wedding, as she rapidly climbed the ladder of advancement and responsibility in business, he became more and more jealous and threatened and reacted with intolerable domination. As a Christian she tried to be patient and loyal, but the situation became unbearable. They had covenanted with each other, but it was not a wise commitment. She finally had to leave him for a while. Ultimately they divorced, the first and only case in her large extended family.

A problem for many is how to reconcile our culture's relaxed attitude toward divorce with the rigorous proscriptions of the Bible. Jesus and the apostles were stringent in their demands. The Pharisees, as guardians of orthodoxy, one day attempted to hang Jesus on the horns of a dilemma, testing him with the question, "Is it lawful for a man to divorce his wife for any cause?" The Mosaic laws permitted a man to hand a wife a certificate of divorce if she had done "something objectionable," "offensive," or "indecent," to displease him. They were pitting him against two rival schools of interpretation — the stringent rabbinic school of Shammai, and the more liberal school of Hillel. "Because of your hardness of heart [Moses] wrote this commandment to you," Jesus answered. Then, deftly rising above legal minutiae, he asked, "Have you not read that the one who made them at the beginning 'made them male and female,' and he said, 'For this reason a man shall leave his father and mother and be joined to his wife, and the two shall become one flesh'? So they are no longer two, but one flesh. Therefore what God has joined together, let no one separate" (Mark 10:5-9; cf. Matt. 19:3-6; Deut. 24:1-2).

Questioned about divorce, Jesus answered about marriage. It was a pointed and courageous stand. In effect, he was championing the cause of women. Some scholars believe that the exceptive clause about "unchastity" is a later addition of the Christian community. No one, however, can contest the stringency of Jesus. It is a difficult ideal, a counsel of perfection for imperfect people, but a guide for a fulfilled life.

In his letter to the church at Corinth, the "Big Apple" of Greece, where mixed marriages were common and cultural conflicts intense, Paul repudiated divorce but made one concession. "If the unbelieving partner separates, let it be so; in such a case, the brother or sister is not bound. It is to peace that God has called you" (I Cor. 7:15). Historically, the church has undervalued and underestimated this emphasis on peace.

Before giving up, however, one should use every resource of grace to reconcile. We should divorce our faults and foibles before we divorce our partners. Forgiveness may not be easy — it is not easy for God either — but the power to forgive and reconcile is one of the great blessings of the Spirit. When all means of grace have been exhausted, however, and the marriage no longer reflects the divine intent, it is already dead. Let couples admit their failure, confess their sin (divorce is not a greater sin than others), and, with God's grace, dedicate themselves to new life in society and the kingdom of God.

Alarmed by the often-cited statistics of failure, many predict that unless we mend our fickle ways the institution of marriage is doomed. This is statistical nonsense. The statistics of divorce are dismal, but not as dismal as many commentators would have us believe. "The prophets of doom could not be any more wrong," says pollster Harris. The American family is surviving. Seven out of ten current marriages, thanks to older couples, are intact. Eighty percent of those surveyed say that their relationship is satisfying. I find that most of my friends and acquaintances are extremely happy in marriage. Christian commitment has much to do with it.

Yesterday's marriages offset today's relaxed trends. Career women and men are also learning how to share the load of caring for home and family. New attitudes of mutual respect and responsibility are forming strong bonds, reassuring us that the revolutionary changes following the devastating depression and the havoc of numerous wars are not wedging all lovers apart. The winsomeness of Christian spouses can have a contagious influence on tomorrow's marriages.

Tending the Fire

The secret of life-long love is nurturing the flame. The enjoyment of companionship, commitment, and compatibility, depends, of course, on marrying the right person. A college friend one time told me that he was not going to marry until he met an angel. Some years later he did meet an angel, but she was a "fallen angel." The misery of adjustment was painful and long-term.

We are all flawed and, at times, bound to disappoint each other. Eros, coupled with philia, needs agape to preserve the romance of marriage. It is the Spirit that enables us to maintain the spiritual glow. Harry S. Truman in describing his long happy life with Bess writes, "We went to Sunday School, public school from the fifth grade through high school, graduated in the same class, and marched down life's road together. For me she still has the blue eyes and the golden hair of yesteryear."[12] Obviously they shared abundant spiritual and psychological resources.

To enjoy lasting love, we need to tend the spiritual-psychological fire. There is something deeply satisfying about pulling your chair up close to a fireplace on a chilly winter night and feeling the warmth of the burning logs surround you with a blanket of coziness.

12. Harry S. Truman, *Memoirs of Harry S. Truman,* vol. 1 (Garden City, N.Y.: Doubleday, 1955), p. 116.

But unless you keep your eyes on it, rearrange the logs periodically, and replenish them when they burn low, you will soon lose your fire. So it is with the romance of married love.

There is a story about an aged couple who lived on the flat plains of the wide West, very much alone, miles from their nearest neighbors. He tended the farm, she busied herself with housework. They rose early each morning, had the same unimaginative quiet breakfast, and then went their individual ways. They went tired to bed each night. Day after day it was the same routine. There was little to talk about, so conversation languished. Expressions of affection also gradually faded away. Life became dull and uninteresting. One day, however, the old codger, noticing his wife's pale and drained demeanor, decided to take her to a physician. An examination revealed nothing organically wrong with her. As they returned to the waiting room, the physician, not being busy, decided to try some old-fashioned country-doctor therapy by chatting with them, hoping to discover the cause of her malaise. But there was little response. Responding to a hunch, he got out of his chair, walked over to her, put his arm around her shoulders in a big hug, and planted a light kiss on her forehead. Immediately he noted a slight sparkle in her eyes. Resuming his seat, he said to her dullard husband, "That's my prescription. Once a day for a month your wife is to receive a hug and a kiss." Dumbfounded, the husband replied, "Well, it sounds silly to me, but you're the doctor, and if you think it will do some good, I will bring her in every day so you can give her a hug and a kiss."

Tend the fire!

CHAPTER FIVE

A Patient Parent

Christian spouses create the spiritual families that offer the only hope for a revitalized society. On every side, we hear calls for the renewal of family values. The highest values remain the fruit of the Spirit, the virtues of Christ, which we have noted at each successive stage of maturing life.

What would family life be without love that seeks the highest good of each other, the joy of shared spiritual experience, peace that comes from clear consciences, patience with the prickles of individual temperament, kindness that respects the dignity of each, goodness that is the climate of spirituality, faithfulness that endures personal foibles, gentleness in delicate situations, and self-control that preserves our harmony with God and each other?

Love (*storge* is the Greek word for family love) is, of course, the primary virtue that nurtures the other virtues that enrich family life, and wise parents will blend *storge* with *agape* and *philia*. It takes effort, but we are not left to our own resources. The Spirit empowers us with both patience and wisdom. "In everything a prudent man acts with knowledge," writes the wise man; "a prudent wife is from the LORD" (Prov. 13:16; 14:18; 19:14). So ordered, family life reflects the personality of Jesus.

When we hear the word *family,* most of us think of parents and children. We celebrate family life. Photograph albums capture and preserve treasured memories of family get-togethers. Costly portraits of fathers and mothers with babies, young children, teenagers, sometimes even the dogs and cats, often grace the walls of our homes.

97

Few experiences are more rewarding than parents and children living together convivially as they grow in grace and character. We also salute single parents who do double duty as custodians of the well-being of their children. Family life retains a profound hold on the American imagination. The radical upheaval in family values in our wider culture may have shaken the family, but it has not dislodged it.

As a mother or a father, you are more than a figurehead. You are, in fact, an important family figure. As a son or a daughter, you are also a significant figure in the family. The paternal love that reflects "Our Father who art in heaven," the maternal love that resembles God's care for us as "a mother comforts her child," and the sibling love that mirrors our status as "children of God," truly model "Spirit-life" (Matt. 6:9; Isa. 66:13).

Some of the happiest families are husbands and wives who have no children. Most married folk, however, desire children. There is a moving story in the Hebrew Bible about Hannah, the barren wife of godly Elkanah. In her grief he endeavored to comfort her: "Hannah, why do you weep? And why do you not eat? And why is your heart sad? Am I not more to you than ten sons?" (I Sam. 1:8). Their patience and perseverance were rewarded. Sometime later a son was born to them, and they named him Samuel after the God who had answered their prayers. Eventually he became one of Israel's notable judges.

Husbands and wives who cannot have children of their own often take into their families by adoption the children of others. In my own extended family they have done so. "Blood does not make a family," writes Lewis Smedes, who, with his wife, adopted several children.[1] Such highly motivated parents think of their adopted children as persons just as worthy of unconditional love as natural children.

It takes a great deal of patience and wisdom to manage a family in our changing times. The family is the foremost character-forming unit and building block in our society. For preeminence, it has no

1. Lewis Smedes, *Caring and Commitment* (San Francisco: Harper & Row, 1988), p. 84.

rival. Nothing can adequately substitute for home, not even church and school. If spiritual attitudes are not rooted here they will not extend to the larger society, and the world will not know that God's way is best.

The Fruit of Love

Children were accorded high worth in the ancient Hebrew and Christian cultures. "The glory of children is their parents"(Prov. 17:6); "grandchildren are the crown of the aged." Jesus valued children so highly that he took them into his arms and blessed them. In cultures where children are not welcome, girl babies especially, as in India, fetuses are commonly aborted, infanticide is common, and wives who do not bear sons are often burned to death.

Loving mothers and fathers nurture the physical, psychological, and spiritual lives of their children. Parents who treat their children with love and dignity as God-created persons are solicitous about both their felt and real needs. "Is there any one among you who, if your child asks for bread, will give a stone? Or if the child asks for a fish, will give a snake?" asks Jesus (Matt. 7:9-10). A loaf of bread in ancient days was shaped like a round stone, and some fish do look somewhat like snakes. Parents who really care seek to provide what is best for their children.

Goodness is the Christlike virtue parents endeavor to foster in their children. As Jesus grew, increasing "in wisdom and in years, and in divine and human favor," so parents, energized by the Spirit, patiently endeavor to produce the same fruit of the Spirit. Make the tree good, said Jesus, and its fruit will be good. "The good person brings good things out of a good treasure" (Matt. 12:35). Fathers who "do not provoke [their] children to anger, but bring them up in the discipline and instruction of the Lord," writes Paul, will have children who "obey [their] parents in the Lord" (Eph. 6:4, 1). In speaking of family matters, Peter counsels: "Those who desire life and desire to see good days, let them keep their tongues from evil and their lips from speaking deceit; let them turn away from evil and do good; let them seek peace and pursue it" (I Pet. 3:10-11).

Through the long period of their children's maturation, parents also patiently teach their children how, in spite of the peculiarities and prickles of individual temperament, to live graciously with others, in order to cope with life's later elbow-rubbing experiences. Patience often must be "long-suffering." To do this it takes a great deal of loving.

But parents can overdo it. Mother-love can become "smother-love." C. S. Lewis writes of the inverted love that prompts parents in the name of loving their families to live for their own gratification. When Mrs. Fidget died, for instance, her family "brightened up." "Mrs. Fidget is now at rest," Lewis noted. "Let us hope she is. What's quite certain is that her family are."[2]

The Challenge of Parenting

Parenting is not easy. To say that it is a daunting and difficult task is an understatement. It involves pleasure and pain, ecstasy and agony. It is the best of all relationships, but sometimes the most trying. Researchers find that many married couples are happiest in the years before they have children, less happy during the emotionally taxing time of rearing them, and then happier again when the last one ventures out on a career. Strong-willed children can be a frustrating responsibility. Ann Landers, confidante to millions, once asked her readers: "If you had to do it all over again, would you have children?" An overwhelming majority answered "No."

I have a feeling that it was mainly negative people, or those who had bad experiences, who answered her the way they did (although some of my minister friends jocularly say they feel that way on occasion!). But it is not the attitude of most of the families that I know. To them children are a joy, a source of gratitude and pride. At Christmas especially, they include letters with their cards detailing the pleasure they have in seeing their children mature and accomplish fine things. I had the good fortune of being reared in a

2. C. S. Lewis, *The Four Loves* (New York: Harcourt, Brace and Co., 1960), pp. 48, 49.

large family that, though not perfect, experienced a great deal of fun and joy. My parents had seven sons (mother wanted a daughter so badly!), but I do not recall a single instance when they expressed regret. Most of my friends have had similar experiences. I have ministered to parishioners without number who appeared to have the same experience. The religious atmosphere of our homes, I am sure, makes the difference.

Children need encouragement to achieve and live at their best. Positive reinforcement of the good fosters kindness toward others, faithfulness to the ideals of family values, as well as self-control of temperament. The by-products for the whole family are joy and peace. Where parents model such virtues, correction, when children make the wrong choices, will be more readily accepted.

Jesus early set the example of respect to parents. After the episode in Jerusalem, when, as a twelve-year-old, he lingered in the temple to talk with the teachers of the law, he returned home to Nazareth with Joseph and Mary, "and was obedient to them" (Luke 2:51). Whatever his awareness of his special divine Sonship was at this time, it did not negate filial duty and honor.

In the prep school of family life, the best learning resource is the wisdom of the Bible. Fifth commandment families are the happiest. Honorable parents and respectful children observe both nature's and God's law. Parents' guidance in such families is not arbitrary if, without being authoritarian, they have earned authority. Longer experience of grace has taught them much about right and wrong. In teaching their children the virtue of self-control, they may at times need to resort to discipline, discipline that may be as painful for them as for their children. But they are prepared to seem cruel in order to be kind.

Kindness and gentleness, however, never violate a child's personality. Spanking is a common means of disciplining children, but a study by researchers at the University of New Hampshire reveals that spanking can be blamed for some of the bad behavior of children. Hostility reappears when they grow up. The university's Family Research Laboratory finds, after thousands of parent interviews, that the more spanking a child suffers, the greater the increase in antisocial behavior two years later. Children who aren't spanked learn to use words, not hands, to settle differences, say the analysts. Paul pithily summarizes the Christian attitude: "Fathers, don't overcorrect your children or make it difficult for them to obey the Commandment. Bring them up with Christian teaching in Christian discipline" (Eph. 6:1-4, Phillips). No psychological technique or social program, nor the legion of self-help books, can compare with the kind and patient firmness of loving parents.

Children who love learn from loving parents. "The single best thing a father can do for his children," says Notre Dame's Fr. Theodore Hesburgh, "is to love their mother."

Religion and family-love must be married. The moral and spiritual life of our civilization depends on this merger. Parents are parenting against today's culture. Only a spiritual family can transform a child's natural sociability into moral sensitivity. "Intentional Christian nurture is necessary," writes Ellen T. Charry of Perkins School of Theology, "because our culture shapes children for a world shorn of God. . . . Unless our children know Jesus," she asks, "what will protect them from hurting themselves and others?"[3]

Money, sex, and power have replaced the classic Christian virtues as social standards of success. Parents who consistently demonstrate an overwhelming interest in material things virtually ensure that their children will desire overpriced sneakers, clothing, jewelry, and the other peer-oriented tokens of being "with it." Many of them will do unconscionable things to get what they consider the symbols of success.

The early years are crucial for giving the attention, instruction, and nurture children need to imbibe a sense of values. "Train children in the right way," says the book of Proverbs, "and when old, they will not stray" (22:6). Parents who are unable to articulate their faith will find it difficult to raise Christian children. Nothing makes a stronger imprint on children than sincere family devotions. As parents read Scripture with them, not first of all to indoctrinate them but for their mutual growth, good things happen. The scant one-hour instruction of weekly Sunday School and the religious void in public

3. Ellen T. Charry, "Raising Christian Children in a Pagan Culture," *The Christian Century*, February 16, 1994, p. 166.

school education (our public schools are graduating a generation of moral illiterates, as though the great moral, religious, and philosophical traditions of several thousand years of civilization have been forgotten) make it imperative that parents talk with their children about the love of God, the grace of Jesus Christ, and guidance of the Holy Spirit.

Occasionally one hears of broad-minded parents who preen themselves on their resolution not to push their religion on their children, but to let them decide the matter for themselves. Of course, one should never push religion. Positive, winsome influence, however, is not pressure. They do not adopt this latitudinarian attitude when it comes to education, whether their children will go to school or not. Nor do they leave it an open question whether or not they will learn a business or a profession. Again, it takes little imagination to see what would happen if they favored freedom of thought and action when it comes to love and sex. Extreme permissiveness undermines family life and a child's moral development. If they are to restore health to the nation, they must end this Spockian period of ultra-permissiveness, teach their offspring moral imperatives, and patiently exemplify the Christlike virtues of goodness and self-control.

Children and young people catch the contagion of a loving home. As I write this, I am thinking of a child, born deformed and defective because of a prenatal aberration, who was the recipient of one family's special love. Her older sister, a beautiful adolescent, always introduced her boyfriends to her, carefully noting their reactions. If anyone did not show friendly interest, it was his last date with her. Eventually she married a young man with a similarly positive spirit, and together they are raising a delightful family of loving, happy children. It takes the Spirit to lift us to such levels of kindness.

I encountered a completely different case in pastoral counseling. A woman who had been horribly abused as an adopted child confessed that for over thirty years she felt she was of no worth, one whom even God did not love. In her depression, she consulted psychiatrists and took all the medicines prescribed, but to no avail. One day, feeling acutely hopeless and entertaining thoughts of suicide, in desperation she threw her life into the hands of God. Immediately, the mental shackles that had bound her slipped away, she said, and for the first time, as hostility to others evaporated, she felt love for God. A sense of worth came in like a rising tide. I listened with empathetic amazement, hardly able to understand her experience. But one thing was incontrovertible. Her religious experience became the expulsive power of a new affection. Continued consultations confirmed that this was no ephemeral episode. At our last session, I sent up a silent prayer that the Spirit would sustain the love she had so long denied herself.

There is no place like home to cultivate the virtues of the Spirit. Caring and committed parents prepare their children for a lifetime of healthier, holier, and happier living.

The Ecstasy and Agony of Adolescence

Young people who carry a fund of happy childhood memories find the transition to adolescence easier for themselves and their parents. The leap from childhood into adolescence — actually a series of little leaps — is more than a chronological passage into the risky unknown; it is a biological and psychological revolution. The hormonal and biochemical changes, coupled with pressures for recognition and acceptance, are awesome.

The time of making this passage is fairly predictable, though each person has his or her own timetable. It generally starts during junior high school years, in the sixth grade for girls and seventh for boys. By the time they reach high school, they face the critical task of synchronizing a sense of self-image with their affectional feelings and sexual potency. By the time they get to college, they find themselves in a culturally charged pressure cooker that propels them toward intimacy before they are ready to marry. M. Scott Peck, in tracing their spiritual development, believes that between the ages of five and twelve, children tend to be psychologically and spiritually chaotic, self-serving, and covertly manipulative, mischievous but not rebellious. "But with adolescence," he says, "all hell breaks loose," and everything their parents stand for is subject to questioning, skepticism, and rebellion.[4] Loving patience faces its greatest test.

For years we have spoken of a generation gap. It is as old as the human race. One witty person composed the ditty:

Said Adam to Eve,
I begin to perceive
That young Abel
Whom we have raised is unstable.
And now it is plain
We shall also have to raise Cain.

Young people may live in different worlds, but they need not be isolated. What they need most from their parents is patient understanding.

Families exhibit striking contrasts. Many young people are from radiantly Christian families, where early commitment to moral and spiritual values is the climate of home life. Troubled families in which conflict and alienation are common, however, foster feelings of low self-esteem, anxiety, anger, and delinquency. The staggering number of runaways, or "throwaways," is traceable to dysfunctional family life. In our large Eastern cities, these young runaways are likely to be the urban poor who roam the streets in search of temporary shelter. In Hollywood, they are middle- and upper-class refugees from everywhere in the country. "Home is hell," explains one of them. In their lonely poverty, they are conscripted by drug pushers or enticed by pimps into prostitution. After six months on the street, the odds of reclaiming them are one in a hundred.

Thanks to Covenant House and similar centers, a network of nonsectarian crisis centers stretching across the nation from Boston to Los Angeles offers to addicted and disillusioned youth food and lodging, and the chance to begin life anew. Dedicated counselors cruise the streets in vans, rescuing young people from the mire of today's moral miasma. They incarnate the Christlike virtues of

4. M. Scott Peck, *Further Along the Road Less Traveled: The Unending Journey Towards Spiritual Growth* (New York: Simon & Schuster, 1993), p. 131.

patience, kindness, gentleness, and generous goodness. "In loco parentis" therapy and counseling enables many runaways to be rehabilitated and to return home as new creatures.

The agony of adolescence is not confined to any one social class. It pervades the entire spectrum of society, from the poor to the rich, from the ghetto to the suburb. The process of alienation may begin when a child brings home a report card with low grades, triggering a torrent of parental abuse. Young people have been beaten with rolling pins, punched until they bleed, even spat upon. Middle- and upper-class parents, educated themselves, expect stellar performances from their sons and daughters. They consider low achievement a personal affront, a reflection on their parenting skills. Instead of concentrating on their own lapses or their overcommitment to work and the social whirl, they react to their kin with rage. They often lose them. It is not the raucous voice, nor the raised fist, but a religious reorientation that is a *sine qua non* for delinquent parents and one of the best answers to the problems of adolescents.

Criminologists trace the violence that shakes the soul of society to the lack of moral nurture in the family. Juvenile crime chronicled on stage and screen encourages similar acts. Parents who batter their children, or incestuously violate them, often with threats to keep them silent, are destroying the moral fabric of society. Nearly three million adolescents, according to a 1991 report, have been physically, mentally, and sexually assaulted by their parents. In some cases, such abuse has triggered a wave of parricide, often by terror-ridden middle-class white teenagers.

When families decay, the nation decays. Rome fell not only because of the barbarian onslaught from without, but also because of the rottenness within. This could happen to America. The pillars of home, school, and church in many places are already crumbling.

A young college girl came often into my church study as she was passing through a terrible transition period in her life (drugs, alcohol, tobacco, temper tantrums), seeking solace from the vehement reactions of her home. One day I suggested to our youth minister that he make a call at her home to acquaint himself with her family. As he approached the front door, he heard her father giving her a verbal lashing that was reducing her to psychological pulp. The emotional thrashing paused only when the youth minister finally rang the bell. As the youth pastor kept a calm spirit and spoke gently and kindly to both father and daughter, the volcanic eruption gradually ceased. It took many contacts by both of us to lead her into a new life. Some time later, her father came into my study to say that he would never be able to thank us enough for what had happened in the life of his daughter. Gentle and patient love has incredible strength! It led her to self-control.

Writing from the campus of Duke University, Chaplain William Willimon laments that with the lapse of the "in loco parentis" policy, which was the alleged modus operandi of colleges and universities until the early 1960s, the emphasis has been placed on the freedom of young people. It is a mistake to treat students as adults, he says, for "at best a student is . . . a novice adult." Few of them are capable of making their own decisions or thinking for themselves. Most of them are submissive to their peers. A better case could be made for in loco parentis in the 1990s than during the 1950s, he claims, because an increasing number of students have been "inadequately parented," having missed interaction with their parents over values. Since universities cannot reinstate in loco parentis, he suggests that they act as wise friends, noting more optimistically that many students seem to be more interested in the search for roots, stability, order, and identity than in freedom.[5]

Not all adolescents are addicted to the herd mentality of prodigality and promiscuity. Athletic celebrities are touting abstinence in many high school assemblies, and thousands of young people are making a pledge that says, "I won't until I say 'I do.'" Many of our major newspapers are carrying the story of a movement sponsored by church-led groups that advocates sexual self-control until marriage. *USA WEEKEND,* for example, reports pro–basketball player A. C. Green telling students at a Los Angeles high school: "I remember my first trip with the Lakers, riding on the bus. Everyone was saying, 'A. C., you're not going to believe how wonderful the girls look who hang out after the game. You won't be talking about

5. William H. Willimon, "Reaching and Teaching the Abandoned Generation," *The Christian Century,* October 2, 1993, pp. 1016-19.

saving yourself for marriage after you see these girls. We'll give you six weeks before you give in, man.'" Shaking his head and laughing, he says, "Well, nine years later, they gave up on me. In the end, I respect myself more than I want to be part of the crowd."[6] While such stories extolling chastity's virtues run counter to the plot lines of today's movies, TV programs, and videos, other athletes for abstinence are signing up, including basketball's David Robinson; football's Reggie White, Darrell Green, and Barry Sanders; as well as Olympic decathlete Dave Johnson.

Abstinence is hip among other groups as well. Across the country, young people in growing numbers are saving sex for marriage, and the mainstream media are taking notice. At least six different studies show that the number of high schoolers having sex has declined dramatically in recent years. The Family Research Council based in Washington, D.C., has launched a "Save Sex" advertisement campaign that features attractive young people who are committed to abstinence before marriage. The evidence is not only that abstinence is safe, but also produces happier marriages. One prominent newspaper said of the campaign: "It is thought-provoking and sophisticated, and it strikes back at the commercial, exploitative rot that the television, music, and movie industry have been perpetrating upon American children."[7]

This is still a minority report, but it is making chastity fashionable again. Church groups have garnered 500,000 people who have signed pledge cards displayed on The Mall in Washington, D.C. "It's time to go back to what works," comments one coed. "We're sick of 'safe sex.' It's devastated a whole generation."

As I think of myself and friends I have known, I am aware of the varying degrees of turbulence and serenity we all passed through. I know hundreds who do not match the sordid model at all. They have progressed psychologically and spiritually in a much more

---

6. *USA WEEKEND*, March 25-27, 1994, p. 4.

7. *The Tampa Tribune*, quoted in *Christianity Today*, December 12, 1994, p. 57. Other newspapers and magazines cooperating with the advertising campaign include the *Washington Post*, *Newsweek*, *The Miami Herald*, and *Rolling Stone*, as well as the Oprah Winfrey Show.

level-headed manner. Some families resemble constant war zones, but there are many others where courtesy, respect, and kindness glow with Christian love.

Prudent parents will take a long, hard look in the mirror. The values of their children and adolescents are often magnified reflections of their own values.

The good news is that many adolescents who have been rebellious during turbulent years, once they reach young adulthood, marry, have children, and occupy responsible positions, turn once again to the values they learned in the family, confirming the ancient proverb that if one trains children in the way they should go they will not be able to get away from that instruction in later years. Many of them think of spirituality quite differently than their parents do, however, since they have been deeply influenced by the social and cultural upheavals of the last few decades. Nonetheless, many of them eventually come to occupy positions of leadership and responsibility in the church.

Polls show that many of the baby-boomers, who were born over the span of years from 1946 to 1964, are reclaiming traditional family values. "They cherish the freedom of individual expression," writes Wade Clark Roof, "yet agree there should be greater respect for authority."[8] Many of them are returning to the fold of the church.

The Nuclear Family Ideal

Vice President Dan Quayle startled the American public by a provocative speech in 1992 in which he declared that the time had come for our churches, synagogues, civic organizations, and schools to renew a public commitment to Judeo-Christian values in the family. The failure of our families is hurting America deeply, he declared. "Children need love and discipline. They need mothers and fathers.

---

8. Wade Clark Roof, *A Generation of Seekers: The Spiritual Journeys of the Baby Boomer Generation* (New York: Harper San Francisco, 1993), p. 1.

A welfare check is not a husband. The state is not a father. It is from parents that children come to understand values." The speech was unfortunately marred by an ill-advised reference to a TV dramatization of an unwed single becoming a mother, but there was so much good in it that it prompted *The Atlantic Monthly* to feature a lengthy lead article with the title "Dan Quayle Was Right."[9]

The Norman Rockwell portraits of yesterday's family life are now obsolete. We look back with nostalgia to the closeness that pervaded family life in the golden age when parents, grandparents, aunts and uncles, cousins and other kin, shared like things together. In most places, such family intimacy, with the church at the center of social life, is a venerated but outdated experience.

But this is not the first time that family life has changed in the United States. In colonial days and up to the mid-nineteenth century, most fathers and mothers worked side by side in or near their homes, farming or plying trades, sharing the responsibility of child raising. With the advent of the industrial revolution (which many sociologists consider the culprit in creating father-absence in families), husbands and fathers went off to work in factories or offices and became the sole producers of family income. Social custom dictated that mothers did not work outside the home but minded the hearth and nurtured the children. Around 1920, the number of working women began to climb. The number escalated during World War II. Immediately after the war, as servicemen returned home, there was a reaffirmation of the traditional family. The new era of prosperity created a baby boom, and wives and mothers were content to relinquish their wartime jobs and have their husbands support their families. Within two decades, however, the pattern reverted to earlier forms, as prosperity cycled to recession, and women (many of them now divorced) heartily plunged back onto the job market. Two-income families are now common, resulting in the absence of both parents from the home for extended periods. To counteract this trend there is a new emphasis on parents reducing their work hours, or working out a

9. Barbara Defoe Whitehead, "Dan Quayle Was Right," *The Atlantic Monthly*, April 1993, pp. 47ff.

time-and-a-half work arrangement, with either parent doing the part-time work.

The importance of father-presence is being reaffirmed today. Fatherlessness is considered by many the most harmful demographic trend in our generation. But fatherlessness can occur even when there is a father in the home if too much emphasis is placed on careerism and materialism, coupled with individualism that exhibits self-interest. In such cases there may be an emotional absence of fathers even when there is co-residency.

Some analysts find it difficult to define the family today, so fluid has the concept become. The census bureau has settled on "two or more persons related by birth, marriage, or adoption who reside in the same household." The Massachusetts Mutual Life Insurance Company, on the other hand, announced that their 1992 survey of randomly selected adults indicated that only 22 percent fit that description, and three out of four chose the broader designation of "a group of people who love and care for each other."

The black community especially experiences a tragic break-down of the family, with dire social problems for all of us as a consequence. In 1940, nine out of ten black families had a husband as head of the household. In 1970, it was six out of ten. Today, it has declined to just over three out of ten. The social repercussions are that drug use, violence, and promiscuity have escalated astro-nomically. Seven out of ten African-American males are now at risk. The effect on the growing young female population is also horrendous. Blacks and whites must work together to accentuate values that will help to bring back families that are more fully functioning.

Don S. Browning of the University of Chicago Divinity School, together with his wife Carol, a student of the family, declares that the family is not only changing; it is deteriorating. Christians, they claim, have strong theological reasons to cling to the mother-father team in its various forms. The principal task of the family is to raise their children to become healthy, responsible adults and, more im-portantly, to nurture them to become members of the kingdom of God. The Brownings reaffirm a limited concept of the family, one that does not include every living arrangement that provides friendship and mutual assistance. The Scriptural ideal of intact first marriages, they believe, provides a better support for raising children than do single parents, stepparents, or unmarried couples. To do this effectively they espouse an equal-regard love ethic for spouses in the postmodern family.[10]

No fewer than 47 percent of all families headed by single mothers (those who are either divorced or out-of-wedlock mothers) live in poverty, which contributes to the declining well-being of children. They quote from Princeton University Sarah McLanahan's definitive research on single-parenthood: "Half of all children born in the 1980s will live with a single mother before reaching the age of 18. Half of these children will be poor. As compared with children from the same social class who live with both parents, children of single mothers are twice as likely to drop out of high school and become single parents themselves, and half again as likely to have trouble finding and keeping a steady job."

Churches have been negligent in paying insufficient attention to these trends, they claim. Mainline churches viewed family problems as private issues, while conservatives failed to understand the complexity of family problems. "Both," say the Brownings, "have been so preoccupied with abortion and homosexuality that they have glossed over the less sensational stresses of people trying to raise children to healthy adulthood." Charles Murray's October 1993 editorial in the *Wall Street Journal,* they note, asserted that the family issue is the biggest public issue of our time.[11]

Many Christian single parents, however, widowed, or, for various reasons, divorced, are heroically facing a challenge that is great, and doing it with remarkable success, thanks to the help of supportive churches and the nurturing they received in their own families. It is in loving, nuclear families that they learned about grace, about loving and being loved, about forgiveness and acceptance — in brief, about unconditional love.

10. Don S. Browning and Carol Browning, "The Church and the Family Crisis," *The Christian Century,* August 7-14, 1991, pp. 746-49.

11. Don and Carol Browning, "Better Family Values," *Christianity Today,* February 6, 1995, pp. 29, 30, 31.

Pockets of nuclear family propinquity retaining traditional values can be found throughout the country. We read about them on the offshore islands of Maine, for example, where families living close to nature are unplagued by the social ills that afflict our large urban centers. For them, the old axiom is still true: families that pray together, stay together. Churches across the country are also filled with families holding to these high ideals. They are raising a generation of young people who are the hope of the religious and cultural life of America.

Whose Happiness?

The widespread dissolution of the nuclear family, most frequently through divorce, is painful for both parents and children, but especially harmful to the children. More than 80 percent of children grew up in two-biological-parent families in the decade following World War II. By the 1980s, however, only 50 percent of the children lived with both of their parents in an intact family. Now, less than half of the children can look forward to spending their lives together with their fathers and mothers, and many will experience family breakup two or three times during childhood.

The emotional effects of divorce on children are long-term and devastating. Some parents endeavor to console themselves with the thought that their children will recover from these painful splits as easily as they themselves do, that within a couple of years they will resume their normal composure. This comforting assumption is being challenged, however, by indications that the traumatic effects linger long. Divorce is a process, not an event, and the wounds are not soon healed.

Sometime in the 1970s, many adults shifted concern for their children to concern for their own happiness. In previous decades, many unhappy marriages were held together for the sake of the children. It was thought that, even though the parents were not happy together, divorce would have a harmful effect on the children, and so they endured the trying relationship. Barbara Dafoe Whitehead notes that the situation has now changed drastically. She cites

Hallmark cards that commemorate divorce as liberation. "Think of your former marriage as a record album," says one. "It was full of music — both happy and sad. But what's important now is . . . YOU! the recently released HOT, NEW, SINGLE! You're going to be at the TOP OF THE CHARTS!" Another card reads: "Getting divorced can be very healthy! Watch how it improves your circulation! Best of luck! . . ."[12] The social stigma once associated with breaking up a family with children has generally disappeared.

But the effects on children remain agonizingly stressful. A mother who remarries no longer has the same name as her children. When children enroll in school, or fill out an application form for any organization or activity, they put down their names as Robert Brown or Jane White, but their mother's new name as Mrs. Mary Dove. There is a sense of fractured identity and canceled continuity that causes the children more suffering than their parents realize. It often takes three to seven years for stepfamilies to blend.

Stepchildren, when there is remarriage, have more developmental, emotional, and behavioral problems than do children of intact families. Step-parenthood does not recreate the nuclear family. More than half of all second marriages also end in divorce, sending both parents and children into another emotional maelstrom.

There are happy exceptions. I have witnessed families held together after divorce by a caring mother or father, particularly in cases where parents have higher spiritual and educational levels, where children are active in church groups and are trained to be citizens of the kingdom of God. But it takes grace!

It is important to underscore this spiritual factor, for without it fractured families face formidable problems. Some young women tell me that they are skeptical about marriage, fearful of being betrayed as their mothers were. I know of young men and women who have entered theological seminaries and the ministry in the hope of finding new meaning and confidence in life. It does not always work. Years later, some still evidence deep-seated hostilities and social pathologies.

The attitudes of uncoupled parents toward each other influence

12. Whitehead, p. 52.

their children's adjustment. They can become fiery foes or remain forever-friends. When both parents remain involved with their children's lives, the children fare far better.

A redemptive factor in many communities is the creation by churches of well-staffed day-care centers. In my own experience a well-ordered church day-care center with spiritual substance has been a positive factor in the religious life of both parents and children.

A new troubling phenomenon is the increase of uncoupled parents who are morally unfit to care for their young, and who, through such dereliction, create a "skip-generation" situation. Fortunately, in many instances, grandparents who have retained a value system of yesteryear are able to give the children the love and nurture they deserve. Such grandparents, noted for their patience, kindness, and gentleness, can nurture the moral stamina to resist or break the pattern of abuse into which these unfortunate children have been born. The "fruit of the Spirit" is the best antidote to the deleterious "works of the flesh."

The Bright Side of Aging

It is no longer true that "life begins at forty"; for many it begins at sixty-five, when they retire. New medicines and cures for formerly debilitating illnesses, social security, pensions, and investment income enable parents who retire to live comfortably and productively in what can be for many a rewarding and fulfilling period of their lives. They have parented their own children; now they also enjoy grandchildren, sometimes even great-grandchildren.

The secret of aging gracefully is affirmation. Aging is not a slow, sad descent to the grave. People who feed their minds with "whatever is true, whatever is honorable, whatever is just, whatever is pure, whatever is pleasing, whatever is commendable," things that are "excellent . . . and worthy of praise" (Phil. 4:8), avoid much of the stress that is harmful to health, happiness, and peace of mind.

Give me a young man in whom there is something of the old, said Cicero, and an old man in whom there is something of the

115

young. Guided so, one may grow old in body but never in mind. Akin to this thought is the affirmation of Marcus Aurelius that a man's life is what his thoughts make of it. Henry David Thoreau added a bit of sparkle to it when he said that none are so old as those who have outlived enthusiasm. Today, in our gender-inclusive culture, we would, of course, include women in these counsels.

Thoughtful parents plan ahead for autumn years, perhaps purchase a condominium, or reserve an apartment in a retirement community, many of which are commodious, equipped for gracious living, programmed for continued intellectual and spiritual enrichment and lifelong support. It has been a joy for me to teach college-caliber courses at a condominium-apartment complex in which many of the residents have been former college teachers, professionals, and business people, who challenge me with their mental vitality. They read, research, and discuss psychological, ethical, cultural, and theological subjects with an eagerness and understanding that would put many college students to shame. They have found the "fountain of age."

Jung affirmed that even in old age we are growing toward realization of our full potential, as his own life illustrates. A biographer notes that his reputation flourished as he grew into old age. Most of his influential books were published in the latter part of his life as his intellectual horizons continued to widen.[13]

Life expectancy in Western countries has increased more than twenty-five years during the twentieth century. Norman Cousins, whose *The Anatomy of an Illness* caused physicians to consider more seriously the psychosomatic aspects of life, and who later became Adjunct Professor in the School of Medicine at UCLA, has written *Head First*,[14] in which he draws upon hundreds of exchanges with physicians, patients, medical students, and research scientists to prove that positive attitudes are not merely moods but biochemical realities, and that faith, hope, and love, plus a will to live, can combat serious disease. He envisions productive lives of 120 years, a prog-

13. Anthony Stevens, *Jung* (New York: Oxford University Press, 1994).
14. Norman Cousins, *Head First: The Biology of Hope* (New York: E. P. Dutton, 1989).

nostication that reflects the pronouncement of the book of Genesis. If one is what one thinks, as it has been alleged, what benefits would accrue to patience, kindness, goodness, faithfulness, gentleness, and self-control!

Parenting Parents

Parents in many instances will be parenting their own parents for many more years. By the year 2000, it will be common for four generations — parents, children, grandchildren, and great-grand-children — to live simultaneously.

An ancient saint once prayed: "Do not cast me off in the time of old age; do not forsake me when my strength is spent" (Ps. 71:9). It is a plea in all generations. The generation that once counseled us not to trust anyone over thirty will begin turning sixty-five in the year 2011. By 2030, one-third of the population of the United States, the 77 million baby boomers, will be senior citizens. The Geritol generation will control the twenty-first century. In the way the rising generation is nurtured, and in the values that control their lives, the values of patience, kindness, and faithfulness, as well as gratitude, will determine the quality of the comfort and care they will give to their aged parents.

An inspiring story of filial love and faithfulness is the dramatic life of Joseph, the favorite son of Jacob and Rachel. He was sold as a slave by his jealous brothers to traders bound for Egypt. There he was purchased by Potiphar, a high government official, and distinguished himself as a highly moral servant. When he resisted the seductions of Potiphar's wife, however, she had him thrown into prison, where he gained a reputation for interpreting dreams. When Pharaoh summoned him to interpret his troubling dreams, Joseph predicted a period of prosperity followed by seven years of drought. In gratitude for this insight Pharaoh made him premier of all Egypt, with a special portfolio on famine preparedness. When the famine eventually spread to Canaan, his brothers came down to Egypt to buy grain. After a series of encounters in which he tested them, Joseph revealed himself to his terrified brothers but assured them that he had no resentment. "You meant it for evil; God meant it for good." He then urged them to hurry back home to bring their aged father with all his flocks and family to Egypt. "I will provide for you there," he promised, "so that you and your households, and all that you have, will not come to poverty" (Gen. 45:9-11). For Jacob, as the long period of mysterious loss ended, it was "the glory of an ineffable sunset through parted clouds at the end of a long, dark day."[15]

In the New Testament, we find frequent exhortations to care for widows, both Hellenists and Jews. James succinctly summarizes the early Christian credo: "Religion that is pure and undefiled before God, the Father, is this: to care for orphans and widows in their distress, and to keep oneself unstained by the world" (Jas. 1:27).

Take a contemporary case of aging parents who had been extraordinarily active in their younger years, especially in the church, who reached a time when familial wisdom dictated the advisability of their moving to a friendly retirement community. The mother, though busy with a large family, had for years chaired the hospitality committee of their church, arranging receptions for weddings, anniversaries, and memorial services. The father, who had served repeatedly on his church's ruling board, through hard work had achieved comfortable financial independence. At ninety, he suffered a mild stroke, and after a few days in the hospital was transferred to a nursing home for therapy, where, between breakfast and his morning bath, he peacefully passed away with a heart attack. The mother gradually suffered memory loss through natural senility and was transferred to one of the finest Christian rest homes in the city. A dedicated staff of nurses keeps her dressed as though constantly ready for guests; her hair is perfectly coiffured, and she is invariably fresh. At ninety-seven, she no longer recognizes her children, but they visit her regularly in the belief that loving contact works in mysterious ways. That man and woman, I am humbly grateful to say, are my father and mother, and all the brothers and their wives, also grateful for their long lives of devout example and service, "do

15. Walter Bowie, "Genesis," in *The Interpreter's Bible*, vol. 1 (New York: Abingdon Cokesbury Press, 1952), p. 803.

not cast [them] off in the time of old age, [nor] forsake [them] when [their] strength is spent."

A quite different story made headlines in early 1992. An old man, his name tag tied to the side of his wheelchair, was taken to a dog race track in Idaho by one of his daughters and, after the race, abandoned. At eighty-two, a victim of Alzheimer's disease, he had required round-the-clock care and, eventually, transfer to a nursing home. The financial and psychological strain on the daughter was too much for her. Her patience gave out. So her father became another statistic in grandpa-dumping. Fortunately for him, the story hit the newspapers and another daughter, who had been abandoned by him years before after a divorce, discovered his picture in her local newspaper and rescued him, though he no longer recognized her. It is estimated that there may be 100,000 aged people abandoned by their families each year, often quickly rolled into hospital emergency waiting rooms and left by weary relatives, maids, household employees, or landlords.

What a difference Christianity makes! Christlike virtues abound where Christian parents take care of their aged parents. They get their inspiration and stamina from the Spirit of Jesus Christ.

CHAPTER SIX

A Contagious Congregant

I f you want to be truly happy, join a joyous church. A loving church fellowship is the extended family of the crucified and living Christ. The New Testament nowhere encourages solitary spirituality. Not to belong to a fellowship of believers is as anomalous as loving flowers but not gardens. "No man is an island, entire of itself," wrote John Donne. The church is composed of individual believers who endeavor to become more and more like Jesus, but it is also the corporate body of Christ in which the many members are mutually related, as organs of the body — in Paul's figure of speech — each dependent upon the other.

Our finest friendships often mature within the life of the church. Romances between members frequently ripen into marriage. Here family life is nurtured. Worship broadens our concern for others so that we become good neighbors and citizens in a widening world. At every stage in our spiritual journey with kindred hearts and minds, our lives are colored by the personality of Jesus.

A church indwelt by the Spirit will manifest "the truly good qualities which only Jesus Christ can produce" (Phil. 1:11, Good News Bible). Its members will manifest other-directed rather than self-seeking love, joy rather than gloom, peace rather than quarrelsomeness, patience rather than short-temperedness, kindness rather than meanness, goodness rather than apathy, faithfulness rather than fickleness, gentleness rather than harshness, and self-control rather than dissoluteness. The transforming power of the Spirit of Christ will be conspicuous in its worship, its study, the living of everyday life, and the way in which it implements its social concern and action.

The apostle Paul was especially exuberant about joy in the Christian experience — joy expressed in the praise of God and doing the will of God. Praise is the joyful celebration of the excellence of another. "There is no such thing as joyless praise of God," writes Yale's Leander E. Keck in his provocative book *The Church Confident*. "Where the news of God is clear and good, it evokes joy in those who receive it." He cites the Protestant Reformation, the Wesleyan movement, the revivals on the American frontier, and the church today to show that "When the greatness of God become real, the church is renewed, and there is joy in the heart and a song on the lips of the people of God."[1] He notes the unfortunate coincidence of a church located next to a restaurant whose kitchen equipment was being repaired by a company whose service truck parked between them carried the sign "Refrigerated Services." Spirit-filled churches are enthusiastically joyous.

The word *enthusiasm* comes from two Greek words (*en,* "in" and *theos,* "god") that mean to be inspired by God. Authentic religious enthusiasm is not artificially whipped by exuberance, like the hype created by pep-rally cheerleaders. It is a spiritual artesian well. Christians in all generations rejoice together because "the Lord hath done great things for us, whereof we are glad" (Ps. 126:3, King James Version).[2]

---

1. Leander E. Keck, *The Church Confident* (Nashville: Abingdon Press, 1993), pp. 40, 41.

2. For a theology of the church see Gabriel Fackre and Dorothy Fackre, *Christian Basics: A Primer for Pilgrims* (Grand Rapids: William B. Eerdmans Publishing Co., 1991), chapter on "The Church," especially the paragraphs on "celebrating." By enthusiasm, I do not have in mind contemporary charismatic movements that are appealing to turnoffs and dropouts from traditional mainline churches by replacing organ music with rock and emphasizing casual dress (jeans and shorts) and folksy worship (with much hugging), coupled with a demanding conservative theology. Churches such as these have been phenomenally successful through a multiplicity of personalized ministries in radically transforming the lives of a significant segment of American youth and the blue-collar population, notably those who have been addicted to drugs, alcohol, and aberrant sex. Many of these churches are paying the unpaid bills of dull mainstream churches. In ministering

Unless God's Spirit lives within a church, it self-destructs. Without the presence of the Spirit of Christ nurturing the fruit of the Spirit, you have no church. You could have the most beautiful ecclesiastical edifice imaginable, but unless the Holy Spirit is active in it, you have not a church but a religious museum, if not a mausoleum. A vital church, however, is a faithful fellowship of contagiously loyal followers of Jesus.

The apostle rhapsodizes on the church as "one body and one Spirit." In one of my favorite passages, he tells the Christians at Ephesus that God has given the church apostles, prophets, evangelists, pastors, and teachers "to equip the saints for the work of ministry, for building up the body of Christ" (Eph. 4:12). Speaking the truth in love, he continues, we must grow up into Christ, who is its head, "From whom the whole body, joined and knit together by every ligament . . . promotes the body's growth in building itself up in love" (vv. 15-16). He uses the same analogy in his first letter to the Christians at Corinth: "the body does not consist of one member, but of many" — feet, ears, hands, sense of smell — all interdependent, so that "if one member suffers, all suffer together with it, [and] if one member is honored, all rejoice together with it" (I Cor. 12:14, 26). And then to counteract their tendency to divisiveness, he follows his counsel with his magnificent poem on love in the thirteenth chapter.

The ideal church includes people of all ages and social status. Children find it to be a spiritual home as much as their parents do, with provision for their care in nurseries and in education and music. Young people in some churches drop out after confirmation and high school, but not in churches that provide vital ministries and fellowships for them. Increasingly, however, young people who have dropped out of church in adolescent days return again when they mature, marry, have families, or simply because they come to themselves and realize that there is something essential missing in their lives. The burgeoning number of singles is a special challenge to

---

to people of a more traditional culture, mainline churches need not mimic the ecstatic aspects of the charismatics, but reclaim the genuine joy and enthusiasm of the early New Testament Christians.

churches today. Many of them are finding a spiritual as well as a social home in the church.

A distinction between "spirit" and "institution" is still a major concern for many. Spirit for them is the inner, experiential aspect of religion; institution is the outer, established form of religion. "The distinction is increasingly pertinent," writes Wade Clark Roof, "because of the strong emphasis on the self in contemporary culture and the related shift from objective to subjective ways of ordering experience."

Some of us belong to downtown clubs that have engraved plaques on their doors, "For Members Only." This you will never find on a church door. The church is not an exclusive club of spiritual elites. The fact is, you will never be a vital member unless, realizing that you have missed the mark of God's intention, you are rescued by the saving grace of Jesus Christ. "Church" in the Greek New Testament is *kyriakon,* the Lord's house, and *ekklesia,* those called out. It is the extended family of Christ, "the household of God" (Eph. 2:19-20).

A twenty-seven-year-old woman once confessed to a pastoral counselor that ever since she had been a Christian she felt that she could face life successfully with the combination of God's help and her own efforts. "Now that has collapsed," she said. "God and I cannot live alone. We both need other people."[3] We need other people to receive God's help; God needs other people to deliver the help.

The Good News of the Glad God

Christians are enthusiastic because we believe that Jesus Christ, "our crucified and risen Lord . . . has come to us and shared our common lot, conquering sin and death and reconciling the world to himself. By the Holy Spirit he calls us into his church to accept the cost and joy of discipleship."[4]

3. Wayne Oates, *Pastoral Counseling* (Philadelphia: Westminster Press, 1974), p. 35.
4. *Statement of Faith,* United Church of Christ, 1957.

Like the apostles, we, too, have been entrusted with "the glorious gospel of the blessed God" (I Tim. 1:11), a message of personal salvation from sin, with implications that are ethical, social, economic, and political. There is "joy in heaven over one sinner who repents" (Luke 15:5) and then reaches out in love to others. We are saved to serve. The New Testament tells us how we can become a positive influence in the world. And the message does not end with the sacred writings. It is a continuing story — *The Third Testament* — in Malcolm Muggeridge's arresting phrase, his account of transformed lives throughout history.

We are not left to our own resources. The fellowship of believers is a "life-support" system. Hospitals use life-support systems for the seriously ill. Like-souled people, often in small groups, are spiritual supports. Christ is the source of interdependent life. "I am the vine, you are the branches," said Jesus. "Those who abide in me and I in them bear much fruit" (John 15:5). Vital linkage with his Spirit creates faithfulness, gentleness, and self-control.

The Radiant Fellowship

A Spirit-animated church is a radiant fellowship. The favorite New Testament word for it is *koinonia,* a warm family of faith and service. The early Christians spoke of it as "the communion of saints." By "saints" they did not have in mind those who wear halos and are found in stained glass windows, but loving believers who look after each other. Thus Paul begins many of his letters "to the saints" — in Rome, in Corinth, in Ephesus, in Philippi, and so on. They knew peace and joy because they experienced the love of God, the grace of our Lord Jesus Christ, and the fellowship of the Holy Spirit.[5]

Fellowship is one of the main qualities people look for in a church. Christians of every denomination love the old hymn "Blest

---

5. E.g., I John 1:3, 4; II Cor. 13:13. Cf. *Theological Dictionary of the New Testament,* ed. Gerhard Kittel and Gerhard Friedrich, trans. Geoffrey W. Bromiley, abridged in one vol. (Grand Rapids: William B. Eerdmans Publishing Co., 1985), on these passages.

Be the Tie that Binds." The fellowship of kindred minds and hearts means as much to the faithful in our secularized society as it did to young converts in the Greco-Roman world. It was an amazing thing then, and it meant everything to those who shared it. "Here you have a Christian love-feast in the catacombs," writes James S. Stewart of Scotland, "and a Roman lady, with imperial blood in her veins, a kinswoman of the Caesars, taking the cup from the hand of a nameless waif of the streets, and both of them feeling it was the most natural thing in the world to do, for there was a love deeper than sisterhood between them now."[6] It is still the amazing experience of millions around the world.

The fellowship of believers is created by fellowship with Jesus. He promised that where two or three are gathered together in his name he is in their midst. Often this assurance has been used apologetically to give significance to a small gathering when a larger one was expected. The words have a higher meaning, however. Whenever we meet in his name we are an empowered community, for he is with us. Our worship, our fellowship, our committee and board meetings are inspired and guided by his presence. Individualism is supplanted by companionship. His unseen presence brings confidence and joy.

The communion is also enhanced by simple, random acts of kindness. A young minister, fresh out of seminary, took on the challenge of a small, declining village church. The old, foot-pedaled reed organ was played by a volunteer with minimal training, but she did her best, and the minister wrote her an occasional note thanking her for her contribution to the worship. One day, happening to call at her home, he saw propped up on her home organ the notes he had written. It taught him an important lesson. People flourish with appreciation. Simple acts of kindness do wonders for the fellowship.

It has been my privilege to minister to enthusiastic, joyous churches in village, metropolitan, and college communities. All responded so positively to the Word preached and taught, uniquely ministering to my soul also, that I hesitate to single out any one for

6. James S. Stewart, *The Gates of New Life* (New York: Charles Scribner's Sons, 1940), pp. 92-93.

special attention. Several of them were devout and dedicated fellow-ships that exuded deep spirituality. Yet one stands out preeminently. It had been considered by some as a large, wealthy, and rather cool congregation, but I found it to be quite different. During the week it became an infectious fellowship. Sunday mornings the spacious narthex resembled a family reunion. In between the two services a large group met to discuss the faith. At worship the congregation, led by a triumphant organ and choirs, lifted their souls as they sang the hymns. Smiles lighted the faces of the worshipers throughout the service; sometimes there was hearty laughter. They loved to hear the good news of the glad God. The fellowship hour that followed in the youth center for younger families with small children and in the parlors for other adults was a "happy hour" of animated conversation with friends and visitors. Members absent for a time were welcomed back with warm embraces. College students home for the holidays eagerly sought out their friends from youth fellowship days. They were a truly contagious congregation.

The apostle Paul knew such churches. To the magnificent church at Thessalonica he wrote: "What is our hope or joy or crown of boasting before the Lord Jesus at his coming? Is it not you? Yes, you are our glory and joy" (I Thess. 2:19). But his favorite church, I am sure, was the one at Philippi, the first congregation he established in Europe. The citizens gave him a rough time at first, but the congregation that grew there knew love and joy in a superlative way. They ministered munifi-cently to his needs, and a deep bond of affection developed between them. His short letter to them, written from death row in a Roman prison, is filled with his finest theology and throbs with his warm humanity. Fifteen times in this choice missive he speaks of rejoicing. "I wish you all joy in the Lord," he writes; "I will say it again; all joy be yours" (Phil. 4:6, New English Bible).

Christian fellowship nurtures all the fruit of the Spirit, but in this chapter I dwell mainly on joy as one of its distinguishing features. Joy, C. S. Lewis reminds us, "is the serious business of heaven." In a world gone mad, the news so often sad, it is good to know love that creates joy. Four features of this joy are noteworthy.

126

1. Christians are the most *joyful people* in the world.

"I don't believe it," says our typical skeptic. "To me," she continues, "most of the Christians I know are a somber and sour lot. Talk about killjoys — they are the most notorious. I don't cultivate their friendship, and I surely would not invite them to my parties."

There is, unfortunately, a modicum of truth in that cynical statement. Some Christians have just enough religion to make themselves miserable, not enough to make themselves truly happy. They are punctilious about their religious duties, attend church very regularly, pay their pledges faithfully, take on board and committee assignments dutifully, and endeavor to live righteously. And they make sure that everyone else does the same! One suspects that they were baptized with lemon juice!

That sort of dour spirituality so repelled Francis Thompson as a young man that he ran away from Christ. In his acclaimed autobiographical poem "The Hound of Heaven" he confesses:

> I fled Him, down the nights and down the days;
> I fled Him, down the arches of the years;
> I fled Him, down the labyrinthine ways
> Of my own mind; and in the midst of tears
> I hid from Him, and under running laughter.

The reason, he tells us, was that he was afraid that in having Christ he would have to give up all else. But when the "Hound of Heaven," as he affectionately calls his Lord, finally caught up with him he learned:

> All which I took from thee I did but take,
> Not for thy harms,
> But just that thou might'st seek it in my arms.
> All which thy child's mistake
> Fancies as lost, I have stored for thee at home;
> Rise, clasp My hand and come!

Friedrich Nietzsche, the son of a Protestant minister, became a militant adversary of Christ because of the negative image created by many of Christ's followers. "His disciples," he said, "should look more redeemed."

These, however, are the exceptions.

The most gleeful Christian I have known was a Portuguese Jew who became a pastor to his own people. His father had been a professor of jurisprudence in Indonesia and had emigrated with his family to The Netherlands just before the outbreak of World War II. As the Nazi armies swarmed over the lowlands, my friend was taken in by a Christian family. They often hid him in between the walls and floors of their home when they suspected a Nazi raid. Many a time he felt the thumping of rifle butts against the ceiling and walls as the German soldiers endeavored to ferret out the protected Jews. He was so impressed by the risking love of his courageous Dutch protectors that, once free after the war, he himself became a Christian. His fiancée, coincidentally, had the same experience. Reunited at war's end, they married, emigrated to the United States, and settled in the greater metropolitan area of New York City, where he became a pastor to the Jews. Not a missionary, he insisted, for Jews are not heathen; they, too, worship Jahweh. Whenever I called him on the telephone and asked how he was, he exclaimed, "Oh, full of joy! Full of joy!" It seemed almost unreal. He had been saved in so many ways that life for him was full of rejoicing.

His joy was not dependent upon external circumstances, for he knew affliction. As a guest in our home in another city some time later, I was amazed at the array of pills he spread out on the breakfast table each morning. "My land, Ernie," I exclaimed, "you're a walking pharmacy!" "No," he smilingly replied, "for months I lived on tulip bulbs fried in candle grease. I'm a human wreck for Jesus Christ."

An exceptional person? But he is not alone in the experience of joy that transcends circumstances.

Malcolm Muggeridge spent some time with Mother Teresa after interviewing her for the BBC. She impressed him as a person from another world. She and the other members of her order seemed to be always smiling. "Is it a put on?" he asked. "Oh no, not at all," she quietly replied. "You see, nothing makes us happier than when we reach out in love to someone who is hurting."[7]

7. Cf. Robert Schuller, *The Be-Happy Attitudes* (Waco: Word Books, 1985), p. 137.

Joyous Christians are commercials for Jesus Christ. They resemble the early followers of Jesus. Those who feed on "the bread of life" become spiritually and psychologically vivacious. Biblically and theologically illiterate folk living on the thin pablum of religion in general, always running after some new idea, have at best a superficial joy. The model life of the members of our mother church was exhibited in their devotion "to the apostles' teaching and fellowship, to the breaking of bread and the prayers" (Acts 2:42).

How does one explain such joy? C. S. Lewis, "surprised by joy" when he became a Christian, wrote: "I had hoped that the heart of reality might be of such a kind that we can best symbolize it as a place; instead, I found it to be a Person." Like the early Christians, he caught the infection of joy from Jesus himself.

2. The secret of Christian joy is Jesus Christ, *the joyful man.*
Jesus began his ministry at a synagogue service in his hometown of Nazareth. Invited to read the lesson, he unrolled the scroll to the words of the prophet Isaiah:

The Spirit of the LORD is upon me,
Because he has anointed me to bring good news to the poor.
He has sent me to proclaim release to the captives
And recovering of sight to the blind,
To let the oppressed go free,
To proclaim the year of the LORD's favor.

Rolling up the scroll, he sat down to speak. Every eye was fixed on him. His next words were like a meteor lighting the sky in their minds. "Today this Scripture has been fulfilled in your hearing" (Luke 4:16-21). He himself was the epitome of the good news he had come to share with all people.

Jesus did so many things that brought comfort and joy. First of all, he went to Capernaum, a lakeside town by the Sea of Galilee, and, strolling along the shore, saw Simon and Andrew casting their nets into the sea. "Come after me, fishermen," he called to them, "and I'll teach you how to fish for men!" Others were also called to join him, and with twelve disciples he proceeded to crisscross Palestine proclaiming, "The time has come at last! The Kingdom of

God has arrived. You must change your hearts and minds and believe the Good News" (Mark 1:14-15, Phillips).

His favorite way of teaching the good news of the kingdom of God was with short stories. "Without a parable he told them nothing" (Matt. 13:34). Today's theologians would call him a "narrative theologian."[8] It was a form of communication that has never lost its appeal. The stories of the lost sheep, the lost coin, and the lost son, for example, climax with the note of joy on being found, calling for a celebration or a party.

The Beatitudes of Jesus are irresistibly appealing. Like a nine-faceted diamond, their truth startles us with shafts of spiritual insight, each one expressing the height of joy. Little wonder that Matthew placed them early in his gospel as an introduction to the summary of Jesus' teaching, the Sermon on the Mount. In effect they say, "O the bliss of being a Christian! O the joy of following Christ! O the sheer happiness of knowing Jesus Christ as Master, Savior and Lord."[9]

Jesus was a master psychiatrist, ministering mind and soul relief to those depressed with guilt feelings. His characteristic assurance to penitents was: "Your sins are forgiven . . . go in peace" (Luke 7:48, 50). Peace-giving forgiveness is the most therapeutic experience in the world.

He was also the great exorcist, casting out demons (psychopathic symptoms, we are told today).

As the Great Physician, he empathized with the suffering, the blind, and the bereaved, healing them and giving them comfort. He understood the anguish of the outcasts, for he himself knew rejection. He wept, once at the tomb of a dead friend and once over a dead city.

Children jumped into his lap. Sinners felt at ease with him in confessing their wrongdoings. He enjoyed weddings and created gal-

8. Cf. Gabriel Fackre, "Narrative Theology: An Overview," *Interpretation* 37 (October 1983): 340-52. See also Gabriel Fackre, "A Narrative Theology of Revelation," and "Narrative Theology in Evangelical Perspective," in his book *Ecumenical Faith in Evangelical Perspective* (Grand Rapids: William B. Eerdmans Publishing Co., 1993), pp. 89-122, 123-46. William C. Placher, "Hans Frei and the Meaning of Biblical Narrative," *The Christian Century*, May 24-31, 1989, pp. 556-59.

9. William Barclay, *The Gospel of Matthew: The Daily Study Bible* (Edinburgh: The Saint Andrew Press, 1962), p. 83.

lons of the best wine at one of them when the supply ran out. Criticized by the pietists of his day for not fasting as others did, he likened his ministry to a wedding reception, he being the bridegroom and his disciples the attendants (Matt. 9:15). "When you fast," he told his disciples, "don't look miserable like those play actors! For they deliberately disfigure their faces so people may see that they are fasting. Believe me, they have had their reward. No, when you fast, brush your hair and wash your face so nobody knows that you are fasting — let it be a secret between you and your Father. And your Father who knows all secrets will reward you" (Matt. 6:16-18, Phillips).

He was, of course, the man of sorrows as well as the man of joy. As sinister forces plotted his death, his anguish at the prospect of the cross pressed bloody sweat out of him in the garden. He was betrayed, denied, and deserted. The sorrows, however, came from without; the joys from within.

His emphasis on joy climaxed in the upper room the very night he was betrayed. At the Lord's Supper table he spoke to his disciples of his great love for them and the love they were to have for each other. He concluded with this arresting word: "I have said these things to you so that my joy may be in you, and that your joy may be complete" (John 15:11). There is in the Library of Congress a document, dated 1514, allegedly written by Publius Lentulus, said to have been Roman Procurator of Judea either before or after Pontius Pilate, a record that purports to give a description of Jesus. "He is a tall man, well-shaped and of an amiable and reverend aspect; his hair is of a color that can hardly be matched, falling into graceful curls . . . parted on the crown of his head, running as a stream to the front after the fashion of the Nazarites; his forehead high, large and imposing; his cheeks without spot or wrinkle, beautiful with a lovely red; his nose and mouth formed with exquisite symmetry; his beard, of a color suitable to his hair, reaching below his chin and parted in the middle like a fork; his eyes bright blue, clear and serene. . . ." There then follows a striking statement that has had a wretched influence on art: "No man has seen him laugh."[10] The

10. Cf. Sherwood Eliot Wirt, "The Heresy of the Serious," *Christianity Today,* April 5, 1991, p. 43.

document is, in fact, a hoax that circulated widely in Europe. The dismal impression persists today.

In a village church on the northeastern coast of Maine such a picture of Christ hangs in the center of the chancel behind the pulpit; it portrays Jesus as sad and pensive, certainly not joyous. For more than three decades as we worshipped there on our summer vacations it cast a somber spell over the hour of worship for me.

We have lived too long with the impression that Jesus was exclusively a man of sorrows. He did indeed know sorrow, as all do, but he was preeminently the disseminator of good news and joy. The gloomy legacy of the medieval mind is a travesty of the New Testament, copied by artists who have bequeathed to us myriad portraits of the sad-faced Christ. Thus the German mind of Albrecht Dürer portrayed him as a young man in his thirties on the cross, head bent sideways and slightly forward, crowned with thorns and ravaged by sorrow. Similarly, El Greco's Spanish Christ portrays him with gray, sunken cheekbones, eyes black, a cold cadaverous face quivering in agony against a thunderous sky. Certain churches and cathedrals major on this one-sided presentation of Christ. Would that we had more portrayals of Jesus in his ministry. The crucifixion was not the last word. Why do we not see more of the glorious Christ of the resurrection? Surely this is the major theme of the Bible.

3. The Bible is the most *joyous book* in the world.

The good news of redemption is proclaimed on page after page of the New Testament. As the apostles and their successors reflected on Jesus years after his resurrection, they decided to preserve what they had seen and heard in what are the epistles and gospels. They all point us to the living Christ. The reality that holds these twenty-seven very different books of the New Testament together is the inspired memory of Jesus Christ, the long-promised Messiah. The Holy Scriptures are the road signs, as Kierkegaard has reminded us; Christ is the way.

The New Testament opens and closes with overtures of joy, and wherever you read in between, joy sparkles even in the darkest circumstances like bright stars studding the midnight sky. The Bible contains enough tragedy to make it the saddest book in the world, yet, in spite of this quality, it is the most joyful. Students comparing it with the sacred writings of other religions invariably reported to me that to them the New Testament stood apart from all others precisely in its note of joy.

If we compare the New Testament to a newspaper, the four Gospels give us the front-page good news, and the epistles present columnists' commentaries on the news. We hear angels choiring their glorias to the shepherds on Bethlehem's hillsides, Mary singing her Magnificat, and Zechariah and Elizabeth, Anna and Simeon rejoicing that the long-awaited Savior has been born. When Jesus began his ministry, "great throngs heard him gladly." Those whom he restored went away rejoicing. He entered the holy city amidst the palms and plaudits of the populace. When he reappeared in resurrection light after his crucifixion, "the disciples were glad when they saw the Lord." Following his ascension they returned to Jerusalem "with great joy," and were continually in the temple "blessing God."

The book of Acts recounts all that Jesus continued to do and teach through his disciples. At a rapturous Pentecost, three thousand were added to their fellowship. The Christian message became a spreading flame of light throughout the Mediterranean world and beyond. Philip introduced Ethiopia's Secretary of the Treasury to Jesus by explaining Isaiah's prefiguration, and he goes on his way rejoicing. Paul, once a persecutor, became the primary propagator of the good news. When he and Silas were incarcerated for their witness in Philippi, they told their terrified jailer, his prison tumbling into ruins in the earthquake, about Jesus, and he and his whole household were baptized and rejoiced. The book is replete with story after story of the same joyful response as churches were established throughout the empire.

The most mysterious book of all, the Revelation of Jesus to John, is the Easter book of the New Testament. Written in coded cartoon language, probably to baffle their persecutors but convey comfort to first-century Christians, it reaches a climax in the triumph song of life, which Handel captured in his Hallelujah Chorus: "Hallelujah! for the Lord God omnipotent reigneth. The kingdom of this world is become the kingdom of our Lord and of his Christ; and he shall reign forever and ever. King of kings, and Lord of Lords. Hallelujah!" The risen Christ is the final conqueror.

4. The good news produced the most *joyful religion* in the world.

"The kingdom of God," wrote Paul, "is joy in the Holy Spirit" (Rom. 14:17). "All life has become a song," declared the ancient church father Clement; "plowing, we praise; sailing, we sing." To Hermas the Holy Spirit was "a happy Spirit." To Barnabas, Christians were "the children of joy."

In our own century, Henry Van Dyke's exuberant hymn "Joyful, Joyful We Adore Thee" speaks of God as the wellspring of the joy of living. All nature sings a paean of praise to the God of glory and the Lord of love, "field and forest, vale and mountain, flowery meadow, flashing sea, chanting bird, and flowing fountain," as we mortals "join the happy chorus . . . in the triumph song of life."

Christianity alone among the religions of the world, James S. Stewart reminds us, knows how to sound the harp. Other religions have noble precepts but their music is plaintive. Christianity, like a mighty organ, pulls out all the stops to glorify and praise the God of creation and redemption.

The church, however, has had its days of compromise and contradiction. Unsanctified Christians have committed horrible acts in the name of God. The Crusaders, the Spanish Inquisition, the Reformation persecutions, the wars of religion have stained our history. They were perverted attempts to impose a limited and twisted faith on others. They were the back eddies, not the mainstream of Christian devotion.

Nonetheless, Christianity ranks supreme among the religions of the world.

I would not be a Christian if I believed that all religions were of equal value. Christianity deals realistically and redemptively with sin and guilt and radiantly with grace and gratitude. God is a great God, greater than any theological system can explain, and the New Testament presents us a glimpse of God in Jesus that is unsurpassed by any other sacred writing. The essence of this revelation is that God is love, a love that creates grateful joy.

The Essence of Joy

The dictionary tells us that joy is a vivid emotion of pleasure, a state of happiness or felicity, exultation of spirit, gladness, and delight. But Christian joy is more. It includes these, but transcends them all.

It is more than happiness and pleasure. Aristotle considered happiness the supreme good. The founding fathers of our nation considered the pursuit of happiness to be one of our inalienable rights. Happiness, however, is dependent upon circumstances, the things that happen to us. The word comes from the little Scandinavian word "hap." Happiness is created; joy is a gift.

Pleasure can be found in good company, good books, inspiring concerts, gourmet dinners, and exciting games. In its lowest sense, it is associated with indulgence and sensual gratification. Before we came to Christ, writes Paul to Timothy, "we were . . . slaves to various passions and pleasures." Pleasures wear off and need to be repeated. They are short-lived vanities, according to the ancient wise man of Ecclesiastes. In our own time, few have depicted their costly pursuit in the upper-world of New York city as vividly as contemporary novelist Thomas Wolfe in his *The Bonfire of the Vanities*. But joy is more than pleasure and happiness.

Joy is more than humor and laughter, though both are healthy and beneficial. Elton Trueblood was so intrigued by it that he wrote a book on *The Humor of Jesus*. Norman Cousins gives his personal story of their healing power in his *The Anatomy of an Illness*. Many a tense board or committee meeting has been relieved by a saving sense of humor. Henry Ward Beecher, Brooklyn's popular and controversial nineteenth-century preacher, championed many causes that elicited bitter criticism from some of his congregants. He was saved by a sense of humor. One week he received a note in the mail with just one word: "Fool!" He took it into the pulpit the following Sunday, held it aloft, and announced that he had often received letters from people who had forgotten to sign their names, but that week he had received a note from a person who had signed his name and forgotten to write the message! A healthy sense of humor can be a saving grace.

Christian joy embraces all these, but surpasses them all with a special quality. "I wish you all joy in the Lord always," Paul wrote

135

to his favored Philippians (Phil. 4:4, Revised English Bible). The determinative phrase is "in the Lord." Such joy is more than joie de vivre, a hearty enjoyment of life. It comes from being accepted by God, belonging to Jesus Christ, inspired by the Spirit, and knowing it. It is God's highest guerdon of grace.

Those of us who were brought up on the Heidelberg Catechism will recall how it summarizes all of Christianity in the carefully crafted, personal, and practical first question and answer. "What is your only comfort in life and death?" it asks, and answers: "That I belong — body and soul, in life and in death — not to myself but to my faithful Savior, Jesus Christ, who at the cost of his own blood has fully paid for all my sins and has completely freed me from the dominion of the devil; that he protects me so well that without the will of my Father in heaven not a hair can fall from my head; indeed that everything must fit his purpose for my salvation. Therefore, by his Holy Spirit, he also assures me of eternal life, and makes me wholeheartedly willing and ready from now on to live for him."

Christian joy, therefore, is a gift of grace, a divine gift freely bestowed on us. Let "grace" in this sense stand as an acronym for "God's Riches At Christ's Expense."

At Christmas time we sing "Joy to the world! The Lord is Come." On Good Friday we sing "In the Cross of Christ I Glory." On Easter we sing "Come, Ye Faithful, Raise the Strain of Triumphant Gladness." At every season we sing "O For a Thousand Tongues to Sing My Great Redeemer's Praise."

The Dark Underside of Joy

To experience sadness and depression, however, is not a contradiction of one's Christianity. Some well-meaning authors assert that Christian commitment and depression cannot coexist, that a depressed Christian is a contradiction in terms. A few categorically call depression a sin. This is a cruel and misinformed judgment.

If it were so, what shall we say about Moses, Elijah, David, Jeremiah, Jonah, and Paul? Anxiety and depression are no respecters of persons. Great theologians and preachers have not been immune.

136

Martin Luther and John Wesley were not strangers to it. London's eloquent Charles Haddon Spurgeon confided that he knew "by most painful experience what deep depression of spirit means."

It is estimated that twenty million Americans of all groups and classes suffer depression at any given time. A prominent New York City minister declared that the sobs of his affluent Park Avenue parishioners mingled at sunset with multitudes around the world. His mission, he said, was to shepherd parishioners with fat wallets and paunches, Wall Street business and brownstone home addresses, in the same way that his colleagues cared for the suppressed in Harlem or in the South Bronx.

Depression is so widespread that the number of therapists is legion. A new resident in the community, a practicing psychiatrist, came to our house to pick up a power mower I had sold him. In our casual conversation I asked him why most people consulted him. Without hesitating he replied, "depression." It has been called the common cold of mental illness.

Historians like to divide time into various ages. Early in the century there was the age of melancholy. A few decades ago there was the age of anxiety. Depression is a subject that also intrigues artists. W. H. Auden wrote a lengthy poem about it, Leonard Bernstein followed it with a symphony, and Jerome Robbins acknowledged it with a ballet.

Somewhere between the 1940s and the 1960s anxiety gave way to depression and despair. Feelings of hopelessness, insomnia, irritability, guilt, fatigue, weepiness, as well as thoughts of suicide, torment its victims. "It is like hell," complained one sufferer.

Depression takes many forms.[11] Clinical depression is a full-scale fall into meaninglessness that may last for months and recur year after year. It can creep up on us as quietly as an ocean fog on the Maine coast, draining us of all energy and zest and making us feel terribly alone. "It is impossible for me to laugh, or find joy in life," commented one counselee. "Think of it, no joy in life!"

11. Cf. David Myers, *The Pursuit of Happiness* (New York: Avon Books, 1992), p. 145. Valuable insights into depression are furnished by the *Baker Encyclopedia of Psychology* (Grand Rapids: Baker Book House, 1985) and *The New Harvard Guide to Psychiatry* (Cambridge, Mass.: Belknap Press, 1988).

Manic depression, on the other hand, may make a person feel as high as a kite one day and plunge the sufferer into the depths the next.

Sometimes we mask it. "Smiling depression" often goes unnoticed by family and friends, even by the one suffering from it. Recently a high Washington official who had given not the slightest inkling of his inner feelings drove to a park one afternoon and put a pistol to his head.

Depression in its many forms, however, is not to be confused with what used to be colorfully called "the blues." This down-feeling may come during the shorter, darker days of winter in northern climes, when a bean-sized part of the brain called the pineal gland produces the hormone melatonin. William Cullen Bryant expressed it for many:

The melancholy days are come,
    the saddest of the year,
of wailing winds and naked woods,
    and meadows brown and sear.

It is a temporary feeling, often treated with medication and additional light, or by getting out of doors more often, or perhaps by taking a Caribbean cruise! Many northerners benefit from going south to a warmer and sunnier climate during the winter months.

The causes of depression vary. In ancient days, it was often considered a spiritual malady. The hermit monks in the Egyptian desert in the fourth century lived solitary and ascetic lives. Since depression attacked them most severely during the heat of the day, they identified it with the noonday demon of Psalm 91:6 ("the destruction that wastes at noonday"). Restless, lethargic, and unable to concentrate in prayer, many entertained thoughts of abandoning monastic life. Thomas Aquinas and other concerned church fathers thought of it as misdirection in spiritual life.

Conscience-distress may be a root cause, as Shakespeare's Macbeth, the writer of Psalm 51, and the Paul of Romans 7 ("wretched man that I am!") graphically portray it. Conscience is the God-created umpire in our breasts, calling out "foul" according to John Milton in

138

his *Paradise Lost*. Sometimes it is overworked, lashing at negative aspects of conduct long after we have repented and been forgiven, robbing us of all peace and joy.

Scientific ethicists recognize that our biology plays a significant role in these moods. The cause may be genetic, sometimes running in families for generations. A genetic link to manic depression, a "marker" on one of the forty-six chromosomes, has been discovered among certain Amish in Pennsylvania. In a quite different case, a minister's wife, writing about her husband's depression, revealed that it was diagnosed as a matter of body chemistry: he had hypoglycemia and couldn't tolerate sugar.

Overemphasis on individualism is another cause for its spread among young people and middle-aged Americans, according to Martin Seligman, research professor at the University of Pennsylvania. Self-absorption and self-centeredness are rife. People used to work hard to get a job done; today many are too much concerned with themselves and their inner feelings. The "California Self," says Seligman, has replaced the "New England Self."

Is there a way out of the pit? Today's therapies are numerous. In certain acute cases a milder use of electroconvulsive therapy (ECT) is again being prescribed. The most commonly sought-out remedy is long, costly periods of psychotherapy. The psychological-medical approach has shown promise. Today, knowledgeable people speak of neurotransmitters, synapses, and dopamine, as well as Prozac and other healing agents. The interplay of biological and psychological factors propels the search for new wonder drugs. The pharmacy has become an adjunct of the psychiatrist's couch. Pills cannot change personalities, but they can relieve the symptoms of disorder. They often correct a chemical imbalance, thereby enabling one's true personality, long imprisoned, to reemerge.

Reality therapy, a new approach to psychiatry founded by William Glasser, emphasizes the importance of concentrating on the present and looking to the future rather than digging into the past with all of its faults and failures. This was also one of the marks distinguishing the psychiatry of Jung from that of Freud. Whereas

139

Freud emphasized the importance of the past and concentrated on looking backward, Jung looked forward and emphasized the importance of concentrating on future goals.

Thought-control therapy is taking a new look at the power of positive thinking. Debunked for decades because of unrealistic emphases, its beneficial effects are now receiving respectful attention from psychologists and other therapists. Martin Seligman finds that optimism can be learned, that "people who have a pessimistic explanatory style and suffer bad events will probably become depressed, whereas people who have an optimistic explanatory style and suffer bad events will tend to resist depression."[12] Psychologist David G. Myers blends his skeptical bent as an empiricist and his biblical faith into a stimulating mix. Religion without science shields itself from new understandings, he claims, but science without religion shields itself from deep understandings.[13]

The role of faith occupies a prominent place in the Bible. "Why are you cast down, O my soul, and why are you disquieted within me?" asks the Psalmist. "Hope in God; for I shall again praise him, my help and my God" (Ps. 42:11). The apostle Paul turns to the power of positive thinking as he writes to his beloved Philippians: "If there is any excellence and if there is anything worthy of praise, think about these things, . . . and the God of peace will be with you" (Phil. 4:8-9).

Better than Medicine

Joy is physically beneficial to us. We now have scientific evidence that a positive outlook and optimism are vitally important in improving health. Our body's immune system fights disease more effectively when we are happy. A study of two groups of heart attack survivors revealed that whereas the first group received only the usual therapy, the second group also received counseling on renew-

12. Martin E. P. Seligman, *Learned Optimism* (New York: Alfred A. Knopf, 1991), p. 77.
13. Myers, p. 22.

ing their religious commitment and enjoying life; the result was that the second group suffered only half as many repeat heart attacks as the first group.[14] Norman Cousins, after ten years of exchanges with physicians, patients, medical students, and research scientists, declares that positive attitudes are not merely moods but biochemical realities.[15] They can combat serious disease. Joy is a medicine.

Christian joy is also psychologically beneficial to us. Here is a person who was born with impaired eyesight. His retinas register only part of what he observes. In the early grades of school he had difficulty with arithmetic: 8 often looked like 3. The result was limited education. While his brothers progressed educationally and professionally, three of them earning doctorates, he contented himself with manual labor. Retirement came early because of further deterioration, but after a brief spell of depression, his effervescent self reemerged. Today he enjoys life to the fullest, travels extensively with a wonderfully supportive wife, and has an infectiously hearty laugh. The secret of his buoyancy lies in his deeply religious nature, an attitude that knows how to "rejoice in the Lord," which keeps him psychologically on top, and equips him with "the peace of God which passes all understanding" (Phil. 4:4-7).

Christian joy is also spiritually beneficial to us. Terry Anderson spent 2,455 days in wretched circumstances as a hostage in Lebanon, blindfolded, beaten, and chained to the furniture of his cell. Reporters who interviewed him on his release were amazed that he showed no resentment or hatred toward his captors. What was the secret of his buoyancy? The support of his fellow captives was a big help, he replied, but more important was the faith and practice of prayer that was nurtured in their private sanctuary that he called the Church of the Locked Door.

Fellowship that nurtures joy creates contagious Christians. At Holy Communion services, I often recall a hymn we used to sing: "O Jesus, Joy of loving hearts . . . from fullest bliss that earth imparts we turn unfilled to Thee again." It was at the Last Supper that Jesus

14. Myers, pp. 21, 76-77, 185.
15. Norman Cousins, *Head First: The Biology of Hope* (New York: E. E. Dutton, 1989).

said, "My joy I give unto you." This joy is enhanced by the good news preached. "I want a preacher," comments Bruce Larson, "who can't wait to tell me the Good News every Sunday morning. Deliver me from the preacher who is going to tell me one more time to shape up."[16] Our hearts yearn for edification and inspiration.

An inspiring church is more than a building; it is a fellowship of people of joy. I confess that I enjoy worshipping in a beautiful edifice. It can be a worthy monument to the glory and grace of God. I have found inspiration in the grandeur of Chartres glass windows depicting scenes from the Old Testament and the New Testament, a radiant chancel with luminous gothic panels portraying scenes from the four gospels, and a glorious rose window above the rear balcony. I thrill to a mighty organ, and banners suspended cathedral-like, symbolizing redemptive events. But, more important, a church is people, people listening intently to the good news, offering prayers of thanksgiving, intercession, and supplication, singing hymns of praise, "sharing in Christ's baptism and eating at his table," and going out empowered to serve a needy world with the love, joy, peace, patience, kindness, generosity, faithfulness, gentleness, and self-control of the Spirit of Christ.

An article in a Nashville, Tennessee, newspaper told about Lila Craig, who hadn't missed attending church for 1,040 Sundays! She was in her eighties. "It makes one wonder what's the matter with Mrs. Craig," commented the editor. "Doesn't it ever rain or snow in her town on Sundays? Doesn't she ever have unexpected company? How is it that she doesn't go anywhere on Saturday night so that she's too tired to attend church on Sunday morning?" What's the matter with Mrs. Craig? Nothing. She has found a spiritual fellowship of enthusiastic believers that help her to "rejoice in the Lord." The fruit of the Spirit is joy.

16. Bruce Larson, *There's a Lot More to Health than Not Being Sick* (Waco: Word Books, 1984), p. 129.

CHAPTER SEVEN

A Beneficent Neighbor

Robert Frost's farmer, in the memorable poem "Mending Wall," says, "Good fences make good neighbors." We instinctively agree. Privacy is proper, we feel. We parenthesize our parcels of property with rails and hedges, some of them spectacularly artistic. The venerable stone walls that embrace wooded domains along the New England seaboard, for instance, evoke a respect for history and instill a sense of privacy.

And yet there is something within us that does not like a wall. It shuts us in as it shuts others out. Seclusion engenders the sensation of separation, even segregation.

Spirit-life nurtured within the church among friends, lovers, spouses, and families reaches out to others in neighborliness. Good neighbors, without being ostentatious about it, are notable for their conspicuous goodness and kindness.

Love without Fences

There are formidable fences that need to be torn down, both religious and social.

Shortly after he had founded Tuskegee Institute, Booker T. Washington, the prominent African-American educator, walking through one of the more exclusive sections of his town, was stopped by a wealthy white woman who, not knowing him, asked if he would like to earn a few dollars splitting her wood. Washington smiled, took off his coat, proceeded to split the wood, and neatly stacked the pieces in the proper place in the kitchen. A servant girl, recognizing him, later identified him to her mistress. The next morning the embarrassed woman went to his office at the Institute and profusely apologized. "I didn't know it was you that I had put to work," she said. "That's perfectly all right, madam," Washington replied; "occasionally I enjoy a little manual labor, and besides, it's always a delight to do something for a neighbor." She shook his hand warmly as she left, and not long afterward he received a check of several thousand dollars from the woman and her friends.

A few years ago Robert Ringer's book *Looking Out for Number 1* became a best-seller and was soon followed by *Winning through Intimidation*. These books appeal to the human ego, getting the best of others, clawing one's way to the top. While most people resent such aggressiveness, many are drawn to such blatant self-interest. The epistles and the Gospels, however, exalt the more winsomely attractive fruit of the Spirit.

There was a day when an advance missionary party of seventy, sent out by Jesus to preach and heal in the district to which he intended to go, returned exuberant about their success. What should really give you deeper joy, Jesus responded, is that your names are written in heaven (Luke 10:20).

At that moment, a lawyer who had been waiting on the edge of the crowd to pose a question, much like a reporter at a presidential Rose Garden press conference, asked: "Teacher, what must I do to inherit eternal life?" Surmising that this was a trick question, Jesus answered his question with a question. "What is written in the law?" The legal expert knew the counter-answer well. In fact, it was inscribed in the phylactery bound around his forehead. He spontaneously replied: "You shall love the Lord your God with all your heart, with all your soul, with all your strength, and with all your mind; and your neighbor as yourself." "Quite right!" said Jesus. Then, more interested in his ethics than in his theology, he said, "Do that, and you will live."

The startled lawyer had been waiting too long for a disputation to be put off so summarily. Recovering quickly, he pressed his question further: "But who is my neighbor?"

A BENEFICENT NEIGHBOR

Jesus dignified his query with an insightful story about a man who was traveling down the precipitous road from Jerusalem to Jericho, and was attacked by bandits, who stripped him, beat him up, and left him half dead. It so happened that a priest came along, and when he saw him lying there bloody at the roadside, discreetly passed by on the other side. A Levite also came by a short time later, and passed him by. But then a Samaritan came along and, seeing him lying there, was touched with compassion and bandaged up his wounds, using oil and wine. Then lifting him up on his own mule, he brought him to an inn, registered him in a comfortable room, and further attended to his wounds. The next day he gave the innkeeper two dollars with the request, "Look after him, will you? I'll pay you anything more that you spend when I come through here on my return." Looking the lawyer straight in the eye, Jesus asked: "Which of these three seems to you to have been a neighbor to the bandits' victim?" (Luke 10:25-37, Phillips).

The parable needs no elaborate commentary. It weaves together all the elements of reality. The steep 22-mile stretch of road descending 3,500 feet between Jerusalem and Jericho, long known as "The Bloody Way," was infested with robbers who hid in the crevices and caves, ready to pounce on solitary travelers. The priest and the Levite may have had religious scruples about being rendered unclean by touching a presumably dead body. One quipster suggests an emendation: "When they saw that he HAD been robbed, they passed by on the other side!"

What startled the lawyer was that Jesus introduced as the hero of the story a despised half-breed Samaritan and deftly rephrased the question: "Which of these three was a neighbor to the man who fell into the hands of robbers?" The question was no longer academic, "Who is my neighbor?" but existentially personal, "Who proved to be neighbor?" "The one who showed mercy," conceded the lawyer. With a telling thrust Jesus responded, "Go, and do likewise."

Performance, not perception, is the important thing. To love our neighbor as ourselves is to love without reservation, motivated by goodness, generosity, and kindness. It is to love as we love God, with passionate hearts, sensitive souls, spiritual strength, and intel-

145

ligent minds. Love of God without love of fellow humans is no love at all.

Little wonder that the parable has come to be known as "The Good Samaritan." *Bene,* the Latin word for well, or good, is used in many combinations: benefit, benevolence, and beneficent. The Samaritan was a beneficent neighbor. He did good.

Neighbor love, according to Jesus, is global. Neither race, religion, nor ethnicity should limit our concern for others. "Neighbor" in the Old Testament generally denoted a person in covenant with Israel, though the later books of Ruth and Jonah broke with this exclusiveness. The New Testament applies the injunction universally to anyone in need. "Neighbor" refers not only to the recipient but also to the giver. We who carry Christ's name are challenged to cosmic compassion. Neighbor is coextensive with humanity. It does not distinguish between Jews and Gentiles, Protestants and Roman Catholics, Asians or Africans, Americans and others whether black, yellow, brown, red, or white. All are created equal in God's sight. All reflect the divine image. Everyone is an "I" or a "Thou," never an impersonal "It." The Samaritan saw a wounded human being and stooped to help. That, said Jesus, is being a neighbor.

Outgoing love, to be sure, may be risky. Abraham Lincoln risked the presidency to emancipate the slaves. Albert Schweitzer, who earned doctorates in theology, medicine, and music, hazarded the contagions of Africa to minister to the sick. Mother Teresa, with first-class educational credentials, stoops to bandage the sores of India. Seamen brave boisterous waves to rescue those in distress. Firefighters choke their way through smoke and flames to save lives. Police brave bullets to quell riots. Surgeons and dentists expose themselves to infection to operate on HIV-positive patients. We are all called upon to risk position, prestige, or privilege to help those in need.

Simple neighbor love sympathizes by writing a respectable check; Christian love empathizes by writing a sacrificial check. Neighbor love rises to its highest stature when it ministers personally to others with hands-on care. In our life in society, we are intimately related to all God's children. We may not live isolated lives.

In Praise of Goodness

Goodness is best defined by what we do. We must be good in order to do good. Casuistry, a literal and legalistic following of prescribed patterns of behavior, persists in certain pockets of both Catholicism and Protestantism, but authentic goodness is a matter of character, not a slavish following of detailed rules. It is easy to follow specific rules; you can check them off one by one. Rule-book religion, however, misses the point. It is too simple. It is casuistry.

Martin E. Marty, church historian at the University of Chicago, recounts an astonishing incident about two sailors in a naval training program at a pietistic college, a story hard to believe were it not told by a scholar of Marty's stature. The draft-depleted campus was populated mainly by attractive coeds who welcomed male companionship. The college was governed by a strict rule book of be-good regulations. A couple of the sailors who had come to know a few of the girls rather well invited a couple of them for a Saturday night date, and asked what they might do together. They could go dancing, one sailor suggested. No, they could not, the men were informed; the rules did not permit it. How about an evening of cards? No, there was a rule against that too. How about the tavern? Not on your life! "We don't want to get into trouble; we keep the school's rules!" "What is there left to do?" the sailors asked. Did the women have any ideas? "Well," they said, "there is a hotel downtown. Why don't we check in for the night?" The sailors were astonished and asked for an explanation. The answer: there's nothing in the rule book against that!

Morality so external shocks us. Change the scene, however, and you can find legalist families and churches that narrowly prescribe certain patterns of conduct but that, like the Pharisees whom Jesus exposed, neglect the more important ethics of the Law. Authoritarianism imposes rules from without. Genuine morality is animated by the Spirit from within. The Law is a guide for living, but, living by the Spirit, we are challenged to live up to our high identity with Christ (cf. Gal. 5:25).

"If anyone is in Christ," writes Paul, "there is a new creation; everything old has passed away; see, everything has become new"

147

(II Cor. 5:17). This is the new life from above that Jesus endeavored to explain to the learned Pharisee Nicodemus. God's Spirit renews us by progressively transforming us into the very image of Christ. Piety, in the best sense of the word, begets practice. Such is the goodness that is worthy of praise.

Profession and Practice

The lawyer's question about eternal life is a paramount concern for everyone, for our chief purpose in life is to know and enjoy God forever. But personal salvation is not an end in itself. We have been saved in order to serve. It reminds one of the old story about a Quaker who invited a neighbor to his Sunday Meeting. After sitting in silence for a long time, the neighbor whispered, "When does the service begin?" To which the Friend whispered back, "The service begins when the worship ends." In the Christian life neither ends; personal experience issues continually into service to others.

The criterion for judgment on the great day of days will be how kind we were to the hungry, the thirsty, the stranger, the naked, the sick, and the prisoner. "Just as you did it to one of the least of these who are members of my family," Jesus declared, "you did it unto me" (Matt. 25:35-40). We are never more like Jesus than when we are good to others.

Some speak of the good life as enjoyment of large homes, luxury automobiles, vacation villas, club memberships, world travel, designer clothes, gourmet foods, ample bank accounts, and swelling investment portfolios. If that is the good life, why are so many who live it dissatisfied and depressed? Self-absorbed people do not have enough to live on! Many who lived through the "Me" decades, with the greed that accompanied them, no longer look back on them as "the good old days." They have become disillusioned with its tawdry values and have become a generation of seekers looking for something that will give greater fulfillment. The things we amass will never satisfy; the good life, as Jesus promised, is to live "abundantly" with the inner resources which his Spirit provides.

I once asked a jeweler how one could tell the difference between genuine pearls and imitations. He replied: "The smooth surfaces of the imitations shine with an artificial sheen; the genuine glow from within." Genuine goodness has a spiritual glow.

Goodness is doing "something beautiful for God," according to Mother Teresa. Human conduct can be considered good, writes Emil Brunner, only when and insofar as God himself acts in it through the Holy Spirit.[1]

The difference Christ makes in human life is graphically depicted by the apostle Paul in his contrast between the "works of the flesh" and the "fruit of the Spirit." The culture of apostolic times had its noble aspects, but it also reveled in wretched depravities. Paul gives us a gruesome catalogue of the deeds of the lower nature: "sexual immorality, impurity of mind, sensuality, worship of false gods, witchcraft, hatred, quarreling, jealousy, bad temper, rivalry, factions, party spirit, envy, drunkenness, orgies and things like that" (Gal. 5:19-21, Phillips). The person who lives the life of the Spirit, however, radiates "love, joy, peace, patience, kindness, generosity, faithfulness, gentleness, and self-control" (vv. 22-23). Good trees bear good fruit, said Jesus; bad trees produce bad fruit.

The Generosity of Goodness

The Christ-life is defined best by those who personify goodness. In the early church, Barnabas stands out as one whose goodness was generosity. "He was a good man, full of the Holy Spirit and of faith" (Acts 11:24). His name means "son of encouragement." Goodness (*agathosyne*) is translated "generosity" in a number of versions. Barnabas was generous because he was good. He would never have made *People* magazine, but he made the New Testament!

For one thing, he had a generous hand. He shared his wealth with the poor in the struggling church. Many early Christians were disinherited by their families and lost their livelihood and their

1. Emil Brunner, *The Divine Imperative,* trans. Olive Wyon (New York: Macmillan, 1937), p. 84.

friends because of their new faith. Barnabas had lands. He sold a tract and gave the entire proceeds to the church. His was no mere capital gains contribution; he gave the entire principal.

Barnabas also had a generous heart. When Paul was converted from terrorism, most of the early church members were suspicious of him. They found it hard to believe that he had suddenly become a true disciple. But "Barnabas took him, brought him to the apostles, and described for them how on the road he had seen the Lord, who had spoken to him, and how in Damascus he had spoken boldly in the name of Jesus" (Acts 9:26-27). Barnabas saved a great man for the church!

Barnabas was a good man because he had a generous outlook. He was a great ecumenist. He was one of the first to break the barrier between Jews and Gentiles. Ordinarily, to be accepted by the Jews, a Gentile had to become a religious Jew by observing the Jewish rituals and customs. When Jerusalem heard that newly converted Hellenists at Antioch had led many other Gentiles to the faith, the leaders of the church dispatched Barnabas to evaluate the situation. When, on arrival, he saw the divine grace at work, he rejoiced and encouraged them all to remain faithful to the Lord with resolute hearts (Acts 11:20-23). Back in Jerusalem he persuaded the Jewish leaders to accept the Gentiles into the Christian Church.

Barnabas was a good man because he had a generous spirit. He was collegial. He was willing to share responsibility and authority. As a team worker he was not threatened by a co-worker's gifts. After evaluating the phenomenal church growth at Antioch, he immediately set out to Tarsus for Paul and persuaded him to join him at Antioch. We would probably not be Christians today were it not for Barnabas. Through his influence, Paul became the great missionary to Europe.

Barnabas was a good man because he had generous goodwill. He was a great reconciler. He healed a rift that developed sometime later between Paul and John Mark, who, for reasons unknown, abandoned Paul on one of his missionary journeys and returned home. Paul was piqued by it, but Barnabas brought them together again. Writing to Timothy years later from a Roman prison, he made this heartwarming request: "Get Mark and bring him with you, for he is useful in my ministry" (II Tim. 4:11). Reconciliation is the master theme of the Bible, and Barnabas is an indefatigable exemplar.

Since the church leaders mentioned in the New Testament were mainly men, many feminists today consider it chauvinistic. The early church reflected the patriarchal culture of its day, yet Paul's epistles are replete with references to the contributions of women in the fellowship. An especially beautiful instance is the story of Dorcas of Joppa (Jaffa), the port city of Judea. She was a good person, one who filled her days with kindness and charity. She has been the inspiration for countless women's organizations that have called themselves Dorcas Societies. Paul also highly regarded Priscilla for her zeal in advancing the Christian cause, making frequent reference to her, often naming her before her husband. There was also Lydia, a dealer in purple cloth, who was the founding member of the church in Philippi. Many of the leaders in the church at Thessalonica were women. Greek women of high standing were also active in the church at Berea.[2]

Goodness continues to be generous today. Many Christians are 10 percent tithers. Some give 5 percent to civic and social causes. I have known several who give to the cause of "heavenly mansions" a sum equal to their yearly real estate taxes. If ministers want to create a storm in their churches, let them suggest in their yearly stewardship sermons that this would be a good norm for each congregant's pledge! A successful businessman told me at lunch that he gives 50 percent of his income to religious causes and lives on the remaining 50 percent. The conclusion of authoritative observers is uniform: the more active persons are in their faith communities, the greater their generosity. Their gifts of time, energy, and money are determined not so much by their income as by the level of their gratitude and commitment.

Recognize with appreciation the good performed by great philanthropists such as the Fords, Rockefellers, Carnegies, Mellons, and others, as well as by our service clubs and the social organizations that help the victims of drugs, alcohol, abuse, teen pregnancies,

2. Cf. Acts 9:36; 16:14, 15, 40; 18:1-3, 18, 26; Rom. 16:3; II Tim. 4:19. Cf. also Acts 17:4, 12.

and AIDS, for the Spirit inspires all human beings with a common grace. Save your greatest applause, however, for Christians who through their churches and religious communities give a far greater portion to alleviate human need. In the last decade alone, one-half of the 100 billion dollars given to charitable causes has come from religious men and women. No less than 57 billion dollars is given each year to specifically religious causes. No church has such limited resources that it cannot do something.

The Theology of the Hammer

Former President Jimmy Carter engagingly exemplifies neighborly goodness in a wide range of social concerns and activities. He and Rosalyn spend an entire week each year, clothed in carpenter's garb, wielding hammers, as they work with others in building houses for the poor with Habitat for Humanity.

They also hammer away at our national health care record and work of preventive care. Now that the Carters are no longer in the White House, and Jimmy Carter does not need to exercise restraint in dealing with senators from the Southern states, they both work to limit the expenditure of federal tax dollars that subsidize an industry responsible for most of the preventable death in our country. Their concern on the tobacco issue is global. "More Colombians are killed each year by tobacco imported from the United States," Carter charges, "than there are Americans killed by cocaine brought in from Colombia." And his Carter Center in Atlanta provides leadership in addressing a wide array of social problems.

He makes it plain that in his social action he is "about his Father's business." He is concerned about his neighbor's welfare because his faith demands it. Eschewing pride, he never ceases to remind his audiences that his humanitarian action is for the glory of God. Little wonder that *Time* magazine described him as our finest ex-president, living or dead.

Kindness: The Dynamic of Goodness

Kindness is the virtue we crave most in other people and the one that they seek in us. It is a beautiful word that expresses a winsome grace. It is the way God treats us. The New Testament Greek word for this Christlike fruit of the Spirit is *chrestotes*. Christians are *chrestoi*, reflecting Christ, who is *chrestos*.[3]

When we recognize it, it warms our hearts. A Swiss girl in her late teens named Ursula came to New York City to live in an American home and learn English in return for doing secretarial work, baby-sitting, and household tasks. She was an ordinary young woman without much money, but, realizing the vast extent of poverty in New York, she decided to buy a dress and give it to some poor child of the ghetto at Christmas. At the department store, she asked the doorman what part of the city was poorest, and with further directions from a policeman walked a number of blocks to Harlem. Eventually she found a bell-ringer for the Salvation Army who offered to help her find a little girl in need of a dress. Hailing a taxi, the two traveled to a certain tenement house. Ursula asked him to take her package to the door, ring the bell, and then leave the anonymous gift. The next day, after some questioning, she hesitatingly told the family with whom she was staying about the journey she had made.

"How do I happen to know all this?" asks Norman Vincent Peale. "I know it because ours was the home where Ursula lived. To this child from across the sea, we seemed so richly blessed that nothing she could buy could add to the material things we already had. And so she offered something of far greater value: a gift from the heart, an act of kindness."[4] By her simple act of kindness she influenced many people: herself, the Salvation Army man, the tenement family, the taxi driver, the Peale family, and people all over the world who hear her story.

3. *Theological Dictionary of the New Testament,* ed. Gerhard Kittel and Gerhard Friedrich, trans. Geoffrey W. Bromiley, abridged in one vol. (Grand Rapids: William B. Eerdmans Publishing Co., 1985), p. 1322.

4. Norman Vincent Peale, "A Gift From the Heart," *The Guidepost's Christmas Treasury* (Carmel, N.Y.: Guideposts Associates, Inc., 1972), pp. 116-21.

A minister friend of mine illustrates kindness in a quite different incident. Going home one night, he stopped for a quick dinner at a fast-food restaurant. After ordering a double cheeseburger and a chocolate milkshake, he sought a table toward the back where he could be more alone, away from the crowd. As he began to eat, he noticed that he was not alone. An old man was sitting in a nearby booth, humped over, tucked inside a ragged overcoat, no food on the table. He was dirty, virtually toothless, his long hair unkempt. The bag alongside of him probably contained his only belongings. Before my friend could marshal his thoughts to do something, a young mother with two children sat down in an opposite booth. Noticing the destitute man, she quietly stepped over to him, gave him a few dollar bills, and said, "Here, wouldn't you like to buy something to eat?" Without saying a word, but with a sense of pride, he waved the woman off. No one else paid any attention to him. As the mother and her children were finishing their dinner, my friend witnessed a remarkable thing. The woman put their refuse in the trash container and then slipped a neatly wrapped hamburger on the lonely man's table. "Here — we couldn't eat everything," she said, and quickly went out of the door. The minister wished that he had been more alert to the human need.

"Random Acts of Kindness" the new movement in the 1990s is called. Several companies have produced buttons and bumper stickers, articles have been written about it, and at least a couple of small books based on the phrase have been published.

Such kindness, Nietzsche thought, made one soft and weak. How wrong he was! It is tender and sensitive, but it is also strong and tough. Kindness is strong because it is active love. It counters the tendency to self-centeredness. Kindness does not look out for number one. It thinks of others. It knows nothing of malevolence or ill will. It is not unfeeling and callous, but compassionate and thoughtful.

I am surprised that Paul should quote a phrase from the Psalms and Isaiah to the effect that "there is no one who shows kindness, there is not even one" (Rom. 3:12). It is hyperbole, of course. He is underscoring the fact that human nature is not naturally good. Yet when he, along with Luke, on their voyage to Rome, were shipwrecked on the island of Malta, Luke tells us, "The natives showed us unusual kindness. Since it had begun to rain and was cold, they kindled a fire and welcomed us all around it" (Acts 28:2).

The virtue of kindness is more fully appreciated against the dark foil of heartlessness, just as jewelers frequently place diamonds on a dark piece of velvet under bright lights in order to intensify their splendor.

Numerous world figures serve as dark foils to kindness. The Roman Emperor Nero, it is said, was kind until he became ruler of Rome. Then, drunk with power, he became a tyrant, recklessly racing his chariot through the crowded streets by day and riding at night through his garden, where pitch-covered Christians tied to stakes lit the way as burning torches. Shakespeare has Lady Macbeth complain that her husband, who shuddered at murder, was "too full o' the milk of human kindness." Vladimir Ilyich Lenin, the revolutionary founder of the Soviet State and propagandist of violent class struggle, had a habit of writing far into the night. His wife, attending her dying mother, was exhausted after long hours of caring for her. Needing sleep, she asked Lenin to awaken her if her mother needed her. The next morning on awakening she was distraught to find her mother dead, and Lenin still writing. "You asked me to awaken you if she needed anything," he retorted. "She died — she didn't need you."

But unkindness is "not the way it's supposed to be." In the movie *Grand Canyon,* an attorney in his fancy sports car, eager to get home after an NBA game, runs into a traffic jam. He thinks he knows how to get around it, so he races down one street after another, losing his way. The streets of the inner city become more and more ominous. Then, like the central character in Tom Wolfe's *The Bonfire of the Vanities,* he runs into trouble in a danger zone. His car stalls. He immediately thinks of the hazard of being caught in harm's way in a gang-infested neighborhood and phones for road service. Before the tow truck can arrive, local toughs surround the car with covetous glares. The kindly driver of the tow truck arrives just in time and proceeds to hook up the sports car. But the toughs move in to stop him for foiling their plans. The driver takes the leader aside and schools him with a lesson on morals. "Man," he says, "the world ain't supposed to work like this. Maybe you don't know that, but this ain't the way it's supposed to be. I'm supposed to be able to do my job without askin' you if I can. And that dude is supposed to be able to wait with his car without you rippin' him off. Everything's supposed to be different than what it is here."

What is the way it's supposed to be? One of the great writing prophets tells us. "God has told you, O mortal, what is good; and what does the LORD require of you but to do justice, and to love kindness, and to walk humbly with your God?" (Mic. 6:8). David as the new king of Israel endeavored to do that. When he ascended the throne (as we noted in the chapter on faithful friendship) he sought out crippled Mephibosheth, and said, "I will show you kindness for the sake of your father Jonathan" (II Sam. 9:7).

"I expect to pass through this world but once," observed Grellet, as we have noted above; "any good thing therefore that I can do, or any kindness that I can show to any fellow creature, let me do it now . . . for I shall not pass this way again."

This takes grace. "The immeasurable riches of his grace in kindness toward us in Christ Jesus," shown by God, is the grace that motivates us to show kindness to others (Eph. 2:7). As we do it to members of his family we do it unto him (cf. Matt. 25:40).

For Christ's Sake

The contemporary face of neighbor-love is social concern. Some Christians are concerned that the church is putting too much stress on social action and neglecting the spiritual emphasis on the salvation of the soul. Careful reading of the Gospels, the epistles, and the prophets reveals that there is a balance of both emphases. Jesus was not just touched by human need and disability; he also fed the hungry, healed the sick, and drew the outcasts into the fold.

Active love for one's neighbor is not optional, therefore; it is linked with loving God. Listen to Isaiah speaking for God to those blind to social need: "Trample my courts no more; burnt offerings are futile; incense is an abomination to me. . . . Cease to do evil, learn to do good, seek justice, rescue the oppressed, defend the orphan, plead for the widow" (Isa. 1:12b, 16b-17). And hear Amos as he speaks for an outraged God: "I hate, I despise your festivals, and take no delight in your solemn assemblies. . . . Take away from me the noise of your songs; I will not listen to the melody of your harps. But let justice roll down like waters, and righteousness like an overflowing stream" (Amos 5:21, 23-24). As we have seen, this was also Jesus' emphasis in his inaugural sermon at Nazareth.

Some Christians are interested mainly in getting to heaven, not in bringing some of heaven down to earth. There is no doubt about it that Jesus came to give his life a ransom for many. But, as we noted in Jesus' first sermon at the synagogue at Nazareth, the planks in his platform were ministry to the poor, the captives, the blind, and the oppressed.

Others complain that we Christians have brokered too many causes that should be taken care of by the United Way and other social agencies. But Jesus had a working theology. He taught us to pray that God's will might be done on earth as it is in heaven. It is one of the glories of the church that it has lit the first of many of our philanthropies.

Philanthropy is a spiritual service. The church should not farm out its concern for alcoholics or drug addicts or poverty victims to secular agencies. It should join hands with them, for many are staffed by professionals. But it should also minister to these needs, and in so doing probe behind the symptoms to the spiritual reasons for people's problems. Christian neighborly and social concern should be theologically funded with love, patience, kindness, goodness, and gentleness. In so doing we will also be faithful.

Archbishop William Temple, esteemed as the most renowned Primate of the Church of England since the English Revolution, maintained that evangelism can take place only against the backdrop of social concern. Social action to him was "pre-evangelism." Moderns would be more easily led to Christ, he believed, if Christians showed love and kindness to those victimized by social conditions. His plea, and that of others, has been heard. Today many evangelicals are taking the lead in what was once considered the province of liberals.

Our growing social sensitivity is evidenced by a renewed emphasis on ethics. What was once a basic course only in theological seminaries is now assuming specialized forms in the curricula of other professional schools. Chairs of medical ethics, legal ethics, and business ethics are now common in many universities. The neighbor-love depicted in the Ten Commandments and the Sermon on the Mount is a timeless guide for "doing what is good."

"Christian" is more than a title, therefore; it's a job description. Seven concerns, at least, deserve our attention.

1. Sensitive Christians, first, seek to *eradicate racism*. The inspiration and the motivating power for breaking and tearing down ethnic and racial walls is the Spirit of Jesus.

The Nazi nightmare of a half-century ago forced the world to recognize the dark underside of goodness, as mass murder on a scale never before experienced exterminated a vast segment of the Jewish population of Europe. Multiplied thousands heroically risked their own lives to save those slated for death. Some sent their own children away for a time to protect them from the danger to which sheltering a Jew exposed them. It was their character, the way they had been raised, and their values that led humanitarian rescuers of the Jews to such feats of altruistic response.[5] They valued all human beings, not just those who shared their own religion and ethnicity. They were motivated by the principle of justice and the norms of family and church.

Today "ethnic cleansing" in Bosnia and rampant rivalries in Africa, the Middle East, and the Caribbean similarly create desperate cries for help.

If we ratchet back into the American experience, we shudder to think of the cruel enslavement of blacks kidnapped from Africa. I find inspiration in sitting in a certain pew in First Parish Church, Brunswick, Maine. Affixed to the back of the pew ahead is a bronze plaque stating that here Harriet Beecher Stowe, at a communion service, had a vision of the death of Uncle Tom. Her book, *Uncle Tom's Cabin,* played a determinative role in ending slavery in the United States. Her social concern was born from deep personal piety, a piety reflected in one of her hymns seldom sung today, "Still, still with thee, when purple morning breaketh . . . dawns the sweet

5. Samuel Oliner, *Altruistic Personality: Rescuers of Jews in Nazi Europe* (New York: Free Press, 1988).

consciousness I am with thee." Such spiritual sensitivity helped her to feel in the mid-nineteenth century what Martin Luther King, Jr., in our country, and Bishop Tutu and others in South Africa, have felt in the twentieth century: that whatever our color, we are neighbors created in the image of God.

I recall the thrill of listening one summer evening at our island cottage on the coast of Maine to Martin Luther King's address "I Have a Dream," proclaimed to the masses that thronged the mall at the Lincoln Memorial in Washington, D.C., and beamed by radio to the nation. With soaring eloquence he decried that "five score years" after the Emancipation Proclamation "the Negro still is not free." But he had a dream that one day the nation would rise up and live out the true meaning of its creed that all are created equal, and that when that time arrived all God's children would be able to join hands and sing the words of the old Negro spiritual, "Free at last, free at last. Thank God Almighty, we are free at last."

The patience and self-control King and many of his followers manifested through their long struggle can be explained by only one quality — their Christian commitment.

When King began his freedom movement in Montgomery, Alabama, he addressed his listeners as Christians. "I want it to be known throughout Montgomery and throughout this nation that we are Christian people," he declared. Today Stephen Carter, an Episcopalian and professor of law at Yale University, notes that when pundits discuss the work of Martin Luther King, the only member of the clergy whose life we celebrate with a national holiday, "the fact of his religious calling is usually treated as a relatively unimportant aspect of his career, if, indeed, it is mentioned at all." Mark Horst also notes that, "King began his civil rights activism as a preacher of the gospel, and it was the gospel that remained his guiding light throughout the next thirteen years of his life. The civil rights movement under his leadership was nothing less than a Christian social movement; it represented the outpouring of the Holy Spirit."[6] But the agenda of the civil rights movement remains un-

6. Mark Horst, "The Unfinished Agenda of the Civil Rights Movement," *The Christian Century,* April 27, 1994, pp. 446-48.

finished. The promise of the civil rights movement rests in the Christian church and the vitality of its gospel. A gospel that reconciles people to God but not to each other cannot be the gospel of Jesus Christ.

Refusing to be patronized as a minority, African-Americans are now emphasizing race as a gift to be affirmed. They celebrate the mosaic of diversity created in human beings of every color.

2. Earnest Christians labor to *abolish sexism*. "Gone is the distinction between . . . male and female. . . . You are all one in Christ Jesus," is the New Testament message (Gal. 3:28, Phillips). Patriarchy was the socially conditioned life-pattern of ancient biblical times, but it takes only one Deborah, one Phoebe, one Mary, one Lydia, and one Priscilla to challenge chauvinistic emphases today. Male and female are both created in the divine image and are endowed with equal status. Residual opposition to equality is exhibited by men who are threatened by the demonstrated competency of women and are often loath to loosen their monopolistic grip on power and position — whether they are physicians, lawyers, architects, clergymen, or blue-collar workers. But sexism marginalizes and impersonalizes half of the human race. Change is, fortunately, in process, and Christians should be in the lead.

3. Christians must work to *alleviate poverty*. "You always have the poor with you" (Matt. 26:11) is one of the saddest things Jesus ever said, but he did not countenance indifference. His parable about Dives and Lazarus depicted gross economic inequality as Dives lived sumptuously in a mansion, while destitute Lazarus sat at his gate hoping for a handout. Dives did not create Lazarus's poverty; he did not rob or exploit him. He simply ignored him when he had more than enough to help him. The dogs that licked the sores of Lazarus showed more compassion (Luke 16:19-31).

Poverty is a worldwide plague. In a trip around the world, my wife and I were not surprised to discover poverty in the Far Eastern countries, but we were shocked by the degree of mass suffering. In Bangkok, as we glided on small boats through the greasy klongs, we observed people with meager facilities taking their baths, performing their toilets, dumping sewage, and washing their dishes in the same polluted stream. Small boys, clad in skimpy swim trunks, eked out a meager living by boarding sight-seeing boats, a string of small brass bells chained about their waists, urging these trinkets upon tourists who did not have the hearts to avert their eyes. We confronted similar situations in Sri Lanka. But it came as an incredible shock to us to realize that even in the United States, with its vast resources, millions live at the poverty level, many because of systemic injustice.

Communism for years was the favorite whipping boy for Americans, but today many Christian leaders recognize that, for all its plus points, capitalism does not wear a halo. It can be cold, selfish, and greedy. In a challenge to Christian capitalists, Richard John Neuhaus argues that economics "should be brought under the Lordship of Christ,"[7] that people who know how to make money should put their skills under the sovereignty of God. Only moral entrepreneurship helps the marginalized and disadvantaged.

Churches increasingly are doing more to alleviate destitution. We need the government to help fight the drug war, to rebuild our deteriorating cities, and to monitor welfare. But we also need individual and personal involvement. We are learning to salvage for the poor many of the things we used to throw away. Furniture and appliances, with a little ingenuity, can be repaired and made available. We have good clothing in our closets that we are tired of wearing and that can clothe those who do not have enough. Instead of staging garage sales to net a meager profit, we can contribute to church networks that judiciously distribute superfluous items to the desperately needy.

4. In addition to alleviating poverty, we must *help the homeless and hungry.* They constitute a conscience-stabbing problem in our large urban centers and even in rural areas. The willingness of the nation to relegate so many poorly housed, poorly fed, and poorly educated to the role of economic and social outcasts, like the memory of slavery, is someday going to haunt us. The cleavage in our society between the admired rich and the disregarded poor cries to high heaven for redress.

In New York City stretch limousines disgorge jeweled wealthy who mince past burrowing street people to enter restaurants where

---

7. Richard John Neuhaus, *Doing Well and Doing Good: The Challenge to the Christian Capitalist* (New York: Doubleday, 1992).

dinner for four with vintage wines easily goes for several hundred dollars. Most are too contented to care.

Some, with a moral twinge, step around recumbent bodies on the sidewalks but feel individually helpless in the face of a problem that has no easy solution. They sidestep a sense of obligation to help by pointing to a long list of contributing factors: rent increases in federal housing, emptying of psychiatric wards, collapsing family life, unskilled job losses, alcoholism, and drug addiction. The list keeps growing. We may not be able to tell in every instance where the blame lies, but all human beings are God's children, and they need help.

Resigning ourselves to the ambiguity of the situation, we often conclude that many are the victims of their own sins, not those of the social system, and excuse our disinclination to help with the suspicion that many of those helped would soon be on the streets again, dissipating their handouts on alcohol and drugs. Ministers tell stories of being ripped off by those who relate pathetic tales, who make the rounds repeating the same stories. The best way of helping is to channel them through social and church agencies that have sufficient data at hand to screen the unscrupulous from the truly needy,

Still, sensitive followers of Jesus are disturbed by the ugly fact that too many Americans are concerned only with their own well-being. Some time ago I heard John Kenneth Galbraith, distinguished economist and former editor of *Fortune* magazine, lecture to a college audience about the complacency of our society. He recapitulated many of the theses of his books, notably *The Culture of Contentment,* in which he maintains that American culture in the past several decades has become a culture run by, and for, people who have become comfortably contented. They regard government programs to assist the less fortunate as an unnecessary burden but government support of their own affluence as a right, and are amazingly tolerant of the frightening income gap between rich and poor, the well-housed and the homeless. We are headed for disaster, says Galbraith, as a greatly expanded, seemingly permanent, underclass of people who do not work and do not vote have become a new caste system that has simply dropped out, a secession from the nation more dangerous than the Confederacy.

When we cannot do the big things alone we can organize to make a difference. Concerned groups convert unused buildings into living quarters, churches and cathedrals open their facilities at night as places for the homeless to sleep, and food pantries feed the hungry. Many, remembering the spirit of caring and sharing in the great depression of the 1930s, are not waiting for some new economic disaster to ignite compassion in an era of glitz and greed.

It took a sickbed visit to the mayor of New York City a few years ago for Mother Teresa to break through the food barrier to relieve the hungry in the world's leading metropolis. While the mayor was recovering from a stroke, she came calling, asking him to help her obtain surplus airline food that could be distributed in food kitchens run by her order in Harlem and the South Bronx. They soon learned that federal agricultural policy barred the distribution of food from international flights, which carried the most surplus food. The Secretary of Agriculture would not waive the rules. But though her first attempt ran into a bureaucratic wall, Mother Teresa did not give up. Together, she and the mayor discovered that there was a produce market that was looking for a way to salvage produce that otherwise would be thrown out. Within days she received her first shipment of vegetables. With the help of the mayor an even larger program was rushed into place, and the surplus of many places was channeled into a system of food pantries and soup kitchens providing over one million meals a day for hungry New Yorkers.

Caring Christians reach out beyond themselves. Nearly half of the forty-one billion dollars Americans give annually to their congregations is for service to others. They outdo others in neighbor-love. They do it for Christ's sake: "I was hungry and you gave me food, I was thirsty and you gave me something to drink" (Matt. 25:35-36).

5. Aroused by the colossal crime wave, concerned Christians seek for ways to *rehabilitate prisoners*. Charles W. Colson, founder of Prison Fellowship, for example, demonstrates that the most effective solution to our escalating crime and prison problem is the gospel, which "proclaims release to the captives." In the center of intrigue as Richard Nixon's "hatchet man," he was implicated in the Watergate scandal of 1974 and served a prison term, a trauma that precipitated a rebirth experience. He tells of his summer night visit with Tom Phillips, president of Raytheon Company, who had gone through a religious reorientation himself at a rally one night in New York City. Through Phillips's sharing of his experience with Colson, as well as his copy of C. S. Lewis's *Mere Christianity,* Colson was led, after much anguish and a conversion, to inaugurate his successful prison ministry.

Prison Fellowship is a nonprofit organization that now works in over 500 prisons across the United States and in over 54 other countries, transforming lives considered hopeless, reducing the number of repeat offenders, and decreasing the prison population through criminal justice reform work — all for a fraction of the money it takes (over $20,000 per inmate per year) to incarcerate them. Through in-prison seminars, Bible studies, prayer groups, and after-care programs, thousands of the toughest, meanest, hard-core criminals have been restored to socially useful living.

In recognition of his work, Colson, at sixty-one, was named in 1993 the recipient of the Templeton Prize for Progress in Religion, the largest prize in the world. It was established twenty-one years ago by John Marks Templeton, a financier, to compensate for the fact that Nobel prizes are not given for religious work. What has he done with the prize? He has donated it to the Prison Fellowship Foundation.

This is but one of a myriad of prison ministries that are being carried out by committed congregants throughout the country. It is work done for Christ's sake: "I was in prison and you visited me."

6. Christians should *love prostitutes*. Jesus did. The legalists of his day, as we noted in an earlier chapter, were shocked by his love for repentant profligates. One Pharisee in particular was disgusted that Jesus would stoop to deal with such a perverted person as the one who slipped in unnoticed at his dinner party to anoint Jesus' feet. He saw the kind of woman she was; Jesus also saw the woman. "Her sins, which are many, have been forgiven," Jesus explained, "hence she has shown great love." To the woman he said, "Your faith has saved you; go in peace" (Luke 7:36-50).

We, too, can assist programs that seek to restore others like her, most of whom hate themselves and their way of life.

Take the case of Marnie as told by a counselor at Genesis House in Chicago. Marnie became a prostitute at fifteen. She came from a severely dysfunctional family. Her father drank excessively. Her mother, constantly abused emotionally and physically, was afraid to leave the relationship. Often there was no food on the table, and sometimes the utilities were shut off because her father could not hold down a job. When she was only nine years old, while her mother was away one day, Marnie's father began six years of sexual abuse, always with the threat, "If you tell anyone, I'll kill you." Her sense of self-worth and self-confidence was destroyed. She did poorly in school. She yearned to be free.

She bought a bus ticket to the big city. Arriving in the strange city bewildered and alone, she accepted the invitation of a "kind" man to take care of her. He fed her well and dressed her in attractive clothes for several weeks, then introduced her to pornographic movies and cocaine. Shortly thereafter he demanded payment for his "kindness" and sent her out on the street, demanding that she return each night with a certain amount of money or face beating and no more cocaine. She was afraid to run away, for he had a network of street friends who would put her life in danger.

Genesis House came to her rescue, offering hospitality, hope, healing, and the possibility of a new beginning.

Similar places, such as Covenant House, form a network that stretches from Boston to Los Angeles, offering similar help and hope. After rehabilitation from drug dependence, they regain self-respect, complete their education, qualify for responsible employment, and find suitable housing. "Most of all," writes Sister Mary Rose McGready, "we give thousands of desperate kids something they've never had before, LOVE. . . . For the first time ever in their lives, some . . . will learn that they are loved . . . that their life is truly worth living."[8] They find the kindness and love that money cannot buy.

8. Sister Mary Rose McGready, *God's Lost Children* (New York: Covenant House, 1991).

7. Finally, and doubtless the toughest assignment of all, we are to *love our enemies*. There is no situation that calls for the repeal or the repression of love, not even war, devilish as it is.

A Scottish chaplain who had been taken prisoner of war in World War II relates how hard it was to hate the enemy en masse once he got to know the camp guards personally. David H. C. Read, preaching minister at Madison Avenue Presbyterian Church in New York City for four decades after the war, says that on his return to Great Britain from prison camp he found that civilians believed that anyone who had been in German uniform was a Nazi villain. No matter how much, as a prisoner, he had detested Hitler's regime, and no matter how much he had helped to plot escapes and spread despondency among the German troops, he realized that the term "villain" was not appropriate for all Germans in uniform. "It is easy to hate an anonymous enemy," he writes, "but it is not easy to hate someone you meet, another human being who shares planet earth with you."[9]

Similarly, Corrie Ten Boom, a Netherlander who sheltered Jews, tells of her suffering in a German concentration camp. After a miraculous release, she traveled extensively, telling of the grace that sustained her through those horrible years. On one occasion, in Munich, after she had finished speaking, a man came up to her whom she immediately recognized as one of her former prison guards, but who did not recognize her. "How grateful I am for your message, Fraulein," he declared, "to think that Jesus has washed my sins away." As he extended his hand, vengeful thoughts boiled in Corrie's heart. Instantly she felt how wrong they were. "Forgive me, and help me to forgive him," she prayed. She struggled to raise her hand, but it remained at her side. Again she prayed, "Jesus, I cannot forgive him! Give your forgiveness!" But then, she says, "as I took his hand, the most incredible thing happened. From my shoulder along my arm and through my hand a current seemed to pass from me to him, while into my heart sprang a love . . . that almost overwhelmed me."[10]

9. David H. C. Read, *Grace Thus Far* (Grand Rapids: William B. Eerdmans Publishing Co., 1986). pp. 7, 8.

10. Carole C. Carlson, *Corrie Ten Boom: Her Life, Her Faith* (Old Tappan, N.J.: Fleming H. Revell, 1983), p. 140.

Joseph Goebbels recorded a quite different story. As a youth, he was a deeply religious and literary-minded Catholic. His first diary, which he wrote as a supplement to the confessional, began, "May this book help me to be clearer in spirit, simpler in thought, greater in love." But gradually he was transformed into a zealous political organizer whose faith was solely in Adolf Hitler, and his diaries began to fume with hatred for the Jews. As Minister of Propaganda for the Third Reich his diaries rage that they "suck the blood from our veins. They are scoundrels, traitors . . . vampires." The diaries end on the day in 1945 when Goebbels and his wife killed first their six children, then themselves, rather than surrender to the Red Army as it swept through Berlin. Forsaking Christ, he jettisoned the virtues of Christ, the fruit of the Spirit.

Jesus startles us, therefore, with the challenge, "Love your enemies, do good to those who hate you, bless those who curse you, pray for those who abuse you" (Luke 6:27-28).[11] He did not say, you will notice, that we have to like our enemies. Nor does it mean that we should condone the evils done, or egotistically and patronizingly tolerate them. Jesus used the strong word of agape. And that means that our love, like God's, is to be nondiscriminating, "for he makes his sun rise on the evil and on the good, and sends rain on the just and on the unjust" (Matt. 5:45). We can achieve this only as the Spirit helps us curb our flawed nature's propensity to animosity, and seek the spiritual good of those who are hostile to us. Our best stance is underneath the outstretched arms of Jesus on the cross as he prays, "Father, forgive them, for they know not what they are doing" (Luke 23:34).[12] Forgiveness means to outlove, outpray, and outsuffer the unloving.

---

11. This love of enemies, not love of man or even love of neighbor, Hans Küng asserts, is typical of Jesus. It has no parallel in other religions, not even in the Old Testament. "The superiority of Jesus becomes apparent, not in the often completely comparable individual statements, but in the unmistakable originality of the whole teaching. The programmatic 'love your enemy' is Jesus' own expression and is typical of his love of neighbor, which now really does know no bounds." *On Being a Christian* (Garden City, N.Y.: Doubleday, 1976), p. 259.

12. The imperfect tense suggests that he repeated the words again and again.

The Triumph of Love

But what if your love is not reciprocated by the needy, or does not make an enemy your friend? You still have triumphed. You have won a battle over your lower nature, and you are better and happier for having tried. It is more blessed to give than to receive, and there is greater blessing in loving than in being loved. Henry Wadsworth Longfellow said it well:

> Talk not of wasted affection,
>   affection was never wasted;
> If it enrich not the heart of another,
>   its waters returning
> Back to their springs, like the rain,
>   shall find them full of refreshment.

Patience, kindness, goodness, and gentleness reap their own reward.

CHAPTER EIGHT

A Concerned Citizen

You have just received word this morning that your daughter and son-in-law have become the happy parents of a baby. You immediately make plans to see them. If you live at a distance, you travel either by auto or plane. You will even fly across an ocean to London or Tokyo to be with them.

What will the next twenty to thirty years hold in store for the young child? And for millions of others? The new generation is facing a rapidly changing world, and parents and grandparents are concerned.

In previous chapters we considered the personal relationships of friends, lovers, spouses, families, congregants, and neighbors. Lives touched by the personality of Jesus also reach out to embrace his world. Our attitude to this divine gift should also reflect all the fruit of the Spirit. We should love it, enjoy it, seek its peace, be patient in dealing with it, be good to it, treat it kindly and gently, faithfully preserve it, and be self-controlled in our use of it.

In our technocratic age the concept of neighbor has been greatly extended. The whole world is now our neighborhood. Isolationism is anachronistic. Our concerns are cosmic. Our stewardship of the good earth that God gave to us needs to be spiritually sensitized.

Some face the future with foreboding as they contemplate the political and ecological eventualities of the next decades. Others face it with the faith that we humans will continue to solve the problems that are currently plaguing us. They confidently believe that all threats to our environment and way of life will be conquered. But

169

whether with faith or foreboding, we are all concerned. If all the inhabitants of our global village were devout, we would feel more at ease. But some are self-centered, others are despots. The demography of demagoguery is disturbing. What can a Christian do?

Ever since our astronauts landed on the moon and took pictures of the earth, we have seen our beautiful blue and white globe glistening in the splendor of sunlight. From a distance it looks so pristinely pure. But back on earth scientists of every sort examine our water, earth, forests, plants, birds, and insects, and they are aghast at what we have allowed to happen.

The story of creation in the first chapters of the book of Genesis asserts: "In the beginning God created the heavens and the earth." Out of the formless void, in a way that is still mysterious to us, God created light, the dome of the sky, the seas and the dry land, fructiferous vegetation, lights in the dome of the sky, swarms of living creatures in the water, everything that creeps on the earth as well as winged birds of every kind, and, finally, responsible human beings in God's own image. Six times, after each act of creation, the writer says, "And God saw that it was good," and summing it all up asserts again, "Indeed, it was very good."

What does becoming like Jesus have to do with concern for the created world? The answer is patent. According to the apostle John's Gospel prologue, "All things came into being through him, and without him not one thing came into being" (John 1:3). Jesus encourages us to look at how God cares for the birds of the air and the grass of the field. "Consider the lilies of the field, how they grow," he says; "they neither toil nor spin; yet I tell you, even Solomon in all his glory was not clothed like one of these" (Matt. 6:28-29). Jesus delighted in the quietude of the Mount of Olives and the prayerful solitude of the mountaintop. He directed his disciples to schools of fish, spoke of arid and fertile soils, gathering up leftovers, and how to respond when harvests were bountiful. "All things have been created through him and for him," says Paul (Col. 1:16).

Back in 1848 Cecil Frances Alexander wrote the words of the hymn:

All things bright and beautiful,
All creatures great and small,
All things wise and wonderful:
The Lord God made them all.

James Herriot chose these words from the British children's hymn as titles for a popular series of books about the life of a veterinarian in Yorkshire, England, that has been made into a popular, often-repeated prime time public television series.

As concerned citizens in a now threatened world we have a responsibility to keep everything bright and beautiful. "This is my Father's world," according to a loved hymn. We are to love the cosmos as God does, treat it kindly, be self-controlled in our use of it, and faithful to the trust given to us. In brief, we are to be as virtuous as Jesus was in living in it.

The Genesis story climaxes with the Lord God putting his image-reflecting human steward in the garden of Eden "to till it and keep it" (Gen. 2:15). I have seen many paintings of Adam and Eve in the garden portrayed as two unclad people with fig leaves, aimlessly meandering through a wooded sanctuary, fruit dangling from tree limbs, with birds fluttering around, and animals contentedly roaming along with them. No one that I know of has made a painting of Adam, perspiration dripping from his brow, hard at work with a hoe in a vegetable plot! And yet, here is his assignment: "till the garden and maintain it."

The original focus was on a small slice of the earth's crust. We now live in a global village, the outgrowth of a scientific revolution. We have created a worldwide civilization of adventurous souls who probe both inner and outer space but prodigally consume the resources of a planet created good, and produce pandemic perils to the myriad forms of life.

Particularly in the most progressive Western industrial nations, writes Hans Küng, "people are becoming increasingly doubtful about the dogma they had believed for a long time: that science and technology are the key to man's universal happiness and that progress results inevitably and — as it were — automatically." The danger is no longer primarily atomic destruction, but the contradictions of international politics and economics, problems that are too great for governments.

Most disturbing are on-the-spot problems, as in New York City, "where . . . behind the most imposing skyline in the world . . . ever increasing air pollution, putrid water, rotting streets, traffic congestion, shortage of dwelling space . . . health hazards, mounting aggression and crime, larger ghettos, more acute tensions between races, classes and national groups hardly resemble the beautiful 'secular city' which theologians dreamed up at the beginning of the sixties."[1] Wherever one looks — in St. Petersburg, or Melbourne, or Tokyo — the same phenomena stand out. These are the negative results of technological development, not mere accidents. If they continue, they will destroy true humanity.

This does not mean that we have to abandon hope, but only "faith in science as a total explanation of reality, in technology as a cure-all substitute religion."

We need to develop a global view of our place in the world, to become interested in more than just ourselves and our children. The world is not only a place for pleasure; it is a bequest of responsibility.

Long before today's environmental movement began, theologian Joseph Sittler wrote about the fragile web, the relationship between ecology and theology. "Touch one small part of the web," writes James M. Wall commenting on it, "and every part will shimmer and move." Everything is connected by a common creator. Our concern is broader and deeper than the existence of a few species; it involves nothing less than "the fragile ecosystem and human inhabitants." You cannot touch the earth's vast spider web, warns Wall, without the rest of the world feeling the impact.[2]

1. Hans Küng, *On Being a Christian* (Garden City, N.Y.: Doubleday, 1976), pp. 40, 41.
2. James M. Wall, "Disturbing the Web," *The Christian Century,* October 26, 1994, pp. 971ff. Cf. also Richard Preston, *The Hot Zone* (New York: Random House, 1994).

Life Trustees

It is a high honor to be elected a trustee of an important college, university, or professional school, or to be made a director of a corporation or a foundation. It assumes that you have the knowledge and wisdom to supervise resources intended for the public good. A key note in the word *trustee* is trust. It means that the organization is confident that you will responsibly care for its present and future affairs. It means that you believe in the institution and are sensitive to its needs and relationships.

God has conferred on us an even higher honor and responsibility. We human beings are trustees of the universe, with "dominion over the fish of the sea, and over the birds of the air, and over the cattle, and over every creeping thing that creeps on the earth" (Gen. 1:26). We are managers of the earth. "Here it is," God seems to say; "see what you can do with it." To have dominion means to be responsible, but over the years dominion over nature has been distorted to mean a domination that misuses, and even uses up, the natural world.

Some environmentalists charge that this despotic view is endemic to traditional Judaism and Christianity. The Westward spread of Christianity, they say, not only paved the way for the development of capitalism and technology but created wanton exploitation. Many of our ancestors, admittedly, have been unworthy trustees. As Dorothy and Gabriel Fackre note: "Christians have a poor record of practicing what they preach about the good earth. If we had done better, the eagles and flowers, the soil and trees would not be in the trouble they are today."[3] We possess a penchant for pillage.

Max Oelschlaeger, professor of philosophy and religious studies at the University of North Texas, argues in his book *Caring for Creation* that a religious orientation toward creation is necessary for a political solution of the environmental crisis.[4]

3. Gabriel Fackre and Dorothy Fackre, *Christian Basics: A Primer for Pilgrims* (Grand Rapids: William B. Eerdmans Publishing Co., 1991), p. 8.
4. Max Oelschlaeger, *Caring for Creation: An Ecumenical Approach to the Environmental Crisis* (New Haven, Conn.: Yale University Press, 1994). As W. Paul Jones observes about his treatment: "Opposing forcefully the environmentalists

Douglas John Hall, professor of Christian theology at McGill University in Montreal, argues that "the deterioration of our natural environment under the impact of a rampant technological society is one of the major crises of our time."[5] Taking his cue from the concept that human beings are created in the image of God, he argues that we must rethink our whole understanding of the relation between humanity and nature. The Lordship of Jesus, he believes, is an authentic model for understanding our human relation to the natural order, a relation that does not conceive of dominion as mastery but as responsible service to and for others.

As trustees we are meant to exercise a spiritual stewardship over nature. We are both a part of nature and transcend nature. We are to care for it as we do our own bodies, recognizing its strengths and fragilities. The old assumption that the land and sea masses are so vast and recreative that nothing we do to them would harm them has been proved to be monstrously false.

Rachel Carson gave us an ecological shock back in the 1960s with her book *Silent Spring*, suddenly alerting us to the damage that years of neglect and pesticide use, compounded by the growth of technology and nuclear power, were doing to natural life. Despite initial ridicule and opposition, her seminal work spawned a voluminous literature, one of the more recent pieces being Albert Gore's *Earth in the Balance: Ecology and the Human Spirit.*[6] In perverse

---

who have either neglected religion or accused it of contributing significantly to the ecological dilemma, the author discerns in all major religions and movements a caring for creation that can evoke and nurture a profound respect to the whole of which humans are an organic part." *Theology Today* 51, no. 4 (January 1995): 636.

5. Douglas John Hall, *Imaging God: Dominion as Stewardship* (Grand Rapids: William B. Eerdmans Publishing Co., 1986).

6. Albert Gore, *Earth in the Balance: Ecology and the Human Spirit* (New York: Houghton, Mifflin, 1992). The bibliography of environmental studies is growing rapidly, indicating the importance of the Christian environmental concern. A select list includes the following: Richard Austin, *Baptized into Wilderness* (Louisville: John Knox, 1987); Austin, *Beauty of the Lord* (Louisville: John Knox, 1988); Austin, *Hope for the Land* (Louisville: John Knox, 1989); Austin, *Reclaiming America* (Abingdon: Creekside Press, 1990); Lionel Basney, *An Earth-Careful Way of Life* (Downers Grove, Ill.: InterVarsity Press, 1994); James Conlon, *Earth Story and Sacred Story*

imitation of God we have become exploitative "uncreators," desecrators who wantonly and thoughtlessly continue to destroy our environment. The wholesome result of all these exposures is a mounting concern about the fate of the earth. Without immediate remedial action, experts warn, we face the prospect of eventual cosmic extinction.

Life is an intricate network of biological, psychological, economic, political, and ethical interactions. The poor of the undeveloped countries in the Southern Hemisphere are now demanding that Northern nations cease the exploitation they have carried on for generations and share their prosperity and riches. We are no longer only national but world citizens, neighbors who have a responsibility for each other's welfare in the world we inhabit.

(Mystic, Conn.: Twenty-Third Publications, 1994); Tony Campolo, *How to Rescue the Earth Without Worshipping Nature* (Nashville: Thomas Nelson, 1992); Calvin De Witt, ed., *The Environment and the Christian* (Grand Rapids: Baker Book House, 1991); Calvin De Witt and Ghillean Prance, eds., *Missionary Earth Keeping* (Macon, Ga.: Mercer University Press, 1991); Langdon Gilkey, *Nature, Reality and the Sacred* (Minneapolis: Augsburg-Fortress, 1993); James M. Gustafson, *A Sense of the Divine: The Natural Environment from a Theocentric Perspective* (Cleveland: Pilgrim Press, 1994); David Hallman, ed., *Ecotheology, Voices from South and North* (Maryknoll, N.Y.: WCC Publications and Orbis Press, 1994); John F. Hought, *The Promise of Nature* (Mahwah, N.J.: Paulist Press, 1993); Shannon Jung, *We Are at Home: Spirituality of the Environment* (Mahwah, N.J.: Paulist Press, 1993); Martin W. Lewis, *Green Delusions* (Durham, N.C.: Duke University Press, 1994); Sallie McFague, *The Body of God* (Minneapolis: Fortress Press, 1993); Richard D. Land and Louis A. Moore, *The Earth Is the Lord's: Christians and the Environment* (Nashville: Broadman, 1992); Bill McKibben, *The Comforting Whirlwind* (Grand Rapids: William B. Eerdmans Publishing Co., 1994); Wolfhart Pannenberg, *Toward a Theology of Nature* (Louisville: John Knox, 1993); Frederick Quinn, *To Heal the Earth: A Theology of Ecology* (Nashville: Upper Room Books, 1994); David Lee Ray, with Lee Guzzo, *Trashing the Planet* (Washington, D.C.: Regnery Gateway, 1990); Rosemary Radford Ruether, *Gaia and God* (New York: Harper San Francisco, 1992); Charles T. Rubin, *The Green Crusade* (New York: Free Press, 1994); H. Paul Santmire, *The Travail of Nature* (Minneapolis: Fortress Press, 1985); Richard A. Young, *Healing the Earth: A Theocentric Perspective on Environmental Problems and Their Solutions* (Nashville: Broadman & Holman, 1994). For a bibliographic resource, see Joseph K. Sheldon, *Rediscovery of Creation* (Metuchen, N.J.: Scarecrow Press, 1992). John Bolt, in a review article, "The Greening of Spirituality," *Calvin Theological Journal* 30, no. 1 (April 1995): 194-211, gives a perceptive evaluation of these works.

We have been quite prone to shirk individual responsibility. We have a tendency to mind our own business, take care of our own interests, and let the rest of the world go by. But when we shuck interest in and responsibility for the rest of creation, under the assumption that the larger and most powerful forces must control things, the result, says Karl Menninger, "is the end of personal responsibility." Then whatever goes wrong is not my fault, but the fault of others — society, industries, corporations, the government. He gibes at this propensity with Anna Russell's sardonic jab:

> At three I had a feeling of
> Ambivalence toward my brothers,
> And so it follows naturally
> I poisoned all my lovers.
> But now I'm happy: I have learned
> The lesson this has taught;
> That everything I do that's wrong
> Is someone else's fault.[7]

The evil of compartmentalization — business is business, religion is religion — cuts the nerve of conscience and integrity even among some Christians. "We are all familiar with the man who goes to church on Sunday," writes M. Scott Peck, "believing that he loves God and God's creation and his fellow human beings but who, on Monday morning, has no trouble with his company's policy of dumping toxic wastes in the local stream."[8] Such "Sunday morning Christians" can do this because they keep their business and their religion in separate compartments and are not troubled by their personal lack of integrity. But, as Aleksandr Solzhenitsyn contends, "Mankind's sole salvation lies in everyone making everything his business." The message is simple, writes Menninger: "It is that concern is the touchstone. Caring. Relinquishing the sin of indifference."

7. Karl Menninger, *Whatever Became of Sin?* (New York: Hawthorne Books, 1973), p. 181.
8. M. Scott Peck, *Further Along the Road Less Traveled. The Unending Journey Towards Spiritual Growth* (New York: Simon & Schuster, 1993), p. 181.

A CONCERNED CITIZEN

To be created in the image of God is our glory, and our responsibility. We have become delinquent saints. Elmer F. Siderman, in his poem "The Smell of Perfumed Assemblies," expresses the bitter thoughts many a clergyman must feel as his self-satisfied, well-dressed congregation assembles on a Sunday morning:

Here they come
my nonchalants,
my lazy daisies,
their dainty perfume
disturbing the room
the succulent smell
seductive as hell.

Here they are
my pampered flamboyants,
status spoiled, who bring
with exquisite zing
their souls spick and span
protected by Ban.
their hearts young and gay
decked in handsome cliche
exchanging at my call
with no effort at all
worship for whispering
God for gossiping,
theology for television.

Baptized in the smell
of classic Chanel
I promote their nod
to a jaunty God
Who, they are sure,
is a sparkling gem
superbly right for them.

There they go
my in-crowd

my soft-skinned crowd,
my suntanned, so so
elegant, swellegant,
natty, delectable,
suave, cool, adorable
DAMNED![9]

Indifference is a terrible sin. Historically the church has called it sloth, or acedia, and listed it among the seven deadly sins. When apathy grips a person, one "believes in nothing, cares for nothing, seeks to know nothing, interferes with nothing. . . ."[10] Only grace can save such a person.

What on Earth Can We Do?

There are serious, high-priority issues that should concern every citizen. In this chapter I will limit consideration to four things we can do: plant trees, clean the air, winnow our waste, and control the population.

1. Plant Trees

A parishioner friend, Alfred B. Swanson, M.D., one of the world's leading orthopedic surgeons, who has trained thousands of surgeons worldwide, is also intensely interested in replanting the "garden" God has given to us by promoting an ambitious tree-planting program. He stresses the urgent need to replenish forests and vegetation that have been destroyed in order to save our atmosphere and provide resources for medicines. He has inaugurated tree-planting programs with many schools and civic organizations to sensitize children as well as adults to our urgent need; he also heads a society called

9. Elmer F. Suderman, "The Smell of Perfumed Assemblies," *Theology Today* 28, no. 1 (April 1971): 50-51.
10. Robert J. McCracken, *What Is Sin? What Is Virtue?* (New York: Harper & Row, 1966), p. 31.

Alternative Methods for International Stability (AMIS). "Trees should be planted around homes, roadways, and hedge rows throughout America," he writes.[11] He envisions a program that will spread to all countries of the world.

Too many citizens resign themselves to a passive role, not confident that they can make a difference, writes Swanson; but citizen action can change history. It can disseminate ideas and desires exponentially through a chain of personal networks. It can require governments to lead in a new and right direction. Sensitive leaders will respond to constructive action. The alternative is depletion of nonrenewable resources that will see us struggling for what is at the bottom of the barrel in a matter of years.

The poet Joyce Kilmer looked and wrote:

I think that I shall never see
a poem lovely as a tree.

Opponents of environmental protection, however, look with a different set of eyes. To them, "a greedy glance at the same scene may mean one sees only . . . lumber."[12]

The earth's forests in all parts of the world, particularly the Amazonian green belt in the tropics, are fast disappearing. Denuded by farming, ranching, logging, mining, and the demand for building materials and firewood, vast segments of the green earth have lost their health-providing potentiality. Fifty acres a second are being destroyed worldwide. At the present rate of consumption, most of the remaining forests, experts warn, will be gone within the next twenty-five years. With them will go irreplaceable resources of medicines, germ plasma, and genetic material that harbor resources for fighting diseases and improving crops. One hundred species of plants and animals are made extinct every day by the destruction of these forests and other habitats, forever obliterating secrets for fighting certain diseases. The tropical forests cover only 7 percent of the

11. Alfred B. Swanson, M.D., *Alternative Methods for International Stability* (Grand Rapids, Michigan, n.d.).
12. Fackre and Fackre, *Christian Basics*, p. 24.

earth's surface, but they are home to approximately 75 percent of the planet's species. Their extinction would be an irreversible environmental calamity.

Ghillean Prance is an activist-botanist, considered by many experts as the foremost authority on the Brazilian forest, formerly on the staff of the New York Botanical Gardens, and now holding the coveted position of director of the Royal Kew Gardens outside London. He demonstrates that it is in a country's best economic interests to save the forests. He and his associates have determined that one hectare of tropical forest, if managed properly, could yield $6,820 a year, whereas a bulldozed plot planted with a single crop would yield $3,184; moreover, if cleared solely for cattle pasture it would yield only $2,960, and that would be for only one year, until the rains would wash the ashes and residue away, laying bare an underlying soil that would not be able to sustain either crops or pasture. Prance is a Christian who holds three degrees from Oxford and endeavors to integrate natural science and theology. When asked what it is like to walk through a rain forest, he rhapsodically describes its luxuriant beauty: "to me, the only thing comparable is the experience of walking into one of the great cathedrals such as we have in England. You are awed, and humbled, and stilled. You walk out purged by an almost sacred beauty. And when you leave, you are determined to defend that building, or that forest, at any cost."[13]

Here in the United States, Nat Wheelwright, professor of biology at nearby Bowdoin College, who has conducted research on resplendent quetzals and tropical trees in Costa Rica since 1979, gives due respect to the economic and ecological arguments, but makes a special case for resplendence. To him quetzals are the most beautiful bird in the new world. The problem is, they are poised to become extinct as the forests they live in and the trees that provide their diet of fruits are rapidly being cut down to create wood products, cattle pastures, coffee plantations, and house lots. Dying species, he argues, foreshadow a dying planet, and humans will be the next to go. "The most convincing case for rain forests," he says, "is simply that the loss of species, like the destruction of a Beethoven

13. Ghillean Prance, *Christianity Today*, July 22, 1991, pp. 26-28.

symphony or a Renoir painting or a Taj Mahal, is a loss of resplendence." Religious leaders and philosophers, artists, writers, and ordinary people, he argues, should promote their preservation.[14]

Who is to blame? Landowners and commercial interests exploit the forests by bulldozing and burning them for short-term income. Resisters have unsuccessfully challenged these interests. Brazilian leaders point to the United States as an example of economic deforestation. The eastern region of our country, once covered with dense forests, has little left of the vast tree cover that once stretched from the Atlantic to the Mississippi and beyond. Even today, the United States continues to clear away its most valuable forests. To Third World leaders, it is hypocritical for us to demand that they halt their economic growth while we continue to practice the devastation we deplore elsewhere.

As I write this, I recall a 1940s parishioner, then in her nineties, telling me that, when she was a child growing up in a mid-nineteenth-century settler family in western Michigan, the entire region was studded with hardwood forests. When they visited their nearest friends, they took hatchets with them to mark their trail through the dense tree growth. Today the region, denuded of the trees that furnished the high grade wood that once made Grand Rapids the furniture capital of the world, has become a produce-farming region dotted with large cities and towns.

In mid-America, the Mississippi River now carries away from the farms millions of tons of topsoil that is gone for good. Iowa used to have an average of sixteen inches of the best topsoil in the world; now it is down to eight inches. The rest of it is somewhere on the bottom of the Gulf of Mexico.

In the Northeast, vast tracts of forest are withering and dying from the acid rain produced by the fossil-burning factories and refineries of the Midwest.

The environmental neighborhood watchword is "Think globally, act locally." We are being summoned to occupy the front lines in protecting the "garden" entrusted to our care.

14. Nat Wheelwright, "Case for Resplendence," *Chronicle of Higher Education,* June 1, 1994, p. 100.

2. Clean the Air

When it comes to the air around us, there is good news and bad news.

The bad news is that the increased emission of certain gases thickens the atmosphere and traps the heat from the sun, heightening the temperature of the earth and creating a greenhouse effect. Unchecked, this process gradually melts the polar ice caps, posing a threat to low-lying seaboard cities as ocean levels rise, but with rising temperatures transforming our productive farmlands into parched deserts. Rivers and lakes will begin to evaporate, experts predict, so that cities such as those along the shores of Lake Michigan will be surrounded by extended beaches and vast stretches of mud flats.

The earth's ozone layer is a shield that protects us from much of the sun's harmful ultraviolet radiation. The thinning of the ozone layer will cause many more cases of skin cancer and cataracts. It will result in tropical insect-born illnesses spreading to formerly temperate zones, increasing suffering and death to those most vulnerable to carbon monoxide and air pollution — pregnant women and their unborn babies, children with developing lungs, people with pulmonary heart disease, asthmatics, and grandparents. It will slowly damage the immune system, leaving many defenseless against infectious diseases. It will also disrupt photosynthesis and plant growth, upsetting the food chain and damaging crops worth billions of dollars. If the warming continues at its present rate, we will find ourselves living not in a blossoming garden but in a withering hothouse spawning hurricanes packing winds up to 225 miles an hour.

The cause of the greenhouse effect is no mystery. It is due to carbon dioxide emissions from factories, industrial power plants, and automobiles, in addition to the burning of the tropical forests. The Forestry Association calls our cities, towns, and suburbs "heat islands," and urges the planting of hundreds of millions of trees, not mainly for scenery, but to absorb the carbons that are the major cause of air pollution and global warming.

The industrial age has been fueled by the burning of coal, wood, and oil, materials that spew wastes into the sky, notably carbon dioxide (CO_2). Another environmental enemy is chlorofluorocarbons (CFCs), the chemical compound used in styrofoam cups and other products, and in the freon used in air conditioners and refrigerators. Nitrogen oxides spewed out of power plant smokestacks and automobile exhaust systems are also pollutants. Methane is another greenhouse gas, the primary component of natural gas but also generated by bacteria, leaving the guts of cattle and termites, the muck of rice paddies, and the rotting garbage of landfills. The air we breathe today is vastly more polluted than the air breathed by Jesus.

It is claimed that the earth's stratospheric ozone layer is being eaten away by these man-made chemicals much faster than predicted. It is no longer only a future threat; the threat is here and now. It is too late to reverse the damage; the best we can do is to adopt measures that will stabilize the atmosphere as soon as possible.

The good news is that government scientists are reporting that the buildup of industrial chemicals most responsible for depleting the earth's protective ozone layer has slowed substantially. If the trend continues, the increase should halt near the beginning of the next century. Then, as the chemicals are gradually destroyed by natural processes, the ozone layer should begin a period of recovery lasting fifty to a hundred years.

Through legislative negotiation, we are learning that we can simultaneously have cleaner air and a growing economy. Measures have been enacted by Congress to control the acid rain that has caused such serious forest and stream damage in the Northeast and Canada. Progress is being made in reducing automobile and truck emissions, the main cause of urban smog. Pittsburgh is a notable success story of a vast cleanup effort. Steps are also being taken to ban the production of CFCs.

The development of nonfossil energy sources, such as solar, nuclear, and wind power, is progressing.

After a slow start, solar power as an energy source is a promising breakthrough. Until now it has been used mainly by affluent homeowners, because of the cost of the equipment. But it already heats and lights more than one hundred thousand homes in the United States, and utilities are getting on the bandwagon to protect

183

their market. For more than a decade, developing countries, notably Mexico, India, and Zimbabwe, which cannot afford fossil fuel or nuclear plants, have been buying two-thirds of the solar panels produced in the United States. Solar power is becoming competitive, and the forecast for the industry in the next century is sunny.

The electric car, an example of cutting-edge technology, is now an actuality. Though too costly for mass use, the solar-powered car will enable people to live in the fast lane and breathe a little easier in the process. Smooth, quiet, and virtually non-polluting, the electric auto is powerful enough to accelerate up to speeds of 80 miles per hour. It costs less than three cents a mile to operate, compared to six cents a mile for the average gasoline-powered car. Its virtue is that it will help clean the air. Yet at $75,000 its market is still limited to the affluent.

Solar energy, however, is increasingly becoming the wave of the future. What was once an exotic new technology is now blossoming into a catalogue industry offering applications to a wide selection of items, including solar homes. In an all-solar neighborhood in Gardiner, Massachusetts, for example, thirty working-class houses and eight commercial buildings are in operation. Experts look forward to the day when solar-run houses will become as popular as split-levels. From Maine to Florida, from the East to the West Coast, houses display roof panels to meet part of their heating needs. In addition, there are composting toilets, solar radios, and even solar panels the size of an attaché case that can power laptop computers. Solar energy may be costly for us now, but by the end of the century it promises to be a highly competitive — to say nothing of moral — way to deal with an environmental problem.

Nuclear energy is also an active option, since it produces no carbon dioxide. Nuclear waste still poses a problem (which is being dealt with, as we shall note in the next section), but, encouraged by the safety record of France, which gets seventy percent of its electricity from nuclear plants, nuclear energy has a brighter future.

Wind power has always been with us, and it is now being harnessed as another nonpolluting energy source. Blowing out of the west to the mountains of the east are proposals and projects to string hundreds of turbines in strategically elevated places. The power created from winds blowing off the oceans and down from Canada can be funneled through high voltage lines to substations across the country, producing a significant percentage of the electricity now produced by fossil-burning plants. Those who object on aesthetic grounds that the sight of turbines on pristine elevations produces visual pollution will eventually recognize their practical beauty as they replace repugnant smokestacks.

Substitutes for CFC offenders are also at hand. HCFCs (hydrochlorofluorocarbons), which break down more quickly in the atmosphere, pose less danger to the ozone layer. Also HFCs (hydrofluorocarbons) do not contain chlorine and are ozone-safe. Hydrocarbons such as butane and propane are inexpensive and readily available. Ammonia is a simple alternative for refrigerators. Water and steam are effective cleansers.

Someday our children will ask why their elders did not do more about greenhouse warming when they had a chance.

3. Winnow Our Waste

Once a week I make a short trip to our town's recycling center with a trunkful of disposable refuse. At the center, everything has a separate stall: cardboard here, newspapers there, cans in another places, bottles in still another, garbage bags in yet another, and garden clippings and other organic matter up the hill to a landfill. Metal products go into a special truck for processing elsewhere. On the hilly, rocky Maine coast environmentalists scrupulously guard against land pollution and toxic seepage into the sea. But nationwide, we are either part of the problem or part of the answer.

Recycling has become one of the best ways to protect and conserve our natural resources. The program has become so successful, however, that it is itself becoming a problem. Cities and towns now collect more recyclable items than the industry can handle, and landfill space is becoming scarce.

Roughly one thousand contaminants have been detected in public water supplies. Virtually every major water source in our country is vulnerable. About half of the people in the United States rely on surface water from rivers, lakes, and reservoirs — most of which harbors wastes and pesticides that have been washed off the

185

land by rain. The other half of the population uses water from underground wells and springs often tainted with chemicals slowly seeping in from toxic dumps.

We are a throwaway society. With our population burgeoning, our landfills are overflowing and the residue of our burning combustibles fouls the air. Bag-piles of waste become mountains at our recycling centers at the end of holidays or at the close of summer vacations. Every person in the United States produces more than twice his or her weight in waste every day. We generate approximately one ton of waste per person per year. Add to this the immeasurable quantity of industrial waste, and it is easy to see that the quantity of toxic chemicals that seeps down into the water table and flows into our lakes and oceans is incalculable.

Recycling may still have its problems, but we are moving forward in properly winnowing our waste. Some materials are more easily recycled than others. Aluminum and steel cans head the list, but progress is also being made with newsprint and plastics. Some of our clothing is now made from recycled plastic! Builders are finding that products made from recycled paper, wood, and plastic are often tougher and more durable than the original materials. The Environmental Protection Agency is inaugurating a "Buy Waste Wise" campaign, noting that goods are not truly recycled until they are used again. Ethically sensitive folk applaud all these efforts to "keep" the earth.

The nuclear waste problem is also receiving increasing attention, with gratifying results. Since Third World countries that do not have the technology or expertise to deal with alternative energy sources are still forced to rely on environmentally harmful fossil fuels, pressure is being put on the developed world to utilize cheaper and safer nuclear power. To cope with nuclear waste, the French have pioneered a vitrification process that mixes radioactive waste with molten glass, producing a material that, when cooled, forms a stable and less radioactive solid that can be buried deep underground.

We can take either the short view or the long view in managing the world's waste problem. The dangers that exist all along the food chain, from our fields to processing plants to kitchens, is an immediate concern. Reports of poisoned grapes and tainted apples, of produce peppered with pesticides, of cans and boxes packed with treacherous additives, of meats stuffed with harmful drugs, of chickens splattered with bacteria, and of fish steeped in toxins have alarmed many people. But experts inform us that these alerts should not produce paranoia, for the danger from them to human health is small, and most people are able to tolerate the present levels of contamination. But since some people may get cancer one day because of what they now eat and drink, we have good reason to demand vigilance and continuing improvements in water safety and food provision.

In the long view, consideration for the welfare of future generations, our children and grandchildren, demands greater caution today and the development of safe waste disposal for tomorrow. The quantity of waste continues to escalate; the development of technology to deal with it must surpass it. It is our only ethical option, if we will be good to, and treat with kindness, the generations that will follow us.

4. Control the Population

It is estimated that at the birth of Christ there were 250 million people living on earth. Eighteen centuries later, the number had risen to a billion. Within two hundred more years, however, with the advent of the industrial revolution and increased control of pestilence and disease, the world's population had tripled to 2.5 billion in 1950. Without drastic control in the next thirty-five years, the number will have doubled to 5 billion.

Population growth has been too rapid, writes Alfred Swanson. When Charles Lindbergh flew the Atlantic, the United States's population was one-third its present size. When Franklin Delano Roosevelt was President, the world's population was one-third of its present size. When John F. Kennedy was assassinated, there were one-third as many cars on the roads of America as there are today.

The underdeveloped nations, with yearly incomes of less than $400 per person, face the greatest problem. Without population control, Bangladesh, which had 42 million in 1950, will likely have

342 million by 2050. At the same time, Nigeria will increase from 32 million to 472 million, Mexico from 27 million to 197 million, and the United States from 200 million to 400 million.

Mexico City, the most populous urban center on earth, has been described as the anteroom to an ecological Hiroshima, struck not by military weapons but by a population bomb. Shanty towns border its outskirts with no running water or sanitation, garbage and human waste pile up with overpowering stench, and rats roam as freely as domestic animals. The city does not stand alone as an example of ecological disaster. The situation is duplicated on a lesser scale throughout the world.

In the poorest countries, growth rates are outstripping their ability to provide the bare necessities of housing, fuel, and food. Trees are chopped down for fuel, grasslands are overgrazed by live-stock, and croplands are overplowed in a desperate attempt to pro-duce more food. Daily, our television newscasts picture the horror of starvation in Somalia, Ethiopia, the Sudan, Rwanda, and a host of other countries. The world's population, say the environmentalists, is sorely taxing the carrying capacity of the earth.

The solution most commonly advanced is family planning, utilizing all the current methods of contraception. In poor agrarian societies, however, numerous offspring are viewed as a source of labor and a hedge against poverty in old age. China and Thailand have successfully launched huge population planning programs, but Muslim fundamentalists in Iran, Egypt, and Pakistan and dominant Christian groups such as Roman Catholics in Mexico, Kenya, and the Philippines often vigorously oppose controls (although the country with the lowest birth rate is Italy!). As the Vatican campaigns vigorously against family-planning controls, the Pontifical Academy of Sciences, a group of more than eighty scientists of different reli-gions and nationalities, suggests that the birth rate should be limited to about two children per couple. Pope John Paul II was infuriated by the report, but the Italian bishops conference declared: "There is a need to contain births in order to avoid creating the insoluble problems that could arise if we were to renounce our responsibilities to future generations." Most Christians agree on the morality of limiting family size voluntarily, without governmental coercion.

Whatever may come from all that, the world's mushrooming population poses troublesome ethical questions. What price should the world-society pay for the survival of all current member societies? Theological ethicists generally maintain that Christians should feed the hungry everywhere in our complex global economy. If "lifeboat" ethics and the right to ration life seem wrong, who should produce more, and who should consume less? The benevolence and charity of rich Americans who continue to consume imported coffee, tea, and bananas grown on land that should produce corn and cattle is not the answer. Reforming the world trade system and the systemic injustice of world commerce that benefits the rich is one answer. Adopting more modest lifestyles as fellow citizens in a global society is another.

But population control is an absolute necessity. The recent United Nations conference in Cairo underscored the fact. Nobel-laureate physicist Henry Kendall of M.I.T. put it in a nutshell: "If we don't control the population with justice, humanity and mercy, it will be done for us by nature — brutally."

On Being a Faithful Steward

We have acted as though the earth belongs to us to plunder as we would. The biblical declaration is clear: we human beings are not masters of the earth but stewards of the creator. Stewards should not exploit the environment, but keep it undefiled. We may not be able to return to the days of innocence, but we do have in our minds and hands the power to save or destroy life on planet earth. The oceans and the jungles cannot save themselves. The task is ours to do, or we will die.

The idea of stewardship of the earth is not a new one. Several centuries ago John Calvin stated it positively: "Let him who possesses a field, so partake of its yearly fruits, that he may not suffer the ground to be injured by his negligence; but let him endeavor to hand it down to posterity as he received it." Would that the generations following him had taken his injunction seriously!

We have created an environmental mess. It is more than a natural crisis. It is a spiritual crisis. The forces of greed, selfishness, and exploitation are powerful. But if we are to love our neighbors as ourselves, future generations as well as our own, it is our religious duty to wage war against the chaos and encroaching extinction in the power of the Spirit. We have not merely inherited our world from the previous generations; we are borrowing it from our children and grandchildren. To bequeath to succeeding generations a polluted world is an unmitigated wrong.

Both so-called liberal and conservative Christians have been so preoccupied with other important agendas — the liberal segment with the poor, powerless, and victimized, and the more conservative with the mission of proclaiming personal redemption and opposing atheistic communism — that not until recently has the environment received the attention it deserves. The good news, however, is that today adherents of both camps consider the welfare of the earth to be a preeminent social and spiritual issue.

In an interview with the editors of *USA WEEKEND*, Vice President Gore summarized twelve steps we can follow to save the earth. Learn more about the crisis — how carbon dioxide emissions contribute to global warming, how some chemicals deplete the upper ozone layer, and how water pollution is best handled by filtering water through natural wetlands. Conserve energy in our homes. Recycle as many different materials as we can. Check with local officials and nurseries about tree-planting programs. Organize neighborhood, waterfront, and park cleanups. Use the power of the pocketbook to buy environmentally responsible products. Vote for officials who responsibly view environmental issues. Speak out by calling or writing elected officials, schools, and community centers when they act irresponsibly. Encourage government to set an example by promoting better environmental practices. Plan environmental vacations by taking family learning trips. Use mass transit or car pools wherever available to cut down on air pollution. Finally, change our ways of thinking by recognizing that we have a responsibility as stewards of the earth, that we have to look beyond ourselves and recognize the effect of our actions today on our children and grandchildren tomorrow. "My Bible tells me that we've been given dominion over the earth," says Albert Gore, "but that demands that we be good stewards."[15]

We have been caught asleep as the world perishes. We must act immediately. The time is short. We don't have one hundred years. We have ten or twenty years at the most. The 1990s, therefore, may be the most critical decade in our history.

Jesus Christ, the Word by which all things were made, who in becoming flesh dwelt among us, showed respect for the created world. He gloried in the beauty of the birds and the lilies, referred to the fertile soil that brought forth harvests, retreated to the solitude of the mountains to be alone with God, enjoyed the quiet serenity of the Mount of Olives, and extolled God's care of it and of us. We can do no better than to follow in his steps in taking care of that which he so generously and lovingly ceded to us in his creation.

Jesus is our example in caring for the created world. We are to be reflectors of his care. And this is no insignificant matter. Example is not the main motivation in influencing others, said Albert Schweitzer; it is the only motivation.

In short, here, too, as stewards and trustees of the created world, we human beings must nurture the fruit of the Spirit, especially goodness, kindness, faithfulness, and self-control.

The French have a phrase "noblesse oblige," a tenet that suggests to us that we, too, have an obligation to live nobly. We know what to do. The question is: Will we have the inclination and the discipline and the love to do it?

15. *USA WEEKEND*, April 9-11, 1993, pp. 4-7.

CHAPTER NINE

A Spiritual Self-Lover

A woman in deep distress paused after a Sunday morning service at a large New York City church to ask the minister to pray with her because she was so wretchedly lonely. She had lost all her friends because of the bitter, hateful, and cutting things she had said and written to them. She admitted that she also had trouble with her landlord, her maid, her grocer, and others. The minister was Dr. John Sutherland Bonnell of Fifth Avenue Presbyterian Church, who also taught us pastoral psychology at Princeton Theological Seminary. After carefully listening to the woman, he quietly asked: "Tell me, why do you hate yourself so much?" He asked if she had done something that she was ashamed of. She then confessed a torrid affair that she had a few years before that she was truly sorry about. Dr. Bonnell was a strong believer in confession and forgiveness. As he led her in a prayer of contrition, asking for God's forgiveness, she felt as though an intolerable weight was being lifted from her heart, and simultaneously resolved to straighten matters out with others and begin a new life. Bitterness, Dr. Bonnell observed, is but a projection of contempt for oneself.[1]

---

1. John Sutherland Bonnell, *Pastoral Psychology* (New York: Harper & Brothers, 1938), pp. 173ff.

An Authoritative "As"

Self-love is not an addendum to a spiritually fruitful life. It is a reverent response to the word of Christ. When the lawyer in quest of eternal life, in answer to Jesus' question about the demands of the Law, responded that one should love God with all one's faculties "and your neighbor as yourself." Jesus declared: "You are right! Do this, and you will live" (Luke 10:28).

The authoritative "as" bonds us with all others. Love of self is not optional; it is a religious obligation. It is more than an obligation; it is a privilege. It is in loving ourselves with the same high love (agape) as we love God and others that we discover the secret of a truly holy and happy life.

This is a psychological law written into the nature of life. Love is a unified act of the mind, emotions, and will. To live at our best, we must keep love in balance. God's love for us begets an attitude of self-worth, which enables us to love others. We are better equipped to have good "foreign" relations when we have good "domestic" relations.

A Sunday school class had on the wall of its room the acronym JOY, which was meant to teach "Jesus first, others next, yourself last." Religiously well intended, it contained a subtle heresy. The Bible uses the same high word (agape) for love of self, others, and God. Love is not hierarchically structured with ourselves at the bottom. The same healthy love permeates all our relationships.

We should note at the very beginning, however, that Christian self-affirmation is worlds apart from humanistic self-assertion. We are dealing here with people who are renewed by the Spirit of God, people who, though by nature sinful, have been recreated and, though not perfect, are on the way of sanctification.

Recognition of Christian self-love confuses some people. They have read Luke's report of Jesus saying, "Whoever comes to me and does not hate father and mother, wife and children, brothers and sisters, yes, and even life itself, cannot be my disciple" (Luke 14:26). How, then, can one legitimately love self? The answer to this paradox is that Jesus does not mean literal hatred but lesser love. Matthew makes this clear in his Gospel when he quotes Jesus as saying,

"Whoever loves father or mother more than me is not worthy of me; and whoever loves son or daughter more than me is not worthy of me" (Matt. 10:37). We must love him supremely, and ourselves as others.

In spite of the approval of Jesus, some still have trouble with the "self" part of the equation. We have no right to love ourselves, they declare, because we are all flawed folk, sinners, who, in the Bible's graphic metaphors, miss the mark of goodness, meander back and forth across the center line of rectitude, and are out of plumb with God's intentions. The claims of ethicists and psychologists that we are not able to love others unless we love ourselves, they say, are the dicta of imperfect sciences.

Such serious folk concentrate more on their shortcomings and failures than on their acceptance by God. As they draw up their ethical accounts, liabilities far exceed assets. They have been conditioned to label any form of self-affirmation as pride, vanity, or arrogance. They undervalue the grace that sanctifies human nature.

Some learned scholars buttress these attitudes. Bishop Anders Nygren, for example, aligns himself with this self-deprecatory attitude. In his magisterial but controversial study of *Agape and Eros* he writes: "Christianity does not recognize self-love as a legitimate form of love. Christian love moves in two directions, towards God and toward its neighbor; and in self-love it finds its chief adversary, which must be fought and conquered. It is self-love that alienates man from God, preventing him from giving himself up to God, and it is self-love that shuts up a man's heart against his neighbor."[2] He quotes with approval Rudolf Bultmann, who also asserts that self-love presupposes a humanistic ideal of ethics, that it is an attitude of the natural man that must be overcome.

Balance is important. If we love ourselves more than our neighbors, we breed egotistical arrogance. If we love others more than ourselves, we develop unhealthy codependence. Frederick Buechner, in his *Telling Secrets*, reveals that his inability to accept and forgive his father's suicide when he was younger made him an obsessive

2. Anders Nygren, *Agape and Eros* (Philadelphia: Westminster Press, 1953), p. 21.

parent to his daughter who was dying of anorexia. He endeavored to take care of her, as his father had not done with him, in such a way that he neglected himself. "The only way I knew to be a father was to take care of her, to move heaven and earth if necessary to make her well and, of course, I could not do that." The only thing that helped both of them was for him to get out of the way. When he did, she got better. "People in the caring professions," he concedes as a minister, "are famous for neglecting themselves with the result that they are apt to become in their own way as helpless and crippled as the people they are attempting to care for and thus no longer selves who can be of much use to anybody."[3] Wholeness and health depend on the triple braided cord of love for God, others, and ourselves.

The Essence of Self-Love

Self-love is a sense of self-worth, which is not self-created but God-conferred. It engenders a sense of self-regard because, loved by God, we do not exalt ourselves; rather God exalts us. It is, therefore, a sin not to love what God loves.

We should form our self-image on the basis of what God thinks of us, not on what others think. If you have ever looked at yourself in the crazy mirrors at a carnival you know what it is to see yourself in distorted configuration. The reflections of social mirrors are often like that. The only reliable representation is what God thinks. You are a child of God.

Humility, like love, is a supreme virtue. One translation of gentleness as a fruit of the Spirit is humility. God, we are told, opposes the proud but gives grace to the humble (James 4:6). We should not think more highly of ourselves than we ought to think (Rom. 12:3), nor should we think more lowly of ourselves than we ought to think. Humility reflects what we really are. But if humility and modesty are insincere, they put a cloud between us and the

3. Frederick Buechner, *Telling Secrets* (New York: Harper San Francisco, 1991), p. 27.

sunshine of God's love. When God looks at us he sees Christ, his "new creation."

Not everything about us is lovable. We are not perfect. We do some pretty terrible things. But, as it has been properly observed, we should love the sinner as we hate the sin.

Genuine self-love, therefore, does not countenance a haughty mien. Arrogance is often a cover-up for an inferiority complex. It makes a person an unattractive, egotistical braggart. Folk who imagine that they are better than others and look down on the "lesser sorts" often mask insecurity.

Nor is self-love, properly defined, narcissistic. As children, we read the Greek myth about Narcissus, who fell in love with his reflection in the pool. Television commercials promise that hair shampoos, skin lotions, exotic perfumes, and diet programs will make you so ravishingly beautiful or handsome that you will become enthralled with your appearance and irresistible to others. Such superficial and synthetic self-esteem has no resemblance to humble self-love.

Self-love does not parade itself, flaunt itself, or show off. It is not given to conspicuous self-advertisement or ostentatious self-glorification. It does not jauntily display all one's ribbons, medals, and trophies. I have seen office walls that were a solid bank of citations, commissions, awards, plaques, and other recognitions. They are contemporary counterparts of the conspicuous phylacteries of the Pharisees of Paul's day. But Paul, who was trained in the foremost school of the Pharisees and had a genealogical, academic, and ecclesiastical dossier that was the envy of all others, writes that "whatever gains I had, these I have come to regard as loss because of Christ" (Phil. 3:4-7). Yet he never engaged in improper self-deprecation. He thought of himself as a "man of Christ."

Such self-love must be distinguished from self-esteem. Self-esteem, properly defined, is pride in oneself. According to the National Association of School Psychologists, self-esteem is "the evaluation which the individual makes and customarily maintains with regard to him- or herself. It expresses an attitude of approval or disapproval and indicates the extent to which one believes oneself to be capable, significant, successful, and worthy." Self-esteem is concerned about what others think. Self-love realistically recognizes that we are a mix of good and bad. Self-esteem, on the other hand, endeavors to cosmeticize one's flaws, creating an image that is superficially attractive and acceptable.

Morally vagrant parents often are so concerned about what their children and others think about them that they blame everyone else for their lapses, unable to face their own guilt. They are regretful, but they are more concerned about what others think of them than what God thinks of them. Self-esteem controls their thought.

C. G. Jung speaks to this condition in making a distinction between the self, the ego, the persona, the shadow, and the animus. It is the persona that controls self-esteem. Just as every building has a facade, so every personality has a persona, a mask akin to that of the ancient Greek actors. Through the persona we present ourselves in a form that we hope will make us acceptable to others. There is an element of pretense about the persona. With it, we endeavor to display our best selves so that people will think well of us, and we hide or repress unacceptable traits. In the same way our "shadow" is our subpersonality, which is hidden away. But, though it is unwanted, we take it with us wherever we go as a dark companion dogging our steps — just like our natural shadows. Though we seek to ignore it, it has an uncomfortable way of intruding into our thoughts, particularly in our dreams. To defend ourselves from this threat and to maintain some semblance of peace of mind, we employ ego-defense mechanisms, particularly repression, denial, and projection. We may do this quite unconsciously, but it is an act of ego-preservation that helps us deny our own badness and attribute it to others, whom we then hold responsible for it. This is behind the general propensity to practice scapegoating. We seek self-esteem at all costs.

Self-esteem is a human creation; self-love is a divine gift.

The Theology of Self-Love

There are several good reasons why we should enjoy a healthy sense of self-worth.

1. First of all, God loves us. Male and female we are *created*

197

in the divine image, the apple of God's eye. God formed us from the chemical dust of the universe (star dust?). He breathed into human nostrils "the breath of life" and "man became a living being" (Gen. 2:7).[4] We are dust athrob with divinity.

If we would understand the image of God in us, let us look at Jesus Christ, "the image of the invisible God" (Col. 1:15). Then note this: "We are being transformed into his likeness with ever-increasing glory through the power of the Lord who is the Spirit" (I Cor. 3:18, Revised English Bible). The writer to the early Jewish Christians rhapsodizes, "Someone has testified somewhere, 'What are human beings that you are mindful of them, or mortals, that you care for them? You have made them for a little while lower than the angels.

4. For a clear statement on the basic theological affirmations in the substance of the following paragraphs see Gabriel Fackre, "A Narrative Theology of Revelation," *Ecumenical Faith in Evangelical Perspective* (Grand Rapids: William B. Eerdmans Publishing Co., 1993), pp. 89-122; and Gabriel Fackre and Dorothy Fackre, *Christian Basics: A Primer for Pilgrims* (Grand Rapids: William B. Eerdmans Publishing Co., 1991), passim. Hendrikus Berkhof, in treating the image of God, analyzes the symbolic, relational, and anthropomorphic language of the designation, and also treats its implied freedom, its christological reference, and eschatological determination, in *Christian Faith: An Introduction to the Study of Faith* (Grand Rapids: William B. Eerdmans Publishing Co., 1979), pp. 69, 135, 179, 182, 187, 292, 531. In asserting that we are created in the image of God, the emphasis is on the bond between God and us. The term *image* in the biblical sense asserts the dignity, responsibility, creative capacity, and active personal relationship God establishes with us. Karl Barth picked up the suggestion of Dietrich Bonhoeffer that the image of God connects with our creation as "male and female," which reflects human relationships. Roger L. Shinn and Daniel D. Williams explain: "It is in our creation in community, as persons made to live with one another in mutual support and communion, that we find the reflection of God's being." In addition, we have the "high dignity of being able to hear the Word of God, and to respond to it, and [we have] the spiritual capacity to use and to misuse [our] freedom." *We Believe: An Interpretation of the United Church Statement of Faith* (Philadelphia: United Church Press, 1966), pp. 45-47. In a brief recapitulation of the relational aspects of the image of God, Douglas John Hall writes: "The biblical usage of this term, as well as the best traditions of Reformation theology in particular, suggest that the relational understanding of the *imago* symbol is the appropriate one so far as the tradition of Jerusalem is concerned; for it corroborates rather precisely the other primary categories of biblical faith (grace, hope, and especially love), which are all relational in nature." *Imaging God: Dominion as Stewardship* (Grand Rapids: William B. Eerdmans Publishing Co., 1986), p. 132.

You have crowned them with glory and honor'" (Heb. 2:6-8; cf. Ps. 8:5-6).

Shakespeare has Hamlet exclaim: "What a piece of work is man!" Numberless are the world's wonders, said Sophocles, but none more wonderful than humankind. We are endowed with minds that can think God's thoughts and perform incredible feats. We did not create nuclear energy, but, having discovered it, we can devise ways to put it to constructive use. We did not create oil and iron, but our world now runs on these resources. Human genius can probe the stratosphere and research the secrets of health and life. All these are gifts of God!

Some scientists today, as they open our minds to the wonders of our creation, see a conflict between science and religion; others find a fascinating world unfolding before them as they study the two great books God has given us, nature and Scripture. According to scientist Howard J. Van Till, "the source of a vast amount of confusion and misunderstanding in discussions on the relationship of natural sciences and biblical exegesis is the failure to distinguish between two classes of questions: those that can appropriately be addressed to the material world (the creation) alone, and those that can appropriately be directed only to the Bible."[5] He seeks to clarify what it means to take the Bible seriously when it speaks of the cosmos as God's creation, what it means to take the creation seriously when it is investigated scientifically, and how to synthesize the views of the cosmos as seen through the spectacles of Scripture and the lens of natural science.

The scientific investigation of our human origin is a kind of detective story, an effort in which physical evidence is carefully gathered, painstakingly assembled, and used to construct a story of what actually happened. Van Till affirms that paleontology, the study of earlier life-forms revealed by the record of fossils, indicates that

5. Howard Van Till, *The Fourth Day: What the Bible and the Heavens Are Telling Us about the Creation* (Grand Rapids: William B. Eerdmans Publishing Co., 1986), p. 190. Similarly, Gabriel Fackre says, "Scripture is for soteric knowledge. . . . Given its soteric purpose, Scripture is not required to be definitive in matters scientific and historical. For such information one turns to the appropriate human disciplines." *Ecumenical Faith in Evangelical Perspective*, p. 12.

differing life-forms have appeared in temporal sequence. "I see no reason, either scientific or theological," he writes, "to preclude the possibility that the temporal developments of life-forms follow from the properties and behavior of matter in a way that is similar to the processes that lead to the birth of the planets, stars, and galaxies."[6] For him, as a Christian scholar, the biblical doctrine of creation provides authoritative answers to questions concerning the origin, value, and purpose of the material world. To other scholars, however, who take a nonreligious view, such as Harvard's paleontologist Stephen Jay Gould, there is nothing that has predetermined our uniqueness and eminence. We are a fortuitous accident, just lucky. Unlike earlier scientific humanists who endeavored to trace the human ascent from bacteria through a long series of diversification to our present state, Gould, as a "post-humanist," standing on the shoulders of the "mistakes" of his predecessors, finds no inherent design or purpose in the developmental process that produced us. We are, he contends, the product of contingent events. It is only by chance, or accident, that we have survived to tell the story — until now.[7]

The biblical position is that "by faith we understand that the worlds were prepared by the word of God" (Heb. 11:3).[8] The vivid, anthropomorphic speech of the biblical writers is language that can be understood by people of every age. On its basis, we believe that God's plan for us is dictated by love, that we can live in the present in that loving purpose and face the future with hope.

Jesus underscored our unique position in teaching us to pray: "Our Father in heaven." Such an address is not meant to be merely a courteous salutation, in the way we begin our letters "Dear John/Mary." He wants us to appreciate that we have special status in a heavenly family, that God cares about us and for us. A reverent sense of self-worth, therefore, is our Christian response to God.

6. Van Till, p. 188.

7. Stephen Jay Gould, *Wonderful Life* (New York: W. W. Norton, 1989).

8. It is interesting that the word *worlds* is used here, since the plural reflects our intellectual situation in the twentieth century. We are part of millions of galaxies.

An East Coast parishioner was visited by his parents from Europe. They had never worshipped with an African-American congregation and asked if I could recommend one. Fortunately, there was one well known to me. The part of the service that impressed them was the entire congregation marching round and round the outer aisles singing a crescendoing refrain, "If anybody asks you who I am, tell 'em I'm a child of God!" With God there are no minorities.

A boy put up a placard on the wall of his room; "I'M ME AND I'M GOOD, 'CAUSE GOD DON'T MAKE JUNK." I like that. Our worth with God is not based on achievements, social status, race, or ethnic heritage. It is intrinsic, not extrinsic.

The conspicuous consumption of accumulated wealth is not an index of worth. Stretch limousines, luxurious condominiums, yachts, club memberships, and designer clothes do not create self-worth. They have nothing to do with the essential self. One could gain the whole world and forfeit life (Mark 8:36). In the great stock market crash of 1929, many plunged from skyscraper offices to suicide deaths. Their fortunes obliterated, they revealed their bankrupt souls. The dollar is not almighty. But the Almighty has conferred upon you a family status as a son or daughter that warrants self-respect.

2. A second reason for affirming your self-worth is that we are *redeemed by Jesus Christ.* God has come to us in Jesus Christ, "sharing our common lot, and conquering sin and death." Our unique ability to think, love, and will enables us to deface the divine image. Human nature has become flawed. This is not the place to spell out all the implications of our fallenness. Suffice it to say that it was precisely because of this catastrophe that good tidings were heralded to the earth that "a Savior" was born, who was named Jesus, for he would "save his people from their sins." We are worth enough to God that a perfect life was lived and sacrificed to restore the divine image within us. As a hymn puts it, "He died to make us good." The more developed our Christology, therefore, the greater our sense of self-worth.

The good news is that God has done for us what we could not do for ourselves. A do-it-yourself theology has no place for the atonement. The atonement is not the whole of the gospel, but it is its heart. There is no healing for us without it. The gospel is not a striver's manual; it is the revelation of the gift of salvation.[9]

Isaac Watts has written many glorious hymns, but one stanza in the original version of one of Watts's hymns has always troubled me:

Alas, did my Savior bleed,
    And did my Sovereign die?
Would he devote that sacred head
    For such a worm as I?

I like worms. They are an ecological blessing to the soil. But I am no worm. No worm was ever redeemed by Jesus Christ. It is better to sing "for such a soul as I," for we are honored children of God.

Though we know its reality, we wonder at the mystery of it. Harry W. Framington has phrased it well:

I know not how that Bethlehem's babe
    Could in the God-head be;

9. Leander E. Keck, *The Church Confident* (Nashville: Abingdon Press, 1993), p. 66. We humans have turned away from right relationship with God and have chosen the ways that lead to death rather than life. In Christ, God savingly deals with us as we actually are. Sin is the corruption of the image of God. We are born into a world where sin is universal, but we are also individually sinners. Sin is both plural and singular. Paul's catalogue of sins, preceding his list of the fruits of the Spirit, names specific acts that horrified him: "fornication, impurity, licentiousness, idolatry, sorcery, enmities, strife, jealousy, anger, quarrels, dissensions, factions, envy, drunkenness, carousing, and things like these" (Gal. 5:19-21). The medieval list of vices named pride, envy, anger, sloth, avarice, gluttony, and lust. These specific acts are symptomatic of the corruption of the soul, which manifests itself in unbelief, spiritual pride (hybris), and concupiscence. God forgives us in Jesus, and the Spirit nurtures the fruit of the Spirit, but sin does not completely disappear. We never become perfect in this life. "So the church keeps the confession of sin and the sacrament of forgiveness at the center in its service of worship." The coming of Jesus Christ "gives the center and key to the whole." "Our faith rests upon the whole meaning and impact of what he did, as that had been experienced first by those who were with him, and throughout the centuries by all who experience the grace and power of his life" (Shinn and Williams, pp. 51-58, 73, 76).

> I only know the manger child
>   Has brought God's life to me.

The incarnation is often described by theologians as condescension and humiliation for Jesus; but it is also the exaltation of human nature.

The parable of the Prodigal Son is the best-loved short story of Jesus because it reassures us that no matter how far we have wandered or what we have done, God loves us and forgives us. The prodigal "came to himself" and returned to the open arms of his waiting father. The good news of the glad God is that we, too, can go home again! "Feelings lie buried that grace can restore."

A story from sixteenth-century Paris fascinates me. A poor, unkempt scholar, desperately ill, was brought to the operating arena of a group of surgeons. As they looked at the destitute creature, one said to the others in Latin, which he was sure the patient would not understand, "Faciamus experimentum in anima vile" (Let us perform an experiment on this vile person). To which the sick man, Mark Antoine Muret, replied from the operating slab, "Animam vilem appelas pro quo Christus non dedignatus more est?" (Would you call one a vile person for whom Christ did not disdain to die?). Christ loves and cares enough to have done that for us. We are thrilled anew each time we read the life-stories of those who have enjoyed the redemptive experience.

Karl Barth, the theologian of our century, gave a lecture in Chicago a number of years ago. In the question period that followed, a student rose to ask: "Professor Barth, you have written so voluminously and profoundly on such a wide range of theology; could you summarize in a few sentences the essence of your thought?" It had to be a student's question! Barth paused, and then with a characteristic twinkle in his eye and a beguiling smile on his lips, he said in his unreproducible, rich German accent: "Ja, I think I can do that. 'Jesus loves me, this I know, for the Bible tells me so!'" It was an inspired answer, and those who knew his hermeneutic appreciated it most.

Our former Surgeon General, C. Everett Koop, confesses that it was not until he sat in the balcony of a Philadelphia church one

Sunday evening that he really understood the basics of the Christian gospel, "that the essence of Christianity was not what we did, but what Christ had done for us." Like many other nominal Christians, he says, "I suppose I had been trying to live as correctly as I could, but like them, I knew in the depths of my own heart that my nature, like everyone else's, was sinful, and my efforts to reform myself were to no avail." But, most of all, he writes, "I understood the love of God. Like many new Christians — and many old Christians — I found the most meaningful verse in the Bible to be John 3:16: 'For God so loved the world that he gave his only begotten Son, that whoever believes in him should not perish, but have eternal life.' I was a believer!"[10] Like all people of faith, he was a new creation in Christ, and he enthusiastically affirmed the wonderful status.

3. A third reason for affirming our self-worth is that we are *renewed by the Holy Spirit.* The Holy Spirit refashions our characters with Christlike virtues — the fruit of love, joy, peace, patience, kindness, goodness, faithfulness, gentleness, and self-control. All the varied ways we have noted this miracle in previous chapters are traceable to this divine act of the Spirit in our lives. To become like Jesus is gracious living. The Holy Spirit provides the spiritual energy to live the Christ-life. It enables us to become humbly self-affirming, not arrogantly self-asserting.

4. Finally, God providentially *sustains us* **in life.**

Some find it hard to believe. Countless times I have heard people complain: "Why does God let this happen to me?"

A beautiful, middle-aged wife was given little hope for recovery after surgery for a virulent breast cancer. "Explain to me how God

---

10. C. Everett Koop, *The Memoirs of a Family Doctor* (New York: Random House, 1991), pp. 85-86. Dorothy and Gabriel Fackre present the two sides of the doctrine of Christ: "Incarnation tells us about the 'Person' — who Christ is. And the Atonement tells us about the 'Work' — what Christ did to make us one with God. Atonement is a very special word in the church's vocabulary: 'It means that God put things together again in the deed Christ did. "Salvation" happened.' . . . Incarnation is necessary to Christ's work, but Incarnation is not its limit. It makes possible the continuing tasks of the Galilean teacher who rescues us from untruth, the Calvary Savior who delivers us from sin, and the Easter liberator who overcomes suffering and death" (*Christian Basics,* pp. 40, 45, 52).

would allow this to happen to such a good person!" demanded her embittered husband. As kindly as I could, I gave the comforting answers: that God does not create evil, that we are bound up in the web of life, that God gives us strength and patience to face tragedy, that by God's grace good can come out of the severest trials. It would have been unkind to remind him that she had for years been a very heavy cigarette smoker. At such a time, he needed to hear the good news that God's grace is adequate for every situation, that every soul is of infinite value.

A few years ago, after the early death of his son from progeria ("rapid aging"), Rabbi Harold S. Kushner wrote a book that became a best-seller. It dealt with the experience of everyone who raises questions about the goodness, the kindness, and even the existence of God. As the rabbi of a large congregation, he had visited his congregants in the hospital, officiated at their funerals, and tried to help them as they passed through painful divorces, business failures, the stress of sustaining senile parents, and the experience of terminal illness. He found it hard to tell them that life is fair, that God gives people what they deserve. Time after time he had seen families and even whole communities unite in prayer for the recovery of a sick person, only to have their hopes and prayers seemingly go unanswered. The wrong people seemed to get sick, get hurt, die young. As a rabbi, he found insight in the book of Job, and concluded his own book with the observation, "I would say that God may not prevent the calamity, but he gives us the strength and the perseverance to overcome it."[11]

One thinks of another Jewish rabbi, who became one of the greatest Christians that ever lived. He wrote of his great labors, imprisonments, countless floggings (often bringing him to the brink of death), being stoned, three times shipwrecked and adrift at sea, living in danger from rivers, bandits, his own people, and Gentiles, as well as knowing many a sleepless night, hunger, and thirst (II Cor. 11:23-28). Besides all this he experienced a mysterious "thorn in the flesh" from which he fervently prayed to be delivered. God's en-

11. Harold S. Kushner, *When Bad Things Happen to Good People* (New York: Shocken Books, 1981), p. 141.

couraging answer to the apostle Paul was, "my grace is sufficient to you, for power is made perfect in weakness." It enabled him to be content with weaknesses, insults, hardships, persecutions, and calamities (12:7-10). He was fit for anything, he said, through the power and love of Christ who strengthened him (Phil. 4:13).

Paul had a rock-ribbed conviction that "all things work together for good for those who love God" (Rom. 8:28). Those who find such a claim too sweeping may find encouragement in a footnote that offers an alternate translation: "In all things God works for good." God helps us find the good in the bad things that happen to us. As Paul affirms, "If God be for us, who can be against us?" (v. 31). Life is often unfair, but God is always good.

Ethel Waters, the popular blues singer, learned that. She describes herself as "a real dead-end kid," a black girl born in an urban ghetto. But she had a voice, and she became a star on the stage and in films. After a spiritual struggle, she turned her life over to God. She inspired millions with the spiritual that became her theme song.

> Why should I feel discouraged?
> Why should the shadows come?
> Why should my heart be lonely
> And long for heaven and home?
> When Jesus is my portion,
> My constant friend is he.
> His eye is on the sparrow,
> And I know he watches me.

She chose one of the lines as the title of her autobiography: *His Eye Is on the Sparrow*.

Dave Dravecky, the former all-star pitcher for the San Francisco Giants, lost his arm to cancer. His arm was to him what hands are to a concert pianist, what legs are to a ballerina, what feet are to a marathon runner. How did he react? "God willed a world that is as mysterious as it is majestic. I believe God rules over that world, but I don't believe he gave me cancer. He allowed it. Why? I don't know. I don't know the purpose of my suffering. But I do know the results. When I compare the Dave Dravecky before cancer to the Dave

Dravecky after, there's no comparison." He emerged from an identity crisis to assume a new career. He now travels the country speaking about overcoming adversity. "I've walked away from this experience," he says, "knowing the value of one day. And in that day I want to be the best husband I can be. . . . The desire of my heart is to please God with my life." He epitomizes patience. He has found peace. And he has learned self-respect and sincere self-love.

God's cradle-to-the-grave care surpasses all social security systems. It was costly, but not for us, as we noted in the acronym for grace: "God's riches at Christ's expense." We matter so much to God that the apostle could confidently write, "My God will supply every need of yours" (Phil. 4:19).

For four good reasons, therefore, we are to love the self that God loves. Created in the divine image, redeemed by the amazing grace of Jesus Christ, renewed and empowered by the indwelling Spirit, and sustained by a loving providence, we are sons and daughters of the Lord God. We have the loftiest family connections in the world!

Too Good to Be True?

Some find this almost too good to be true. How can we love ourselves when we do so many things that are wrong? C. S. Lewis for a time thought that the old adage "love the sinner but hate the sin" was silly. How could the two be separated? But one day, looking into the mirror while shaving, the truth hit home. He hated the wrong things he did, but all the while he kept on loving himself. God treats us in the same way.

We do not have to be perfect to be accepted by God. A young woman who regularly attended our Sunday morning study class was troubled by Jesus' statement: "Be perfect . . . as your heavenly Father is perfect" (Matt. 5:48). "I can't do that; it's impossible!" she declared. It made her question her Christianity. When I assured her that Jesus gives us goals and ideals to strive for, but that none of us actually attains them, she leaned back and breathed the sigh, "Thank God!" Acceptance is not a human achievement; it is a gift.

This was Martin Luther's great discovery. No one tried more diligently to win God's favor. He fasted. He flagellated himself. He exhausted his soul in confession. He read the writings of the masters. Finally, he read the Scriptures and discovered that he could be made right with God by grace through faith. He was accepted by God. It became the diapason note of all his preaching and teaching. It is still the nerve center of all Christian proclamation.

To be able to say, "I was wrong," however, is a mark of healthy maturity. Confession is good for the soul. It does not destroy a positive self-image, but opens our hearts to forgiveness, the finest therapeutic promise in the world. Unconfessed sin, by way of contrast, can make us ill or depressed and rob us of peace of soul.

Confession must be sincere, however, whether in private with God alone, or in a liturgical setting. Worshipping in a socially average church one Sunday, I was startled by the unison prayer that lamented our neglect of the poor while we slept on designer sheets! Cleverness cancels contrition. As Scotland's James Denney once put it: no one can simultaneously give the impression that he is clever and that Jesus Christ is mighty to save.

If you want to enjoy a healthy sense of self-respect and self-worth, join a church that proclaims grace. Religious masochism drives some folk to churches that constantly harangue people about their sins. A new parishioner explained why he resigned from his church to join ours. "I got tired of having gravel thrown in my face every Sunday," he said. The good news of the glad God is that there is forgiveness and acceptance for us, that sin-sick souls can be delivered from despair to enjoy the happy status of sons and daughters of God. As the hymn states it: "To those who fall how kind thou art, how good to those who seek."

The Athletics of the Spirit: Self-Control

All self-respecting believers will endeavor to enhance their spiritual, psychological, and physical natures by self-discipline.

The apostle Paul knew about the Olympic games that were held a mere hundred miles from Corinth. Given their particular religious character, I doubt that he ever attended these spectacular events, but the rigorous self-discipline that was required of all contestants furnished him illustrations for healthy Christian living. "Do you remember how, on a racing track, every competitor runs, but only one receives the prize!" he asks. "Well, you ought to run with your minds fixed on winning the prize!" Every competitor in athletic events goes into tremendous training, he says — for a fading crown of leaves. But "our contest is for an eternal crown that will never fade." Then, changing the figure and speaking for himself, he says: "I am no shadow boxer, I really fight! I am my body's sternest master" (I Cor. 9:24-25, Phillips).

What is self-control? It is more than temperance, a kindred New Testament word meaning moderation, today often misunderstood as abstinence. Properly understood, it has a moral sheen of its own; it is used more than a dozen times in the New Testament. The Greeks esteemed it as one of the four cardinal virtues. For Plato it was mastery over the desires of the lower nature achieved through reason by superior people. Aristotle considered it the middle way between the excesses of self-indulgence and deprivation. For Paul it meant nothing in excess. Some scholars sense in his pastoral counsels a blend of Hebrew, Greek, and Christian virtue. Actually, he had in mind something more demanding.

For him self-control (*enkrateia*) is much more arduous than temperance (*sophrosyne*). It means mastery, mastery of one's whole personality, a firm grip on one's thoughts, emotions, will, and desires. Such control creates a positive attitude about ourselves. It elevates our morale and develops a healthier soul and body.

Physical fitness is the "in thing" today. Everyone admires a slim, sleek physique. Health counselors are constantly encouraging aerobic exercise, and many of us have a regular regimen of walking, running, swimming, or engaging in other sports that produce healthy bodies, wholesome minds, and longer life.

Exercise is a sacred discipline, one that needs more converts. Christianity never deprecates the physical. God wants control of the body. It is his by right of creation and redemption. "You are bought with a price; therefore glorify God in your body" (I Cor. 6:19-20). It is the temple of the Holy Spirit. Our bodies influence our psyches, and both influence our spirits. We have long been acquainted with

209

psychosomatism; we need to become aware of what I like to speak of as "psychosomapneumatism" — the interaction of mind, body, and spirit.

In our leisure age, however, too many still opt for a softer religion of the body. They race to the reclining chair, exercise without sweating, and diet without giving up cake. Bookstore shelves groan with the weight of diet and nutrition books, but cookbooks with exotic and tempting recipes outsell them all. A flabby body creates a flabby soul. Without self-restraint, we lose a sense of self-respect.

Three elemental and dominant hungers call for control: food, sex, and acquisitiveness. Sex and food create and sustain life, but can also corrupt it. Add greed, and you have a triple agenda for monitoring self-discipline.

1. First of all, *food*: we need to eat to live. And what a delightful way to stay alive! God gave us five senses, one of them taste. A fine palate is to be appreciated as well as fine music and good literature. "That a man should eat and drink and enjoy himself, in return for all his labors," observes the wise man, "is a gift of God" (Eccl. 5:12, New English Bible). Jesus came eating and drinking, relished wedding receptions, frequently enjoyed dinner parties, and taught us to pray for our daily bread. We have been bombarded with messages on what this means in terms of a balanced diet: plenty of vegetables and fruits, plus carbohydrates, but keeping low on fats. It is a good Christian guide.

No self-respecting person, however, will overdo a good thing. Americans eat and drink so much that 30 percent of us (58 million) are obese, a condition that is defined as being 20 percent over our ideal weight. And that in a nation where thirteen million are undernourished! Health professionals consider it a national disgrace, and churches now are hosting Overeaters Anonymous groups.

The extra baggage is not just unsightly, but unhealthy as well. It increases the risk for diabetes, hypertension, heart disease, stroke, gout, arthritis, and some forms of cancer. The peril looms larger for the rising generation, which consumes even more junk food, uses more sedentary technology, and exercises less. Restraint has never been America's long suit. But there is hope if more will adopt moderation and self-control as virtues to be practiced.

But a word of caution. Sophisticated biologists note that in some cases etiological factors such as "genetic predisposition, endocrine and biochemical disorders, abnormal neuroregulatory mechanisms, and early adipose tissue development" contribute to the onset of obesity.[12] That is, some inherit a biological predisposition to be overweight however much they control their diet.

In New Testament times, the Roman bacchanalian banquets were gargantuan and gross. The affluent ate, imbibed an emetic, and ate again. "Their god [was] their own appetite" (Phil. 3:19, Phillips). It is an unruly temptation in every age. A woman paused in a restaurant to admire a friend's new baby. Her friend asked her when hers was due. "I just sat down and cried," she said, and immediately went on a weight control program.

We should treat beverages the same way. Eight glasses of water a day foster a healthy body, but coffee, chocolate, and carbonated drinks require circumspection.

Alcoholic beverages introduce a separate category. The controlled use of wine is nowhere condemned in the Bible (distilled spirits were unknown at the time). A psalmist praises God for "wine to gladden the human heart" (Ps. 104:16). When the wine supply gave out at the Cana wedding reception, Jesus changed the water in six 20- to 30-gallon stone jars into the very best wine (John 2:3-10). At the sacred moment in the upper room, as he instituted the Lord's Supper, he took the cup, blessed it, and said: "Do this in remembrance of me" (Luke 22:17, 19). In a letter to Timothy, Paul advises his associate to take "a little wine for the sake of your stomach and your frequent ailments" (I Tim. 5:23).

But while the Bible commends its discreet use, it vehemently condemns its misuse. "Wine is a mocker, strong drink a brawler, and whoever is led astray by it is not wise" (Prov. 20:1). Similarly, the New Testament declares, "Do not get drunk with wine, for that is debauchery, but be filled with the Spirit" (Eph. 5:18). Even in morally indifferent cases, a considerate Christian will not flaunt freedom if

12. H. Bruch, *Eating Disorders* (Cambridge, Mass.: Harvard University Press, 1979); quoted by J. D. Guy, Jr., "Obesity," in *Baker Encyclopedia of Psychology* (Grand Rapids: Baker Book House, 1985), p. 767.

it harms the weaker believer (Rom. 14:21-22). Every self-loving follower of Jesus, therefore, will exercise caution.

Some physicians suggest that a drink a day is good for the human heart. Heavy drinking, however, creates a greater incidence of strokes and cancer. Some trace the complex psychology and sociology of excess to genetics, others to social conditioning.

Alcohol consumption has been declining every year for the past twenty years, except among young adults. The extent of alcohol abuse on campuses is a cause for concern. There is a market component to students' consumption; the beer industry targets young adults as its best hope for increasing sales. William H. Willimon, chaplain and professor of religion at Duke University, notes that the money generated for the university by TV revenues are beer revenues, and that college athletics is financed by the breweries. He laments that students, who ought to be among the nation's most thoughtful, are being manipulated by economic forces of which they are mostly unaware.[13]

The perils of alcohol use during pregnancy are medically well-documented, and the literature of pathology is plentiful. What is not always known, however, is that alcohol is often a gateway drug. It leads to the use of marijuana, cocaine, and crack. It is estimated that 3,000,000 use marijuana every day (20,000,000 occasionally), that cocaine use has skyrocketed to twenty million affluent professional and high school users, and that the more concentrated crystallized crack, once the "junkies'" curse in depressed urban centers, now, at higher prices, has become the plaything of the upper middle class.

13. Willimon, "Reaching and Teaching the Abandoned Generation," *The Christian Century,* October 2, 1993, pp. 1016-19. Studies reveal two trends on campus drinking: one, that remorseless drinking is as much a ritual of university life as football, final exams, and frat parties; two, that there is a new force for change among students who are tired of paying huge tuition fees for going to college and suffering all the indignities of their inebriated peers, such as vomiting, vandalism, and sexual assaults. Restraint may be a tough sell among young people who have just escaped their parents' watchful eyes and are eager to become free spirits, especially when those who do restrain are made to feel that they are antisocial. The campus temperance movements have been encouraged by the good results of the antismoking movement, however: "enough is enough, say the campus rebels who want to stay sober." Cf. *Time,* December 19, 1994, pp. 66, 67.

While some see a decline in drug use and addiction, others point to new forms of usage. The epidemic continues. It was painful for me as a college teacher to observe bright students from respectable homes sit in class with dazed looks, bloodshot eyes, and runny noses, oblivious to the ways in which they where destroying their lives. I met some of them a few years later completely changed, married, and often the parents of happy children. Yet precious years had been wasted beyond recall.

It still surprises some that a drug far more lethal is tobacco. While crack claims about 300 lives a year, the death toll of nicotine exceeds 350,000. One thousand people quit smoking every day — they die. Smoking is no longer the "heathen vice" only of the stricter fringe of the Christian community, it is a health concern for all, since the smoke of tobacco users also affects the health of those who inhale it secondhand. A cardiovascular physician friend categorically states that a large percentage of our hospital beds would be emptied if people stopped smoking. His graphic slide-presentations at our Wednesday night church dinners stunned even broadminded congregants with the revelation that virtually every organ in the body is harmed by nicotine.

To love yourself is to say "no" to gluttony, intoxication, and drug and tobacco addiction.

2. Self-love and self-respect include appropriate control of our elemental *sex* drives. To say that Christianity frowns on sex is towering nonsense. Christians are not prudes; they celebrate sex because God created it and encourages it. The ancient church father Clement of Alexandria declared: "[We] ought not to be ashamed to mention what God was not ashamed to create." Eros married to agape can integrate personalities in the rapture of psychological, physical, and spiritual fulfillment. It can be sacramental, not merely animalistic titillation of nerve endings.

The uniform declaration of the Bible is that sex is to be enjoyed within monogamous marriage. Within marriage it is much broader than genital sex. It is eminently psychological. "Any two persons who are living a full life together as persons," writes Lewis Smedes, "know that their sexual relations cover a lot more ground than a few moments of intercourse. Sexuality is involved in the quiet hours of

213

communication and contemplation as much as in the volcanic moments."[14] "Rejoice in the wife of your youth," writes the wise man of Proverbs. "Let her be your companion. Her love will satisfy you at all times and wrap you round continually" (Prov. 5:18-19). Love's kindness, gentleness, patience, and loyalty create joy inexpressible as well as peace of mind and soul.

Our structured moral universe exploded with a bang in the sexual revolution of the 1960s and 1970s. Of all the sixties' revolutions, writes Wade Clark Roof, "none had a greater long-term impact than the gender revolution. The changing sexual rules and relationships of the period mushroomed into a major social movement that had radically altered marriage, family, parenting, and career patterns."[15] The consensus of Western society until mid-century reflected fairly closely the biblical ideals, however imperfectly they were observed. What shattered it was the idea that uninhibited permissiveness is a boon to human fulfillment, especially among the rapidly growing number of unmarried or divorced adults and gay activists.

The jettisoning of traditional moral guidelines was also fostered by chemical breakthroughs that made penicillin available as a cure for venereal disease and the pill for the prevention of pregnancy. Freed from these fears, people felt more liberated in their sexual behavior. Casual affairs, freewheeling rituals in singles' bars, and relationships the outcome of which remained insouciantly negotiable became de rigueur for many. "The joy of sex" became the current refrain.

Self-control can be an arduous discipline for those who have spent long periods of their lives reining in their sexual impulses and drives, trying to live discreetly. Suddenly, upon achieving success, position, and power, or facing a mid-life crisis, that part of them that they have tried to suppress overwhelms them and pulls them and someone else down. Almost without warning, they are brought face-to-face with their shadow-side.

14. Lewis B. Smedes, *Sex for Christians* (Grand Rapids: William B. Eerdmans Publishing Co., 1976), p. 39.
15. Ward Clark Roof, *A Generation of Seekers: The Spiritual Journeys of the Baby Boomer Generation* (New York: Harper San Francisco, 1993), p. 48.

A recent landmark study by University of Chicago researchers, however, in what is considered the nation's most authoritative survey of adult sexual behavior, paints a picture that shows our society as less libertine than many have supposed. Unlike the Kinsey reports in 1948 and 1952, the Masters and Johnson study in 1966, and the Hite reports of the 1970s and 1980s, which relied solely on volunteers to collect data, Chicago's National Opinion Research conducted interviews with over 3,000 randomly selected women and men between the ages of 18 and 59. The study finds that Americans have less promiscuous sex than the other reports indicate. Furthermore, 75 percent of the married men and 85 percent of the married women say they are faithful to their spouses, and those who are happiest with their sex lives are monogamous couples.[16]

And yet our society idolizes sex. Virtually every magazine on the newsstand, most of the stories in the tabloid press, the majority of television entertainment, as well as movies, depict sexual philandering as a common pastime. Rock musicians and sports heroes who advocate unchecked recreational sex often become role models. When Wilt Chamberlain boasts of sexual liaisons with 20,000 women, and Magic Johnson boasts of hundreds, adherents of liberal culture without a moral compass have no guide for moral decision making. Anyone who watches five hours of television a day sees nearly 14,000 sexual encounters in a year. As freedom of expression is encouraged, perversion flourishes. Monogamous couples wandering this Sodom and Gomorrah feel "out of sync" with their proclivity to propriety.

The spotlight may be on the young, but the young are not the creators of the sexual revolution. They are the inheritors of changes that reach back several decades. Parents and others often expect teenagers to behave in ways they themselves rejected during their teen years, but teenagers are quick to see through the hypocrisy of adults who still live according to the myths of the dominant culture, and then slap their children's hands when they reach for a share of the forbidden fruit.

16. Edward O. Laumann, John H. Gagnon, Robert T. Michael, and Stuart Michaels, eds., *The Social Organization of Sexuality* (Chicago: University of Chicago Press, 1993).

Teenagers are bombarded with mixed messages. "Just say 'No.'" "Use a condom." "If it feels good it's OK." As AIDS becomes pandemic, warnings escalate, yet many junior and senior high kids are as sexually active as ever. Negatives by themselves often create defiance.

"Kids can't say 'no' if they don't first learn how to feel good about themselves," declares Surgeon General Joycelen Elders. If there is one point of agreement among all parties, it is that sex education has to be about more than the anatomy lesson. It must come in a larger context of building relationships based on integrity and respect.

So-called mainline churches that espouse a culturally conditioned interpretation of Scripture, in distinction from literalist churches, as well as the traditionally strict Roman Catholic Church, ardently debate the question of how flexible and relative the biblical tradition is in today's permissive society. Broadening churches fracture over the issue as traditionalists within their fellowships form protest groups that call for a return to stricter positions. Students of church history note that the family-oriented sexual ethic of the early Christian communities won to Christ many of the disillusioned in the promiscuous and decaying culture of Rome. "Wouldn't it be wonderful for the Church," writes Episcopal Bishop Frey to his fellow prelates, "to find such counter-culture courage today?"

The message is clear. If we love the self that God created, redeemed, and renews, we will respect our sex drives by expressing them in responsible and properly self-regarding ways. This is the road to the highest happiness.

3. The desire for *possessions* is a third great hunger — and a legitimate one. It enables us to maintain a decent standard of living. It becomes an ugly thing only when it becomes unbridled acquisitiveness. It is not money that is evil; it is the love of money. "Take care! Be on your guard against all kinds of greed," said Jesus, "for one's life does not consist in the abundance of possessions" (Luke 12:15). Self-love and self-respect dictate self-control.

Nonetheless, prosperity, according to the Bible, is a blessing of God. Abraham, included in the Hebrews 11 Hall of Fame, was "very rich in cattle, in silver, and in gold" (Gen. 13:2). His son Isaac had

216

such great wealth that he was the envy of the neighboring Philistines (26:14). God-fearing Job was very wealthy, and twice as rich after he emerged faithful from the devastation that had stripped him of family and fortune (Job 1:1; 42:10). Solomon's legendary treasures made the Queen of Sheba exclaim: "not even half has been told me!" (I Kings 10:7).

At Christ's birth the Magi brought treasures of gold, frankincense, and myrrh. Jesus frequently feasted with the affluent. His warnings were not against wealth but the idolizing of it. You cannot serve GOD on Sunday and GNP on Monday.

The Holy Spirit on Pentecost created a church that was a spiritually vital, sharing fellowship. Barnabas, we have noted, was a dedicated, prosperous member who turned over the entire proceeds of a sale of land to the benevolence program of the Jerusalem church. Such a worthy sense of stewardship, which does not covetously clasp everything to one's self, begets a feeling of self-respect.

The earth and all that is in it does not belong to the devil, nor does it belong to us. "The earth is the LORD's and all that is in it" (Ps. 24:1). We are trustees of it. It is our attitude toward possessions that either curses or blesses us. Australia's Frank W. Boreham stated the case clearly:

> Dug from the mountainside, washed in the glen,
> Servant am I or the master of men!
> Earn me, I bless you; steal me, I curse you!
> Hold me and grasp me,
> A fiend will possess you!
> Live for me, die for me, covet me, take me,
> Angel or demon, I am what you make me.[17]

If the dollar bills in your billfold and the stubs of your checkbook could write their autobiographies, what stories would they tell?

Enough is enough. In Aesop's classic fable about a man and his wife who had a goose that laid a golden age every day, cupidity

17. Frank W. Boreham, *Mountains in the Mist,* quoted by Louis H. Evans, *Youth Seeks a Master* (Westwood, N.J.: Fleming H. Revell, 1964), p. 46.

prompted them to kill the goose in order to get at the gold treasure they imagined was stored inside. When they opened the goose, however, they found that it was an ordinary goose. They lost not only their goose, but also the daily dividends it paid. The simple tale describes how inordinate desire is both demonic and destructive. One of the chief narrative patterns in literature, past and present and in all cultures, is the disaster that occurs when people grasp for possessions beyond their legitimate and reasonable needs.

Spiritual self-love, therefore, inspired by the faith that our creation, redemption, and renewal are gifts of God, is our best guard against gluttony, sensuality, and greed. Body and soul, we belong to Jesus Christ. This confidence begets a sense of self-worth, fills us with zest for life, fosters positive attitudes, and encourages us to cultivate Christlike virtues. Healthy self-affirmation is a reflection of God's affirmation.

This is the good news of the glad God: we can become like Jesus. True joy in life, a peaceful conscience, patience in plenty and in want, kindness that shares with the needy, faithful observance of the rules of health, and self-mastery that maintains moderation in all things beget wholesome self-respect and spiritual self-love. But what is fully as important is that this spiritual fruit is a seal of the life we dedicate to God, and, through God, to our neighbor.

EPILOGUE

Poems by Barbara M. Van Dyken

Each of us writes a spiritual biography as we journey through life from childhood to old age. I have endeavored to show that in each relationship, though our human nature is flawed, the good news of the glad God is that we can, by the energy of the Holy Spirit, realize God's intention that we become more like Jesus.

The wind of the Spirit is sweeping through the country today, creating a new interest in spirituality. Spirit-life progressively supplants "the works of the flesh" with love, joy, peace, patience, kindness, goodness, faithfulness, gentleness, and self-control — the fruit of the Spirit. These virtues enrich all our human relationships.

Rather than following the common scheme of dealing with each fruit in serial succession, which often makes them more abstract and disjoined, I have chosen to relate them to human experiences in life's progressive relationships, thereby rendering them more personal.

And yet, the spiritual value of each fruit can be contemplated individually in various literary forms. Poetry expresses feelings as well as thought in special artistic fashion. The poems on the fruit of the Spirit composed by my wife Barbara hopefully will say some things to your heart that prose has not been able to do.

S.V.D.

Love

"Greater love has no man than this,
that a man lay down his life for his friends."
John 15:3

For Christ to give his life, you say,
Was vast, but you are merely man.
You cherish your breath, you watch your way
And try for virtue as you can.

Love is
    a basket filled with meat and rice
    a word blown out — hold on,
    a hand to grip in wresting vice,
    a durable smile when days are wan.

Love
    does when it would rather not,
    takes when it prefers to give,
    cools the tongue when words are hot,
    stretches limits that one may live.

For ardent man may love his friend
By giving ear or time or heart,
With adversary he will rend
The wall, that no one, withheld, depart.

Joy

". . . God my exceeding joy."

Psalm 43:4

In fog-swamped seas the channel fades
And hope, unless the compass aids.

The onslaught of an irate wind
Does not bring loss if the skiff is pinned.

When rising breakers claw the shore,
The house on granite withstands the more.

Voracious rains eat loose the tree,
Save roots fed deep in security.

With God as guide all ways are joy.
The anchor struck in him saves joy.
If Christ be rock how strong the joy.
My roots through him sustain that joy.
As God becomes my full employ,
No factor shall destroy my joy.

Peace

"My times are in thy hand."

Psalm 31:15

Stillness is a part of peace.
Its revelations teach release:
The eye instructs the soul.
It sees the leaf in quiet burst the branch,
Or gale shiver down to zephyr dance.

Stillness only is not peace —
From hate to give the heart surcease.
"My peace I give to you."
To listen as he tunes the complex airs
Admits regard for an other one's affairs.

Stillness can masquerade as peace,
Mock sedation of caprice.
When the body craves repose —
Its cancer edging up on waves of pain —
The end in him returns his calm domain.

Stillness tells the worth of peace.
The patience of "not yet" will cease.
God's way disquiets death.
The eye and heart and breath inform the whole:
Such peace will see the Savior's peace control.

Long-suffering

". . . let us not be weary in well-doing."
Galatians 6:9

To walk the second mile
is a many miles' walk
up the hill of tolerance.

To turn the other cheek
pulls the face away
from the magnet of revenge.

To ply seventy times seven
burnishes
the iron of amity.

The lag of dreams,
the again of human foible,
the stabs toward perfection,
the wait for supernal time,
all hone the edge of endurance
that prunes the insistent self.

A graft to the Master
enables
the miracle.

Kindness

"What does God require of you . . .
to love kindness."
Micah 6:8

He had a habit
Of caring
For the passing strange —
   His host up a tree,
Or the hungry,
   even five thousand strong.

He gave heed
To the unseen need
Of the alien
   Parched in thirst,
Of the cripple bent
   With truncated sight,
Of expectant guests
   Without wedding wine,
Of two sisters
   Whose tears sealed a tomb.

     Here as ever
     The importunate ones
     Want grace on grace.

     To do for them
     In prodigal wise,
     Does for Jesus' sake.

Goodness

". . . I will make all my goodness
pass before you."
Exodus 33:19

Through centuries and nations
The germ of virtue grew.
It swelled in those who bloomed
With alms and colleges and cures.
It sprouted mercies that
Fed need and freed slave.

Unworldly source of the seed
Surely from the womb
Of revelation sprang.
Its issue across ages heaps
Our earthen bowls of charity
With pregnant seeds of purpose.

Faithfulness

"Only be faithful till death. . . ."
Revelation 2:10b

The robin will sing at dusk
After rain,
The crocus will purple
The snow.
So the dawn will rouge
The sky
Routinely.
These jewels rotate the facets of
His faithfulness
Forever.

The axis
Of the soul
Rotates the self in its turn.

If it turn
In whim roulette,
The axis must tip from the source.
Let the soul turn true
In him,
Allegiances vagrant
Will spin in,
Align,
And spin on
Forever.

POEMS BY BARBARA VAN DYKEN

Meekness

"Blessed are the meek: for they
shall inherit the earth."

Matthew 5:5

The world's demands are tough commands
If one would be its king.
Pursue those codes and withstand
Every tender thing.
Craftiness wields insurance.
Resistance counterfeits endurance.

The Savior's meekness mortified weakness.
Patience through injury is strong.
Humility is not less.
Its quietness outrages wrong.
Those malleable by God endure.
Their hold on courage ensures.

Who follows his heart, not the world's plan,
Shall know all things and have the land.

227

Self-Control

*"But godliness with contentment
is great gain."*

I Timothy 6:6

I

The animus that brings anguish on nations,
That strikes the course of man in relation
To fellow man, unleashing turmoil,
Is rampant hunger after spoil.

Wars would die without diets of greed.
A man would coerce none for his need,
Nor take his love nor fill his frame
Too much, were reins on wanton aims.

II

Prune desire and the tree of the self
Yields mellow fruit that reaches well
Toward the Sun. Trimmed life
Grows free of wild strife.